DI132376

MICHAEL PENNINGTON

Over the last twenty-five years Michael Pennington has played a
variety of leading roles in the West End of London, for the Royal
Shakespeare Company, for the Royal National Theatre, and for
the English Shakespeare Company, of which he was co-founder
and Joint Artistic Director from 1986 to 1992. His Shakespearian
roles include Hamlet, Macbeth, Leontes, Coriolanus, Richard II,
Henry V, Angelo, Berowne and Timon, and he has played central
parts in the works of Euripides, Molière, Congreve, Vanbrugh,
Tolstoy, Chekhov, Dostoievsky, Bulgakov, O'Casey, Granville
Barker, de Filippo, Shaffer, Mortimer, Pinter, Rudkin, Stoppard,
Harwood, Brenton, Edgar and Poliakoff.

In 1991 he made his directing début with *Twelfth Night* for the
English Shakespeare Company, going on to direct the same
play for the Haiyuza Company in Tokyo and for Chicago
Shakespeare Theater. These productions form the starting-point
for this *User's Guide*, the second in a series which began with his
successful *Hamlet – A User's Guide*, published by Nick Hern Books
in 1996. Pennington's *English Shakespeare Company – The Story
of the Wars of the Roses* (co-written with Michael Bogdanov) was
published by Nick Hern Books in 1990. As well as pursuing an
active television, film and radio career, he has presented his one-
man show *Anton Chekhov* at the Royal National Theatre, at the
Old Vic Theatre in London and extensively on tour and abroad.

Michael Pennington

TWELFTH NIGHT
A User's Guide

Limelight Editions
New York

First Limelight Edition, October 2000

Published in the United States by Proscenium Publishers Inc., New York,
by arrangement with Nick Hern Books Ltd., London.

Library of Congress Cataloging-in-Publication Data

Pennington, Michael, 1943-
      Twelfth night : a user's guide / Michael Pennington.-- 1st Limelight ed.
        p. cm.
      "First published in Great Britain in 2000 as a paperback original by
    Nick Hern Books Ltd."--T.p. verso.
      ISBN 0-87910-950-5
      1. Shakespeare, William, 1564-1616. Twelfth night. 2. Comedy. I. Title.

PR2837 .P39 2000
822.3'3--dc21
                                       00-056929

Contents

Introduction

English Stage Company, 1991   1

Part One

     Act One   35

     Act Two   75

Entr'Acte

Haiyuza Company, Tokyo, 1993   111

Part Two

     Act Three   145

     Act Four   181

     Act Five   197

Conclusion

Chicago Shakespeare Theater, 1995   225

INTRODUCTION
English Shakespeare Company, 1991

INTRODUCTION

English Shakespeare Company, 1991

Duke Orsino's appetites are all taken up by Countess Olivia, to whom he seems barely to have spoken. He used to be a powerful and aggressive prince, knocking pirates about on the high seas; now he listens to the same few bars of music all night and uses the channels of government for sending love-letters. His misappropriation of bureaucracy is a running joke: in this story, noble characters will make proud speeches to each other as if discussing the partition of kingdoms, but in fact they are debating erotic fancy.

Orsino is so deafened by his own obsessive verbalisations that he overlooks everything that is really happening to him. He thinks he loves Olivia and must have her, but his real need is for friendship, which he finds in the unexpected form of a woman dressed as a pageboy. He doesn't exactly desire the pageboy, but what he feels for him turns out to be the basis for marriage. It is in fact Viola, an aristocrat from another country: under the aphrodisiac influence of grief, she has fallen for Orsino and is prepared to wait an eternity for him. Meanwhile she models herself on her lost twin brother Sebastian, who is 'yet living in my glass': she imitates his 'fashion, colour, ornament'. So her male costume is not a joke, but shows her need both to feel like her brother and to fool Orsino's establishment, who would not take her seriously otherwise. She succeeds in this until she has to duel with a foolish and intemperate wooer of Olivia, Sir Andrew Aguecheek, at which point her manliness deserts her; nothing comes of it, but Andrew is punished for his challenge later when he mistakes Sebastian for her, and is thoroughly beaten.

The duel has been set up by Sir Toby Belch, Olivia's uncle, who is witty and unkind. Since accidents can happen, to make two incompetent fighters face each other in this way is a very dangerous thing to do. But Toby's continuous drinking has sharpened his instinct for meaningless revenge – even on Andrew, who has more money than sense and believes anything he is told. The sour military joke might have gone badly wrong had not a friend of Sebastian's, the brave Antonio, turned up to interrupt it. Antonio eventually realises he has made the opposite mistake to Andrew's and taken Viola for Sebastian. He is reunited with his friend, who marries Olivia, who has previously fallen for Viola in disguise; Orsino discovers who his pageboy has been and marries her; and Andrew, left out of the generally happy ending, must return home with a sore head in more ways than one.

Andrew says that he has been adored by someone in the past: but it is a long time ago and no use to him now. His life is cold and unloved, and he has developed a dangerous fantasy about Olivia. So of course has Orsino, whose problem, Viola sees, is that he lacks the stability of real affection, even though he is the Duke. She offers him this quieter devotion, but it takes him a long time to recognise it. Throughout, emotional security is most unfairly distributed – Toby Belch, who seems completely selfish, has inspired the devotion of Maria. All the unloved people yearn for someone, as do those who have lost part of their families; even Olivia's Fool Feste, a great loner, cares for something, though it may only be his dog.

Olivia is proud, vulnerable and perhaps rather spoilt. Too much has descended on her too suddenly: her father and brother have recently died, and an ambitious steward, Malvolio, is hastening to fill the power vacuum in her household. Like Orsino and Andrew, he dreams of Olivia's favour. He stands, apparently protectively, between her and the people who need to get in touch with her: Feste, with whom she has a confused relationship based on child-hood affection; her lady's maid Maria and her Gentlewoman; and Fabian, another member of her staff, who perhaps works in the stables, fuming at Malvolio and in awe of Toby. Fabian is easy to bring into a plot to humiliate Malvolio by exploiting his secret desire for Olivia.

The Elizabethans would have understood that, for many of these people, the alternative to service was blank destitution – and perhaps we new Elizabethans have an inkling of it too. The difficulty is not con-fined to working people: Toby, who must have drunk away several pensions, is hanging on by his fingertips to his niece's protection and, currently, to Sir Andrew's profligate purse. He risks the former and brings Olivia's wrath down on himself, but then somehow survives by marrying Maria. She has been throughout in the most delicate position, but Fabian saves her from disgrace by pretending that the joke against Malvolio was his and Toby's idea, not hers.

The other thing the rulers do instead of ruling is to listen to jesters. Feste survives through expert effrontery, as entertainers will, remarking to Olivia that her beloved brother is probably in hell and telling Orsino he is unstable. He may have some of the performer's hollowness, but his singing in particular goes to the heart of things. Everyone understands his yearning, fatalistic songs, and Orsino, who loves broken-hearted stories, specially likes them. We learn very little about Feste, except that he never forgets a grudge and sees through everybody: when Andrew brings up the subject of Feste's sweetheart, he replies with dazzling incomprehensibility. Wherever he is, he knows exactly how long the odds are, and he specially sees the danger of Malvolio.

Malvolio is still very much around, stopping the fun. As a character in the play, he has a right to his dreams of Olivia, tawdry as they may seem, and the rhapsody that enters him when he believes she loves him is as beautiful as Orsino's, certainly. Unfortunately it turns him into a blundering giant in ridiculous clothes, so blind to her reality that he might rape her and imagine it love. The revenge taken on him is extreme because what he stands for is so dangerous, starting as it does with his denial of all tolerance and humour. Malvolio kills the good feeling that leads to art, not because he altogether condemns it, but because he patronises it with shallow judgments, listening to Feste and an 'ordinary fool' before deciding that the ordinary fool is better. Feste never forgets this bad review and, on behalf of all dismissed entertainers, torments Malvolio in prison in the form of a vengeful cleric. When Malvolio leaves the play vowing revenge on the company, they know he will be back in a moment, the original audience knew it and so should we. Malvolio is the one who cuts the grant, tears up the agreement, won't lift the tax. He is for Section 28 and against a national lottery. He certainly doesn't want you to sit in a theatre.

★

To begin at the beginning. As you can read in any self-respecting introduction to *Twelfth Night, or What You Will*, its first recorded performance (not necessarily its actual first) was on the Feast of Candlemas, February 2nd, 1602, in the Middle Temple Hall of the Inns of Court, off London's Fleet Street: for this intelligence we have the casual diary entry of a young barrister called John Manningham, who attended it. He thought the play rather resembled Shakespeare's earlier *Comedy of Errors* and the *Menaechmi* of Plautus, which also feature identical twins, and he specially liked the trick whereby Malvolio is led to believe that Olivia is in love with him by a letter 'prescribing his gesture in smiling his apparraile &c'. The thought of this wintry candle-lit premiere is enticing, partly because the beautiful Middle Temple Hall is largely unchanged today – the portraits of Charles I (by Van Dyck), Charles II and James II obviously came later, but the double hammer beam roof was carved from the oaks of Windsor Forest by Elizabeth I's carpenters; from its huge Bench table she welcomed Francis Drake on his return from circling the world, and the cup-board nearby was made from the wood of his ship, the *Golden Hind*. There is an attractive series of drawings by C. Walter Hodges imaginatively reconstructing the performance – close your eyes and you're halfway there, amidst the happy laughter of the young barristers and the echoing voices of Shakespeare's colleagues, he himself perhaps playing the passionately loyal Antonio. The company had a new clown, Robert Armin, apter at impersonations and more musical than his predecessor Will Kempe: Feste, who sustains an assumed role as Sir Topas, is the first of a new sequence of Shakespearian fools who sing (*King Lear*). The play seems to have gone down well with its rather specialised audience; we are short of accounts of other performances in Shakespeare's lifetime with which to compare it, and are left with the lineaments of the published play, in the First Folio of 1623.

Twelfth Night's title, with its odd alternative (a unique ploy in Shakespeare), is forever vexatious. What is the reader supposed to think? Conventionally, a play might be named after its hero (*Macbeth, Hedda Gabler, The Misanthrope*), describe its main action (*The Taming of the Shrew, Death of a Salesman, Six Characters In Search of an Author*), or make some suggestive comment on its theme (*Life's A Dream, The Way of the World, Closer*). But *Twelfth Night*? Perhaps the story is to take place on, or have something to do with, January 6th, the Feast of the Epiphany, when Christ was baptised and when nowadays Christmas is over and the cards come down. But there is no reference to this feastday within the play, nor in fact any religious matter at all apart from Feste's clerical satire, and few other works in the canon exude such a strong sense of the summer – half of the action (its 'midsummer madness') is played out in a garden, with a tree sufficiently in leaf for three people to hide behind.

Perhaps then the title is circumstantial. There is a view, hotly propounded by the detective-scholar Leslie Hotson in his *First Night of Twelfth Night* (1954), that the play was written as a celebration of the visit of one Don Virginio Orsino, Duke of Bracciano, to Queen Elizabeth around Twelfth Night in 1601 (a year before its Middle Temple appearance). The theory has fallen out of favour, with good reason: for one thing, though Bracciano's visit is well documented, there is no extant record of such an important performance.[1] It would in any case be an odd proceeding to name a work not after its own business but the date of its first night. Then, even if Shakespeare and his company could have written and got the play up between Boxing Day 1600 (when the Duke's visit was in fact announced) and January 6th 1601 (Shakespeare's lifetime average being two plays a year, not one a fortnight), to present the royal visitor as anything like the erratic Duke Orsino of the play – let alone the Queen as the self-indulgent Olivia and the Comptroller of the Royal Household as the pompous Malvolio, as Hotson also argues – sounds like the perfectest way to land them in jail. Elizabeth I's volatile reign hardly marked a high-day for free speech or political satire, and actors lived on a narrow ledge between patronage and disgrace. a few weeks later, in February 1601, a revival of *Richard II*, a play questioning the divine right of kings and so always a risk, was suspected of being an incitement to the Earl of Essex's rebellion, nearly landing its leading actor, Augustine Phillips (though not its distinguished author) in very hot water indeed.

The possibility that the title is a thematic hint is more fruitful. The Feast of Epiphany has been a curiously adaptable occasion, trading elements of paganism and Christianity: intended to celebrate the coming of the Magi to Christ, it had by the middle ages assumed

---

1   Shakespeare's company had in fact been advised to provide something for this occasion 'furnished with rich apparel . . . of a subject that may be pleasing to Her Majesty'; and Don Orsino wrote to his wife later that he had seen that night 'a mingled comedy, with pieces of music and dances'. The recent *Much Ado About Nothing* with its two dances (*Twelfth Night* has none) must be the better candidate.

enough aspects of the ancient Roman Saturnalia to occasion an annual Feast of Fools. In English villages, a Lord of Misrule (elected by drawing whichever portion of the Twelfth Night Cake had a bean in it) presided over a single day of lawless opportunism: in one Lincolnshire town, the peasants would fight to capture the land-lord's leather cap, and the winner was awarded land.[2] These rural holidays had their equivalent at every level of society: John Stow, in his account of pre-Elizabethan life, *The Survey of London*, confirms that at this season

> there was in the king's house, wheresoever he was lodged, a lord
> of misrule, or master of merry disports; and the like had ye in
> the house of every noble man of honour.

For one day, the masters allowed themselves to be bettered, just as officers in our armed forces traditionally serve Christmas dinner to the privates.[3] At the Inns of Court there was in any case a lively tradition of Revels: later on in the seventeenth century it became necessary to build the double-leaved doors into Middle Temple Hall to keep boisterous young lawyers from occupying it and 'keeping Christmas' well into January.

At first sight there seems to be strong support for this explanation in the play's action, especially in the humiliation of the pompously self-admiring Malvolio by a group that includes his subordinates Fabian and Maria: the play's status quo is nudged by this, and then more or less restored as the rulers consolidate their power by marriage. However, Malvolio is not a master undone by his staff, but a *parvenu* forced in the end to appreciate his proper place as a servant; and the conspiracy is driven by Sir Toby Belch, who is a knight related to Olivia, assisted by Maria, a trusted maidservant, and by Sir Andrew Aguecheek, who is from out of town and nothing to do with the household. Meanwhile the Fool Feste, a candidate if ever there was one to be Stow's 'master of merry disports', is generally an absentee, weaving adroitly through the play and avoiding its main developments. And whereas the events of a traditional day of toler-ance would be forgiven and forgotten with the morning light, the

2   The festivity was also linked to the seasons, the trunks of the apple-trees being whipped in hopes of a good harvest.

3   A one-day holiday is either a matter of benevolence or social control, depending on where you're standing: in eighteenth-century London the child chimney-sweeps, bewigged and rouged and powdered white, were allowed their Festival on May Day – but it was not till the end of the century that Parliament thought to alleviate their wretched conditions.

people of *Twelfth Night* have to survive the consequences of what they do: at the end Fabian restores the conspirators – just about – to the Countess Olivia's favour, but you should feel that his job is at stake, and in fact she leaves the question of forgiveness open. Certainly, if the steward does get reinstated, life will be forever tougher for Fabian and the rest. In other words, the beneath-stairs rebellion in *Twelfth Night* is heavy with danger – and little sense of festivity infects the lives of Orsino, Olivia or Viola, Sebastian or Antonio. All in all, the vapours of this play are too unsettling to be slept off overnight.

At a certain point scholarly speculation should be left to chase its creditable tail. Icons as they have become, it does seem that, in the years around *Twelfth Night*, Shakespeare couldn't be much troubled with his comedy titles, preferring a kind of disingenuous deprecation: in contrast to the earlier *Comedy of Errors*, *Two Gentlemen of Verona* and *Midsummer Night's Dream* (and the later *All's Well That Ends Well*), *Much Ado About Nothing* (1598) and *As You Like It* (1599) seem to brush aside any idea of celebration or summary. The very existence of a subtitle (and oddly enough a plagiarism – another *What You Will*, by John Marston, was probably written about this time), seems especially like an authorial shrug of the shoulders.[4] Perhaps we should allow ourselves the same.

However, another contemporary title was *Hamlet*, either on its way or, very probably, just written – and in the foothills around this peak there is a decided change of scenery. By the turn of the century, Shakespeare's comic writing had become bold enough to cast long, strong shadows. Malvolio threatens to return for revenge and you believe it as you don't of Shylock; Feste's enigmatic imprint is not only on the action of *Twelfth Night* but, unnervingly, on the very nature of language and theatregoing. And within the general gaiety the play's characterisations are surprisingly bleak – harsh pride in Olivia, cruelty and exploitation in Toby Belch, misogyny disguised as romanticism in Orsino, amoral malice in Feste, meanness of spirit in Malvolio but an even greater meanness in those who hound him almost to madness. At the same time, some of the play's preoccupations anticipate the next stage of Shakespeare's career: the miracle of reconciliation after mistakes and sufferings, of impossible second

---

4   Worth noting that the Elizabethan sense of 'will' was quite active, as in 'what you will into being': it is used often in the Sonnets, with an overtone of sexual impulse or passionate whim – and as a reference to the poet's name.

chances and redeeming accident, will soon animate *Cymbeline, Pericles* and *The Winter's Tale*.

The fact is that Shakespeare was not an author who would surprise his audience with an uproarious farce after a major tragedy and vice versa. The Romantic concept of autobiographical literature lay well ahead, but it is quite reasonable to trace a cautious line through his life: his prodigious imagination and ability to respond to market demand don't contradict the fact that he wrote from the heart, and some of its movements are traceable. In the five years before *Twelfth Night*, he had lost, as well as his uncle Henry Shakespeare and his father John, his eleven-year-old son Hamnet (the twin of his daughter Judith, who by the way lived to seventy-seven); and though one of the conventional sources of *Twelfth Night* does propose identical twins for farcical purposes, it does not insist on their mortal separation. Even if such detective efforts feel uneasy, there is an obvious deepening of Shakespeare's tone on the way to the great tragedies, which themselves modulate into the late 'romances' – even if the brilliant unclassifiables (*Troilus, All's Well, Measure for Measure*) tend to muddle the neat equation. *Twelfth Night* sits on a bend in the road: near enough ten years' playwriting done, with ten to go (though production is to slow up a bit from now on), it touches on both past and future. The conventions of mistaken identity and sexual ambiguity (*The Comedy of Errors, Two Gentlemen of Verona*) are still a comic *lingua franca* with the audience: but now they are also an alibi for mortal thoughts. Arguably, this play marks the last time Shakespeare was to give his spectators anything like what they wanted: now, their smiles faltering, he leads them into the compassless dark.

This development is also reflected in the way he handled his sources – in the deviations more than the debts. Shakespeare was both a trawler of literary precedents and a re-cycler of his own best ideas,[5] which he would transform according to fashion and his temper. A number of sixteenth-century Italian light comedies feature the joke of a woman disguised as a man who woos on behalf of someone she herself is in love with – in one such, indeed, she is

5   It is remarkable to observe the dazzling self-plagiarism by which Antipholus of Syracuse (*The Comedy of Errors*) reacts to the same wonderful overture as Sebastian receives from Olivia in this play; or to compare Proteus instructing the adoring Julia (disguised as his page Sebastian) to woo for him in *The Two Gentlemen of Verona* with Orsino and Cesario. And Andrew Aguecheek has a not-so-distant cousin in Slender in *The Merry Wives of Windsor*.

called Cesare, and in another Fabio. A sort of novella called *Apolonius and Silla*, first published in 1581 as part of Barnaby Riche's anthology *A Farewell to Military Profession* – and popular enough to be reprinted twice – tells the story of a wealthy widow wooed by a lord, of a storm at sea and a sea captain who tries to rape the heroine during it; the heroine then enters the service of the lord, whom she has always loved, and finds herself wooing the widow for him, only to be fallen in love with by her. Her twin brother then arrives and is immediately taken to bed by the shortsighted widow: the result is a pregnancy, which the lord suspects to be the work of the disguised heroine.

Quite obviously, Shakespeare cleaned up this racy tale: there is none of the lyricism of *Twelfth Night* in Barnaby Riche, and none of the emotional undertow. Also, the Toby–Maria–Malvolio–Aguecheek–Feste plot is completely original to Shakespeare – proof, if proof were needed, of his subtle instinct for making one story work against another. Much of the comic suspense of *Twelfth Night* depends on the potential impact of one world on its opposite. So does its music, since the counterpoint between the comics' easy, flexible prose and the aristocrats' self-conscious verse is of a wit and subtlety that no writer before Shakespeare, and perhaps none after, has mastered. When Malvolio's planet collides for a moment with Toby's in the scullery, when the Countess Olivia is subjected to the whiff of pickled herrings, when Orsino is forced to witness the foolish Aguecheek with his broken coxcomb, you hear magnificent harmonies.

In practice, the innovations win out, by miles; and, rather than any romantic conventions, it is the single figure of Malvolio, the pitifully officious steward battling against the devils of disorder while nourishing a rich fantasy life of his own, that has kept the play theatrically afloat. Even Toby, Andrew, Maria and Feste owe much of their vitality to their relationship with him. In 1623 the play was presented by what had been Shakespeare's own company under the title *Malvolio*; and Charles I wrote this name as an aide-memoire in the margin of his copy of the 1632 Folio edition.[6] And like many Shakespeares, *Twelfth Night* only survived the next three hundred years in any recognisable form because of the egos of actor-managers attracted by a fine part. There were many worse fates dogging it, such as piecemeal theft of the plot (by Wycherley among

---

6   He also wrote 'Pyramus and Thisby' in the margin of *A Midsummer Night's Dream*: serious fellow as he was, it is clear what sort of thing he liked most in the theatre.

others, for his savage *Plain Dealer*) and various 'improved' versions, presumably pleasing to the public but scorned by the good writers of the day – Samuel Pepys, seeing one such, thought this a 'silly play'. In 1771 Olivia sang a song, and in 1818 Sebastian did as well; 1820 saw a fullblown operatic version, with numbers such as 'Cesario, By the Roses of the Spring', as well as inclusions from other plays and the Sonnets – 'Who is Silvia?' and 'Full Many a Glorious Morning Have I Seen'. In 1894 there were not one but two shipwreck scenes, preceded by a song, 'Come Unto These Yellow Sands' (brought in from *The Tempest*), as fishermen and peasants strolled along the shore; 'Who is Silvia' became 'Who is Olivia' in a setting by Schubert, and in 1901 Orsino and Viola were married in Illyria Cathedral.

More loyally, Charles Macklin brought the original play back into the London repertoire in the mid-1740s after an absence of thirty years, and in the nineteenth century both Samuel Phelps (a great Shakespearian who gave a wary public thirty of the plays) and Henry Irving sustained it by applying their gifts to Malvolio. At that century's end, Herbert Beerbohm Tree, who combined a crass over-pictorialism in his productions with genuine innovation in his own performances, played the part against a gigantic garden set (copied by his designer from an illustration in *Country Life*), complete with staircase, which he duly fell down; he was followed around throughout by four identical miniature Malvolii. I'd like to have seen all these performances, but thank the Lord for the arrival in the early years of the twentieth century of the great Harley Granville Barker to establish the pre-eminent roles of director and ensemble which we now take more or less for granted. His version (1912, Savoy Theatre, London) cast Henry Ainley strictly as a Puritan Malvolio, quietly spoken and discreet, dour and somehow even modest.[7] That might not have given rise to much fun, but it brings us closer to the authentic colouring of the man: and making Malvolio an equal part in a team obviously gives the audience a chance to look at the play as an organism, not just as a star's ticket to ride.

Doing so, we can see that Shakespeare has pulled off a remarkable thing, against the most ticklish of self-imposed odds: nowadays we might call it magic realism. On the one hand, Olivia's household is

---

7   'The first Malvolio of his generation that does not seem to have walked onto the stage from some municipal museum of theatrical bric-à-brac' – John Palmer, *The Saturday Review*.

detailed only a degree less explicitly than it might be in a Chekhov: its hierarchical domestic politics give the play its anchorage. On the other, a magic world is delivered in which lost twins can come out of the sea and meet again. Binding these two extremes together – and entangling various satellite worlds between them – is a cat's cradle of sexual desire, its filaments criss-crossing class and gender. Such a net of misplaced hopes could become as ominous as that of *Phèdre*; but here, as the actors play their dilemmas with all the intentness of tragedy, the audience often picks up a telltale whiff of symmetry and experiences their tensions as funny.

Deeply funny, that is. Many *Twelfth Night*s have relied on a certain dire cheerfulness, the play's corners uncritically softened: not so long ago a critic described Illyria as 'the land of total bosh' in which Olivia 'carries inanity to the extreme'. There is a sense in which this is true, since theatre, suspending the normal rules of life, can open the door to dreams: certainly, through the barely controlled vertigo of *Twelfth Night*, you glimpse an alternative, unreferenced world. But on the whole its madness is tethered to the everyday. Though the name Illyria reminds us of delirium or illusion, it was in fact part of the old Yugoslavia, and a ship from Messaline (Marseille) could quite logically be wrecked there; while the play's wildest fancies celebrate familiar truths, such as our tendency to be as blind as bats in love – and to nourish to fantastic lengths a belief that something lost might be restored. Without these touchstones, the audience wouldn't stay; and Shakespeare's comic practice, which anatomises human behaviour under fantastic exemplary circumstances,[8] is always moderated by morality, danger and social conditions.

With the same creative self-consciousness, Shakespeare often reminds you of the artificiality of his medium as he transcends it. Thus Macbeth at his greatest despair speaks of being a poor player on the stage, the child actor of Cleopatra complains that some 'squeaking Cleopatra' of the future will 'boy' her greatness, and Prospero foresees the great Globe itself dissolving. When in this play Fabian declares 'if this were played upon a stage now, I could

---

8   Even in the rare virtuosic sequences (there is one in the second half of this play) when Shakespeare feels like a simple farceur, he still allows moral consequences to nag. After their fantastic eavesdroppings, Berowne has to reason his colleagues out of real moral chancery in *Love's Labour's Lost*. When I first saw *The Comedy of Errors*, early and slight as it is, I was shocked by the initial agony and later paternal rage of old Egeon, by the hurling of Antipholus of Ephesus into a prison like Malvolio's, and that a harmless quack, Doctor Pinch, is burned, beslimed and scissored half to death.

condemn it as an improbable fiction', Shakespeare is daring us with a quotidian thought – 'if you put this in a movie you wouldn't believe it' – while mocking his own trade. It is an absurdist technique ahead of its time, without the absurdists' alienation, making us complicit and oddly enriching the material. When the same character reports later, more or less by the way, that Toby has married Maria, we recognise the loose end being tied up, as we might sense the gathering momentum in a last movement of music; at the same time we catch another, severer meaning – Maria's and Toby's efforts to secure their tenure in the household. As always, Shakespeare could do a number of things at the same time without apparent effort: a fantasy which is also a documentary and a joke about the theatre causes him little strain.

★

I didn't at first recognise the voice on the phone, which was surprising as I used to hear it a couple of times a day. In 1991 I would almost know it was Michael Bogdanov from the timbre of the bell: but I had never heard him like this, as the relative at the bedside the night before a touch-and-go operation. How was I feeling? Yes? Was I sure? I declared that I was as ready as a human can be, which is hardly ready at all; and I did know *Twelfth Night* inside out – if that helped. He laughed wanly.

I had been earning my living as an actor for twenty-seven years. Bogdanov had been a director for the same length of time. The company we ran together, the English Shakespeare Company, had arrived with a bang five years earlier with our seven-play Shakespearian History cycle (sometimes performed in a single weekend) *The Wars of the Roses*, which Michael had directed and in which I had played many kings. Although our shows since then had been a bit uneven, we were still working in a way I don't think you could see anywhere else – at its best combining the fastidiousness of traditional Shakespearian production with an unabashed modernism. We were not afraid of strategic drolleries – a newspaper seller announced the death of Edward IV with 'King Shuffles Off Mortal Coil' – but we also laboured for long hours over the pastoral intricacies of the Bohemian scenes in *The Winter's Tale*, and our attitude to verse-speaking was religious. I also know that many people will not forget the armour-encased figures of Richmond and

Richard, gold and black, slugging it out like medieval dinosaurs to Samuel Barber's *Adagio for Strings* at the climax of *Richard III* – or the Falklands campaign hooliganism with which we underscored Henry V's invasion of France. On the touring theatre circuit, the ESC, together with Kenneth Branagh's Renaissance, were pretty much kings of the road; in parallel we had run a wide educational programme, and were ahead of the field with such initiatives as fully participatory prison performances and an improvised tour of African villages with *Macbeth*.

However, after these bright beginnings, funding insecurities were squeezing the sense of adventure out of our main repertoire. A timely *Coriolanus* (1990), implicitly set in revolutionary Bucharest, had just lost us a packet, and we were rather resignedly settling on two popular favourites, *Macbeth* and *Twelfth Night*, for 1991-2: an unfriendly observer might have asked what kind of trailblazing that was. There were many reasons for this retrenchment, none of which we liked; but as it was, I was telling myself (with perhaps a degree of cunning), that we should mix our shots a little. All the same, when I announced to Michael that it would be best if I were to direct the *Twelfth Night*, it must have struck him much as it would have me if he had suddenly decided to play Hamlet.

King Umberto I of Italy said that escaping assassination was one of the incidents of his profession. Metaphorically, it is of ours too, and since England is a bit suspicious of the all-rounder, you can find yourself looking down the barrel of a gun if you change your usual job. At the time of writing, David Hare has been acting on Broadway, and Harold Pinter has always succeeded as both director and actor as well, but still – actors who direct, writers who act, directors who also design: there is something disorderly about it, a deadly whiff of dalliance. The arts press were reasonably interested in my own new hat, and soon I faced an eager reporter from *Time Out*, I think it was. His first question came rolling over the hilltops like an approaching stormcloud. What made me think I could direct? I drolly pointed out that people had so often told me that I ought to, that, although I felt a little like an electrician being recommended a carpentry course, perhaps they had a point. Tactical interviewer silence – I think he found the conceit rather fragile. At least I would understand the actors, I hurried on, perhaps protesting a little much: as an artistic director of the ESC I was on stage with the company every night, caretaking the shows as well as acting in them. Apart from a moment when a new Pistol lay on the floor in Chicago and refused to re-rehearse *Henry V* for me without Michael Bogdanov, this ambiguous role was taken by the company in good sort – I was at least sweating the same sweat as them. Very well, what was it that drew me to this *particular play*? I sensed a triangular trap: if the choice of play was untypical of the ESC, and the choice of director experimental, was the choice of play at least typical of the experimental director?

Good question. I had never been in *Twelfth Night* and hadn't necessarily seen it as a friend. In my teens, hopelessly stage-struck, I had gone to more Shakespeare than perhaps ever since; and my father, who often mixed his love with a nice line in provocation, used to lament that this had caused him to become intolerably acquainted in his middle years with this *particularly* silly play. He was at the time building for me (I put it that way because I did little but march around the sidelines barking specifications) a model theatre, a metre square and a metre-and-a-quarter high, complete with fly-tower, four battens of lights with dimmers, vomitorium entrances, Juliet balconies and fully rouched miniature curtain – at the same time hoping desperately that I would get over this mania for the stage. A few defensive jokes were the least I could allow him.[9]

I liked everything I saw in those days (and sometimes sought to emulate it – the photographs are under lock and key), though I was pitifully determined to be harsh and discriminating in my judgments. Generally, I preferred the Old Vic in London to Stratford-upon-Avon: it was something to do with the more overpowering whiff of size that came billowing off the stage as the curtain went up – one of theatre's great forgotten smells. But I did see Laurence Olivier play Malvolio (with Vivien Leigh as Viola) in *Twelfth Night* at Stratford in 1955 – and straight away judged the production's

---

9   When Life Took Over and this remarkable object fell out of use, it languished for some years in a garage, where mice ate the hardboard, the gold beading fell off, and the facing crumbled more or less to dust. Not so long ago I rebuilt it, as a homage I suppose. I had to buy three new hardboard stages, having misjudged the measurements as my father would never have done: I repainted, oiled the pulleys and blew dust off the brittle wiring. It seems you can't get 6.5 volt bulbs any more, so I worked with 5 volts and a new plastic transformer. I turned it on. After a small delay, as if an elderly man was heaving himself out of an armchair, a brown light began to glow and grow, blessing the stage once more: the wiring was intact. There it sits, in a remote corner of my house, covered with a vegetable-garden crop blanket: the politely composed features of visitors, not only of children, usually melt with pleasure at the sight of it.

broken-hearted Feste too sentimental, not far enough from Jack Point in *The Yeomen of the Guard*. I could also see that this was not one of Olivier's big hits, and approved the critic J.C.Trewin's view that his Malvolio seemed to have lived on a diet of green apples: but I liked that he kept being betrayed by social insecurity, hesitating over the pronunciation of 'slough' ('sluff?') – it was a subliminal reminder that his could have been one of the 'tinned minds' in John Betjeman's jeremiad on the Buckinghamshire town of that name.

Meanwhile, at the Vic in the same year, Judi Dench followed up a spectacular professional debut as Ophelia by playing Maria, and I was there: I have a picture of John Neville as Aguecheek looking winsome in a barrel, somewhat like the Dormouse in *Alice in Wonderland* – I dread to think how he came there. Despite its lack of Old Vic aroma, I could then see that Peter Hall's revival at Stratford in 1958 was something of a benchmark: Geraldine McEwan was a gorgeous Olivia, and Dorothy Tutin's surpassing Viola was twinned with Ian Holm as Sebastian. The show was also distinguished by Lila de Nobili's ravishing gauzy sets, which included a striking front-cloth of Feste, melancholically capering. However the production didn't please everyone: when it was revived at the height of the Cuban missile crisis in 1960, the august critic Harold Hobson declared that this 'perverse and displeasing' version, which paid 'both too much attention to words and too little' (whatever that means), had caused him as much anxiety that week as had Mr Khrushchev.

My big memories remain these early ones. I have missed many distinguished revivals since, though I had a good time at Ariane Mnouchkine's in 1982 for her radical Théâtre du Soleil at the Cartoucherie, on the outskirts of Paris, a disused munitions shed that sometimes feels like the city's theatrical centre. Under its French title, *Le Nuit des Rois*, it brandished an affronting mixture of *kathakali* and *kabuki* influences, and was irresistible. Contradicting everything you know to be true about Shakespeare – the emotional chiaroscuro, the humanity, the sense of travel – it would have been dull were it not for the dazzling virtuosity of the staging and performances, brilliant arpeggios played on a single string. Orsino had one painted tear on his chalky face, and a handkerchief longer than himself held to his other eye; Aguecheek was played by an actress with the looks and clowning skills of Giulietta Masina. Aguecheek is the only part in *Twelfth Night* I have ever fancied taking myself. I haven't done so, but my son has, in an entranced account of the play on a summer evening the same year in the walled Ashburnham Garden at Westminster School. Amidst the straw wigs, the garish make-up and the under-rehearsed young blunderings, Shakespeare was somehow at large, taking new prisoners. Such unexpected beauty is quite common when actors on the edge of adulthood (and not believing themselves actors) share unselfconsciously in an effort as great as football or choir singing. Their burgeoning testosterone and adolescent melancholy served the play's painful lyricism as touchingly as I have ever seen.

In the small hours of self-knowledge, I had to admit that all this didn't add up to a great start. If my best memories were of a school production and a French deconstruction, there might be a gap still to be closed between myself and the most complex of Shakespeare's classic comedies. I could imagine all the full-time directors I knew curling the lip, and Michael Bogdanov's long-suffering face – not to mention the critics. Meanwhile, *Time Out* was tapping his pencil, waiting for an answer. I looked him steadily in the eye and said that, like that of Viola and Sebastian, this was to be a great voyage of discovery.

★

I saw quickly that the play is difficult to cast, difficult to direct, and specially difficult to design: it defies any single image imposed across its grain. A director might insist on Feste presiding over the proceedings like an omniscient Puck, or even dreaming up the action out of nowhere, as Christopher Sly does *The Taming of the Shrew* – but I don't like it much. On the other hand, the fundamentalist fallback – a bare Elizabethan stage and no context – is a blankish choice for a modern audience, especially in the magic-box theatres in which, for better or worse, we usually work. Something has to be done: and it seemed to me that *Twelfth Night* could only benefit from as documentary a starting-point as it could bear. All the more so since such reality is constantly battling with the ungovernable: indeed, in the second half the sense of location becomes so delirious that Antonio seems to be arrested simultaneously in Olivia's garden and Illyria's main square. While I retreated before the approach of John Draper's *The Twelfth Night of Shakespeare's Audience* (1950), which precisely analyses Olivia's house in its progress from feudalism to economic modernity (and each character in terms of social status, psychology and even astrology), I felt there was a lot to be said for his cast of mind. Practically, we would have to design a set with enough realistic detail to suggest that Olivia's world is the play's central structure, but not let it immobilise us – in the early stages the location alternates at great speed between there and Orsino's palace, the seashore and the street. We would be touring to many different venues, not all with efficient overhead flying, not all with much wing space. So we needed some adaptable machine, its components sliding or being drawn aside. If that could be done swiftly, we would get reasonably close to Shakespeare's inspired jump-cutting from scene to scene, which sometimes resembles that of a screenplay. The deeper question remained: where should we be, and at what time?

The weary old debate about non-Elizabethan settings for Shakespeare seems to have quietened down, its arguments worn smooth at last. Most people would agree that it is as futile to choose 1600 as the starting-point for a modern production as it would have been for the actors of 1600 to dress in the period of four hundred years before that.[10] But straightforward modern dress, apparently the quickest route to an audience, is a little problematic all the same. If a director encourages his actors to reach back to an Elizabethan temper of mind, but at the same time abandons puffed trousers and the constricting farthingale, the improbable consequence may be a man in a copied Armani suit pirouetting with the passionate vehemence of Mercutio, or a girl in Doc Martens trying to sound like Beatrice. In each case, their linguistic fluency puts any image of contemporary life, with its jargonistic, image-led Babel, to shame. At the ESC, we looked for parallels with any period or culture almost as a matter of charter, but our choices were generally volatile and allusive, a series of implications only. Sometimes we would start with what the actors pulled off a costume rail: with some canny adjustments, their choices would resolve into images of conspirators in combat fatigues, Bonnie Prince Charlie kilts and civilian suits, all sitting round the same campfire – a witty and chaste assembly with the players looking to the manner born. This allusiveness suited the tapestry-work of the History plays very well, but it worried me for *Twelfth Night* –

---

10   We know they didn't, from the only extant illustration of a performance in Shakespeare's own lifetime. This is a drawing by Henry Peacham, in what is known as the Longleat Manuscript. It shows the actors in *Titus Andronicus* in their own modern dress, with token togas and tabards thrown over it.

I feared to see, say, an Elizabethan country-house for Olivia with a jolly Toby-jug Belch, a fin-de-siècle Orsino, and a Dungeness-like wasteground for the shipwreck. The play's moral tensions would be better served by some consistent world not too far from the audience's experience; at the same time Shakespeare's vulgar, super-articulate grace might find an enlightening equivalent in another culture than ours.

It is not unusual for a director to retreat from the present day,[11] and at the same time to incline towards the mediterranean, especially in comedy – it's an astute double alibi. Sure enough, I too was heading south, hoping this was a true response to the play. Where is the heart worn on the sleeve as clamorously as it is by Orsino, or as proudly as by Olivia? What about the fatalism of Viola? Or the reckless friendship of Antonio and Sebastian, who would presumably travel the streets in a walking embrace? In Andalusia, in southern Spain, so little seems to have changed: you could be at any moment in the 1920s or the 1990s, and there are still great estates, *latifundia*, held by absentee owners who know little of the land. On them, a hired administrator can gain disproportionate control, as Malvolio does over Olivia. Here, one side of the street can be sunlit and the other in deep shadow, an effect spiritually acknowledged in the phrase *sol y sombra*: and there is no bright surface in *Twelfth Night* without a shadow running alongside it. No shortage of licence in the Spanish Festival calendar either: for instance, a special Day for Fools and Bellringers, the great Tomato Battle in Buñol in Valencia, and a day in Segovia when the married women take over the town, elect their own Mayor and harass the men. Perhaps it is this world – fierce sun, dark interiors, fiesta gaiety, morbid introspection – that Viola and her brother have fallen into, travelling not east to the Dalmatian coast but west towards the Balearic Islands. In a culture as extreme in economics as in climate, they see dispossessed peasants tilling the soil by hand, and a distribution of wealth so uneven that many people have to hold down two jobs in order to live. Antonio, a poor man, loves Sebastian so much he gives him the little money he has. Feste's begging for tips can come across to a modern audience as just so much fun, but it reflects a bitter reality in which virtually nobody is safe: he, Fabian, Maria and her staff must hang on to their positions or end up in a doorway.

11   But no further back than the Victorian period, before which clothes look like remote costume to us.

I was foolishly excited, as if I had stumbled on the answer to a crossword clue without checking the number of letters. I also knew that Shakespeare always leads you into this sort of discovery, and then slips the knot, leaving you looking flashy. It would be a matter of seeing if it worked with the actors in rehearsal, commonsense to hand if we struck the gong too loudly. Feste with a little cigar and a pale young Priest, his biretta parked by his side, might well play cards in a bar, but there was no question of flat-hatted policemen wildly blowing whistles. There should be no *Concerto de Aranjuez* on the soundtrack, nothing from *Sketches of Spain*, and if any tango, then only for the lightest of self-mocking purposes. With caution, it would all fit. Toby Belch could once have been a Francoist officer: there is a martinet energy in him and he might dance the military *paso doble*. Andrew Aguecheek could be from up-country, the gauche heir to a sherry fortune perhaps, looking for a bride. Malvolio has often enough been played as a would-be Spanish grandee – Charles Lamb complimented Bensley's 'old Castilian' (1777), and Henry Irving (1884) was said to look like 'some great Spanish hidalgo' out of a Velasquez painting. Above all the idea would work for Feste, an entertainer with a name like a carnival, who would sing a raw *cante jondo* but pass in a crowd as a butcher; for the conservative ceremoniousness of Olivia's household; for Orsino's intertwined savagery and lyricism; and perhaps Goya's portrait of Doña Isabel de Porcel – black mantilla, creamy lace, her costume all middle-aged propriety but her young eyes alert for something new – is close to the châtelaine Olivia herself.

★

We couldn't afford the mantilla, so Doña Isabel ended up on the poster instead; meanwhile Claire Lyth designed heavy burgundy brocades for Orsino's quarters and black lace draperies for Olivia's sorrowful mansion; for the exteriors, high dark green Moorish towers, some with long narrow windows and others tessellated with tiny translucent grilles, their verticals casting deep shadows; black ironwork furniture on a floor of diamond-patterned gold and green Spanish tiles; and, spectacularly, when the play moves out into Olivia's garden, a triptych of lightweight iron trees, furiously contorted but held within rectangular trellis panels. The sky was at all times as high and wide as the variety of venues permitted, having been designed for the highest and widest. The whole look, though less brooding, was remarkably like the angular abstracts that used to be designed by Edward Gordon Craig, and receptive to the steep light which Michael Bogdanov would design for it.[12] A changing world of street-alleys, courtyards and interior corridors was to be created through a crafty combination of textures.

In Notting Hill we found an improbable and presumably unrepeatable orange raw silk suit for Andrew Aguecheek which shouted Tourist – or perhaps Superannuated Rock Star:[13] he progressed in the second half to Hawaian shirt, shorts and sandals. After an early flirtation with suede, Viola as Cesario ended up in a delicate grey flannel suit enlivened by a burgundy waistcoat and jaunty buttonhole. As if she was stepping cautiously into sunlight, Olivia moved from deep Edwardian mourning to light black lace over white satin, and Orsino from designer *déshabillé* to designer-floppy black suit. Toby borrowed a guards uniform from our *Wars of the Roses* to officiate over Andrew's and Cesario's duel, its tunic clanking with unearned medals. For some time we were stumped by the special problem of Malvolio in his yellow stockings and cross-garters. This essentially Elizabethan image is certainly funny, but with the passage of time has lost much of its embarrassing quality, its hint of inappropriate sexuality. One morning in the tube I looked along a row of identical pinstriped legs to see that one pair resolved into outrageously garish socks: I mentally rolled up this gentleman's trousers and imagined a glimpse of suspenders above the hectic legwear – reflecting how these always look both silly and sleazy, especially with lots of black hairs around them. Panning back down, I imagined not fashionable slip-ons but heavy black brogues to round it all off, and sent the unwitting commuter on his way, satisfied that I had met Malvolio in love.

Twelfth Night requires an ensemble of a dozen actors of more or less equal power, carefully balanced and appreciating their dependence on each other. This is untypical of Shakespeare: if you leave aside *Troilus and Cressida*, another wonderful team play (for the men, at least), and the infinite variety of *Henry IV*, only *A Midsummer Night's Dream* offers such a range of leading parts. Orsino, Toby,

---

12   In a style which the *Evening Standard* was, unaccountably, to call 'harsh Adriatic'.

13   There's the rub. Andrew needs longish hair because of Toby's jokes about it, and in modern dress may look like a restaurateur, a pirate or a doleful Rod Stewart. Tie it up in a pony-tail and it looks worse. I don't have an answer to this.

Andrew, Feste, Olivia, Malvolio, Viola, Maria and, I would argue, Fabian, are all absolutely central, and Sebastian and Antonio can't let matters down either: it comes as a surprise to find that on a straight line-count Toby Belch is probably the biggest part, and even this is hard to prove as he is all in prose and so it depends which edition you're using. It is difficult enough to get all this balanced up at the best of times; I was setting out under the curious circumstance that the company would go on in the New Year to do Michael Bogdanov's production of *Macbeth*, essentially a two-character play in which I was to be the Thane. Not so easy to explain to your Olivia that she is going to have to be a Witch after Christmas, or that Caithness is worth the attention of a Toby Belch.

The casting of the twins, Viola and Sebastian, causes many anxieties, most of them pointless. There have been occasions when Viola has contrived to double as her brother,[14] but it takes too much stage management and draws attention to itself, like casting Hermione and Perdita together in *The Winter's Tale*. If you choose a period when, as they say, you can't tell the boys from the girls – the Caroline (long hair for the men), or our own (short hair common for the women) – you can halve the problem; but it's a pity to make the choice for that one reason. The fact is that if the actors have much the same height and colouring, the difference in bone-structure matters surprisingly little – identical male-and-female twins are in any case a biological impossibility, and they tend to be alike in physical proportions only. Sebastian and Viola need to be close enough for the cast to mistake without too much kindness from the audience – how accurately does anyone register a face anyway? – and much more important is the sibling gene: a touch of tenderness in the manly Sebastian (he weeps as soon as we meet him), and a good fist at masculinity learned from him in Viola.

Jenny Quayle was born to play Viola; and though Vivian Munn was not as close a lookalike for her as other contenders,[15] they were to find an instinctive kinship, mirroring each other's temperament and body-language so well that they became like the two halves of an egg. Maria (Tracey Mitchell) was young and black – unfashionably,

14 Kate Terry did it in 1865 at the Olympic in London, and Jessica Tandy in 1937 at the Old Vic (when Laurence Olivier played Toby Belch 'like a veteran Skye terrier' – J.C. Trewin).

15 What a tiresome part to audition for – you know that you are being compared to someone who is probably already hired, and judged for things you can't control.

the audience was not asked to be colour-blind but to take the precise point, so that her involvement with Toby seemed unequal but tender, somehow forbidden – this was to be an Hispanic society that gives its minorities servant roles, no rights and a permanent need for male protection. Michael Mueller would be a Monaco brat-pack Orsino, pursuing Ally Byrne's impulsive Olivia, who was certainly young enough to have had greatness thrust upon her. She would also be a good victim for the *apparatchik* Malvolio of Timothy Davies, on whose hatchet face I could foresee a permanent rictus of discomfort – owing something to shame and pride, and something to the heaviness of a black woollen suit making him a little malodorous in the southern sun. Derek Smith (who was acting before I was, let alone directing), would make a peppery and intelligent Toby; James Hayes, who had done Autolycus for us, would be ideal for Andrew; Alan Cody, a Cornishman, had the clear-eyed honour of Antonio, and Sean Gilder an equally unforced chippiness for Fabian. In an ESC tradition, we had three professional debutants in a cast of fifteen, one of them (Ed Little) plucking ravishing arpeggios from a Spanish guitar. Feste, who at that time I imagined as something like Manet's *Spanish Singer*, but later desentimentalised into braces and beret, would be the innocent but very experienced Colin Farrell: thirty years earlier he had been one of the best Justice Shallows I have ever seen, at the age of eighteen, in the Youth Theatre, and was recently a brilliant trombone-playing Bardolph in our *Henry IV*. Now he would have to learn the accordion. Giving a local habitation and a name to Shakespeare's extravagant abstracts was a great relief: now they *had* to be these people and none other. It all began to feel like a reality.

I at first rehearsed with more punctiliousness than flair: the sessions seldom overran, but you win no Oscars for that. I had known for a lifetime that a director has to go round to work: an offhand remark may provoke a creative riff better than an hour of discussion. And you must know when to let be for a bit if the actor is cooking up on his or her own. Choose your moment to nag; encourage even when you're infuriated (frightened horses bolt); come down heavily only on laziness; if you're an actor too, don't demonstrate. These skills generally take some time to learn: I had five weeks. For the first of them, we tested the Spanish idea to see if it fitted – a genial collusion in a *fait accompli*, as the set was already being built. That was fine, but I think in other ways the cast felt a bit constricted – not because I was dictating, but because there just wasn't enough carnival in the air: I hadn't mastered the sleight of hand that pretends there is lots of time to play about in. However, developing the music with Terry Mortimer, who understood exactly the necessary yearning quality, I felt on song. Two kinds swiftly developed: plangent rhapsodies for Orsino to languish to, and then Feste's folk music to excite him. The latter would be guttural, harsh and bluesy, not so much *flamenco* perhaps but the more fatalistic Portuguese *fado*: however, listening to it issue from Colin Farrell's open throat and heart, you could hear the wind howling across the central Sierra. As we insinuated a hint of *Viva España* into the Keystone Cops chase of Viola and Malvolio through the Madrid traffic – horns, streetcars and bicycles – and then hit on Scarlatti's *Stabat Mater* (the one non-original theme) for Sebastian's union first with Olivia and then with his sister, it struck me that I might be better at directing a musical of the play than the original.

We opened at the beautiful Theatre Royal in Nottingham, where the proscenium is significantly higher than wide and there is plenty of room for a cyclorama to be lit from behind, so that the set looked terrific (and the actors rather small). This was a miracle as, built at a distance from London and consequently difficult to supervise, it had turned up painted not in green metallic car paint as ordered, but in some supposed scenic equivalent ideal for panto: each horrible inch had to be re-done by any available hand, and while this was going on Orsino's metal chair was stolen. From there we moved on to Newcastle, Northampton, Wolverhampton and Blackpool, to Leeds and Plymouth and Hull, on a familiar ESC ticket, until Christmas. In a small pool of light like a prison cell, Michael Mueller, barefoot and spreadeagled on the floor, began the play with a single, exhausted musician, his new chair thrown down behind him. The scene dissolved through heavy draperies (built on gauzes) to the spotlit figure of Viola on the seashore – the first of several editorial devices linking the two characters. Where possible, each new arrival – Viola as Cesario, Feste, Toby and Sebastian – was pinpointed for a moment like this in the change preceding their appearance, initialising their scene. Toby Belch broke in with his disgruntled comments on Olivia's mourning as he watched the household's solemn return from church (led by a Priest who would remain in constant attendance on her, finally marrying her to Sebastian) while black drapery corridors closed in from every side.

Weaving his way through these, Feste arrived to something like the Harry Lime theme from *The Third Man*. The tolling bell that had accompanied the procession announced the main arrival of Olivia, at which point the whole picture seemed to slide into monochrome – a bit too much so, I later decided, for any comedy. Toby and Andrew, having danced their way into town, returned to this mausoleum with much mock trepidation for a nightcap, bedecked with the balloons and ribbons of a street fiesta, and carrying – a cultural liberty – panettones. They sang an aria from *Carmen* to enrage Malvolio in his nightshirt, and on their way to bed got one of their bigger laughs blearily watching the set reorganise itself around them. Malvolio, promenading in the garden, got Maria's letter stuck to his foot as if it were something left by a dog – we abandoned this joke later as only the Dress Circle could see it, but for a while it was a pleasure to watch him stride obliviously to and fro. On the same spot, Olivia, out of mourning, shockingly kneeled to beg Cesario for love. Feste entertained the house during the interval by teaching himself the bongos. Andrew's challenge to Cesario 'in a martial hand . . . curst and brief', was written on a scroll that, unfurled, was as tall as he was: the duel that followed was attended by Maria and a Gentlewoman dressed as Red Cross nurses, but no blow was struck since neither party knew at all what to do. In his prison, Malvolio's seemingly disembodied head peered through the grille of a specially narrow tower like a vertical coffin, and he arrived for his showdown with Olivia pathetic and proud in long combinations. By now Spanish lanterns hung on the ironwork trees to lighten the dusk. Much of the action had taken place in a single day – it had begun with Feste singing 'Come Away Death' in an uncanny whooping falsetto, and as his mood intensified, a violet sky had turned to bright white, as if you were looking into the eye of the rising sun. This sun began to set flaming red as Sebastian fell in love with Olivia. The lanterns were taken indoors at the end and the house closed up by the united couples, leaving Andrew to make his way home and Feste to sing alone in a cold night light. At the end of this final song Malvolio returned as he had promised, very quietly and seriously, that he would, looking somewhat like an Arts Council officer of the time (the ESC was arguing about its grant – what did I have to lose?). Accompanied by two removal men and carrying a clipboard, he sneered at Feste's proffered cap, dismissed the set, and snapped his fingers to turn off the lights and close the theatre.

For this I was duly chastised by certain critics who believed that Shakespeare should always 'speak for himself'.[16] I can only say that it is not Shakespeare's fault that he occasionally needs a translator. Malvolio commonly goes off nowadays to a pleasing small shudder of apprehension, but the Elizabethans would have been scared stiff of the puritannical bigotry he represented – it would soon close the playhouses and damage their cosmopolitan culture almost beyond recovery. Some of us sensed that in 1991, too, Malvolio was a figure who stretched beyond the play; so I call it licence in a good cause.

So far so good; but as the weeks rolled by, the show remained no more than serviceable, and the performances curiously constricted. I more than anybody longed for some demon of misrule to disrupt it all. I blamed myself and the cast by turns, at one date cheering them on, at the next rather self-consciously carpeting them: neither approach made the damn thing shift. The press and public responses were indeterminate ('One should be grateful. And yet . . . ' – *The Times*). That we were still very provisional was borne out by a visit from the directors of the Chicago Festival: they had bought the show for the following spring sight unseen, on the strength of *The Wars of the Roses* five years earlier, and they now threatened to withdraw. Having talked them round, I had the rare pleasure of seeing the production bloom into one of their hits. Approaching the Christmas break, we rehearsed again for a couple of afternoons a week and re-designed a few of the clothes: though tired, the actors welcomed it, and the play's floor began to ease open, revealing some of its depths at last.

In the New Year the production got an unexpected boost with the arrival in the rep of *Macbeth*: after the stress of playing that darkest of tragedies, to return to *Twelfth Night* two or three times a week was a tonic, and the performances began to sing. In February we went abroad with both plays, again on a familiar ESC route through Tokyo to Chicago, but this time to Seoul as well, the first time the company had visited Korea and the first time I had myself been since 1975, when the capital was still patrolled by American troops. At that time a midnight curfew sent people scuttling nervously home through the streets of their own city; I have an indelible image of amateurish prostitutes huddled in the doorways of international

---

16   One of them complained that I misunderstood the play's hierarchy because I let Feste put his feet up on Olivia's table – as if this had just happened by default rather than being entirely planned, as an illustration of Feste's exceptional licence in the house.

hotels, making split-second decisions – in for a chancy foreign investment of their own or home without being arrested. By 1991 the military had shrunk back to the north-south border and Margaret Thatcher was hailing South Korea as a triumphant model of capitalism, though I doubt if it had done much for the female slaves. Even with Hyundai and Samsung in the international top twenty, the air of prosperity hanging over the capital (mingled with severe pollution and the pervasive smell of garlic and pickled cabbage) was tentative, as if a colony of skyscrapers had been built on a shanty-town. Like a final symbol, a huge and filthy river, the Han, flows through Seoul with hardly a boat on it, ever – it comes out into the sea precisely at the trigger-happy borderline and so is useless for trade. A commuter stuck in the daily traffic jam on the bridge can reflect on this baulked opportunity as he prepares another day of economic marvels and struggles to breathe.

Humiliation brutalises, in matters great and small. The Korean Broadcasting System had invited the ESC: they'd never handled such a big company before, didn't know how to do it, and weren't about to be told. It was quite something to see inexperience combine with an absolute refusal to lose face. A first visit to the performance hall, forty-eight hours before we were to open, revealed that though KBS had offered to build a duplicate set rather than paying to fly ours out, construction hadn't been started. By a true economic miracle, our crew swiftly built one in conditions of high tension in local workshops, while the British Council stood hopefully by, their feet in perpetual motion from side to side. Meanwhile the antagonists in the showdown – our production manager and myself on one hand, their head of production and director on the other – screamed at each other like banshees, re-enacting in little the bullying transactions that have so scarred the history of this beautiful country.[17] Of course, everyone ended up in drunken embraces after the opening, all brought together by Shakespeare in action. As in so many unhappy cultures, there is a heartbeat here that defies global puppeteering, war and poverty – a hungry response to art, be it their own beautiful ceramics or some

---

17   At one point in these tussles, the KBS master carpenter threw his fist in the air as if he were going to take a swing at us, but in fact to demonstrate an armpit damp with the sweat of exhaustion, yelling: 'Look! Am I not depraved?' Once the set was built, KBS, sensing an advantage, managed to sell it back to us, and then dispatched it to Chicago significantly the worse for wear.

touch of nature sensed under the incomprehensible language of a four-hundred-year-old Englishman. So somehow we got on, got through and got out; and since in most matters between Japan and Korea, Japan has always looked worse, unacceptably worse, it felt odd, the following week, to rush with relief from all the hostile duplicity into the solicitous arms of Seiya Tamura at the Tokyo Globe Theatre.

We went from Japan to the Blackstone Theatre in Chicago, where Helen Hayes and the Barrymores used to play,[18] and reached London in early summer, where the show was warmly welcomed by some members of the press who had never been friends of mine as an actor. The common link between all the foregoing dates was a series of increasingly ominous faxes coming my way: the ESC was beginning to nose-dive. The Arts Council of Great Britain, on whom we depended for subsidy, had appointed as new director of its Touring Department a pleasant enough man from the British Council in Paris with no discernible qualifications for the specialised job. He worked under a Chairman best described as an opinionated dilettante,[19] but was really led by the hand by an ambitious deputy in his own department who, like Malvolio, demonstrated what fills a power vacuum. Noisily chomping sandwiches at our Board meetings, these doubtful characters insisted that, even though the ESC had proved itself several times over, we must now, if we were to qualify for continued support, supply a detailed three-year plan budgets, schedules, the lot – not to mention principal casting and the design concept twelve months ahead of any new production. Any fool can do this speculative exercise, dreaming away, but any fool knows that it is miles away from the natural rhythm of theatre, and therefore undeliverable. Tying up our staff in miles of paperwork, I obediently went away and returned, in good faith, with a season that included Simon Russell Beale as Hamlet and Adrian Lester as Pericles, on a budget that, for certain good reasons, would surely make a profit.[20] This was a partial means of subsidising (so that we would need less from the Arts Council) a brilliant but

18   Where I had the odd experience of having to go on, because of some understudy foulup, as Valentine for a few nights, and so had the pleasant impression of being in the stokingroom of some great ship of which I had lost command.

19   And who was also on the Board of one of the touring companies competing with us for funds – the Arts Council is either weighed down with too much middle management and too few artists, or has too many artists with vested interests.

admittedly expensive Michael Bogdanov plan – Goethe's two-part *Faust* (music by Michael Nyman, translation by Howard Brenton, set by Pina Bausch's designer Peter Pabst) which would answer the Council's demand that the ESC become big-scale and unexpected again: like jaded libertines, that wanted us to turn exciting tricks while still fumbling with their wallets. The plan wasn't approved – nor was *The Seagull* ('a boring choice'). As we struggled through the circular conversations, vainly pointing to written promises now broken and wondering why we were once again auditionees, it dawned on us that we were, in code, being shown the door – as was Compass, the Council's other dedicated touring company in the big regional theatres. It was cheaper for them to tour units half the size of ours, or to ambulance-chase the RSC or the National – that is, by guaranteeing them against occasional losses while taking public credit for the association.

Altogether, it was a dismal time in the arts, with bad faith all over the place: ousted Arts Ministers tried to get on the side of the angels by denouncing their successors, arts organisations faced obviously unmeetable criteria. Next to the best European models of subsidy England remains an absolute disgrace, and these local troubles did symbolise the Tory government's utter indifference to culture – what flickering energy it felt was being devoted to the idea of dismantling the Arts Council altogether and devolving its brief to regional arts boards ill-equipped to handle the extra burden. What a pity the Council didn't share their anxieties with their clients instead of defensively blaming them, or quietly advise us to save our time instead of shuffling around emptying the ashtrays.

Taking the deep hint, I prepared a noisy resignation, without consulting my chairman, Luke Rittner, or even Michael Bogdanov – an act of treachery which short-cut a lot of pointless discussion and which both of them have, I think, just about forgiven by now. I felt that we had reached the end, and that a genuine sense of public grievance would be a witty enough way of masking our own battle-fatigue. Most good ideas in the theatre have a metabolic life of about five years, at which point they should either stop, institutionalise or – marvellous euphemism – redefine. I didn't think we should do the latter – though it must be said that the ESC has survived with Michael as its sole director and myself as the kind of picky board

20 I see you smile, but it can be done. If the cast is small, the play big enough for the major stages and the company has the following we still had, you can't really fail.

member we both used to dread. At the time, my gesture did provoke, by way of embarrassment, a few more pence from the Arts Council, and I was relieved on every score: after six years on the road, I was myself beginning to feel like the itinerant actor described by Ben Jonson in the 1590s, 'shoes full of gravel, going after a blond jade and hamper . . . to stalk upon boards and barrel heads, to an old cracked trumpet'. The touring life is both austere and haphazard, and I had no further stomach for the compromises – fit up fast on Monday, do your best on Monday night, spend the rest of the week getting the show steady again, before travelling on and starting all over. I wanted to feel that the stage I had left on Saturday I would find at the same temperature, in the same light, with the same acoustic, on the Monday.

The ESC has left a strangely faint mark on the profession, but our unspoiled and desirous audiences had been supremely rewarding; and I have a lasting pride in having done something to help young actors trained for television to conquer a new 1500-seat theatre every week without effort. Also, I knew producers' problems as well as I did actors', and am now maddeningly fairminded when the latter condemn the former as exploitative devils. *Twelfth Night* had put something unexpected into the ESC's pot – colour, unabashed romance, festivity – but it was in quite steep contrast to our typical style, and for a maverick company perhaps a consistent style is all. Turning these changes over, I would look in on the production in London, simply for pleasure – it was like drinking long draughts of clear water after the stewed tea of theatre politics. We were *Time Out*'s recommended choice throughout the run and I hoped my interviewer had noticed. Having taken so long to cook up, the show had reached a conclusive point where I could assess what had and hadn't been achieved. The balance-sheet was rather surprising. As an untrained actor thirty years before I had been at great pains to prove myself *technically* adequate; and now, as a director, I had been much concerned to master light, sound and choreography, which were where the main strengths seemed to lie – the highly-drilled scene changes were a pleasure to watch, and one or two were quite virtuosic. The musical reprises were witty – a wobbly version of Viva España for the drunken knights, and very *legato* restatements of 'Mistress Mine' and 'Come Away Death' for the gentler transitions. Built up from such details, much of the show was infectious, definitely uplifting, and the curtain call was great fun.

On the other hand I had perhaps helped the actors only a bit – and mainly to disguise their particular weaknesses rather than to find anything unexpected; and as ever, stage experience showed. Too often I hadn't found the magic word, or the magic silence. And the Spanish setting, though it was justifiable and entertaining, was an imposition, of course – you were watching a version, not quite the unmistakeable *play*. I don't altogether know what you do about this: a choice of milieu in Shakespeare always has some limiting effect, and yet I no longer want to see the plays 'speaking for themselves'. This sort-of-Spain was not, after all, organic: it arose from my homework rather than the actors' associations, an exotic alibi that everyone had to aspire to as well as rising to a great text. Similarly, most of the gags (and some were a bit self-conscious) arose from predeterminations of mine rather than the actors' inventions. And Malvolio's return at the end now seemed heavy-handed. Too many times, the play seemed to have been subdued to the concept rather than released, tent-pegged where it should have flapped freely, especially if the playing was ever a bit slow. I had certainly been thinking in a fresh way about Shakespeare – even my father might have enjoyed it – but, for all the hard work and good days we'd had, I could see that I hadn't (who has?) quite caught the evasive grace of this play, its deluded eroticism, its profound sense of fugue. What I didn't know was that our visit to Tokyo had given Seiya Tamura of the Globe Theatre an idea, and that the following year I would be getting another chance.

PART ONE

ACT ONE

Act 1 Scene 1–Act 1 Scene 5

1.1. He starts with the authority of a king but with a rather un-kingly instruction:

> If music be the food of love, play on . . .

This is Orsino, though it will be some time before we learn the name. We could be indoors or out, by day or by night: a concert is in progress, and there has been a pause between items. Orsino clearly expects a lot of the occasion:

> Give me excess of it, that, surfeiting,
> The appetite may sicken, and so die

– which seems tough on his musicians, who are likely to be practical people. His words are smooth, but his feelings, clearly, less so: he wants the beautiful music not for its own sake but to kill off a painful need.

  The players count themselves in and start again – but then Orsino notices something and tells them to go back a little:

> That strain again; it had a dying fall . . .

It is another difficult order. The musicians confer, decide from which bar to start, then get going in unison once more – whereupon they are stopped altogether:

> Enough, no more;
> 'Tis not so sweet now as it was before.

What a life.

  There is another way of doing it, and it is less absurd. Orsino's opening line could be a grand cue for the beginning of the concert, and 'that strain again' not be an order at all, but his quiet appreciation of a phrase as it is repeated in the tune. In this sweeter version, many silences lap around the lines for the music to play in, and the musicians don't have to keep stopping and starting. In fact, you hardly notice them, but get a strong impression of the romantic hero, languishing in the appropriate key. If the musicians' dilemmas made for a little comedy the first way, this is a rhapsodic colour-wash.

Satire or stardust, or how much of each? In this play, the choice will present itself every few minutes.

Either way, Orsino's abrupt order marks the end of the beginning, and in the silence all attention swings onto him. He will surely explain himself, and begin a story: but instead, he apostrophises about the 'spirit of love'. It is, for him, 'quick and fresh', but it also strips all value out of everything it touches:

> . . . notwithstanding thy capacity
> Receiveth as the sea, nought enters there
> Of what validity and pitch soe'er
> But falls into abatement and low price
> Even in a minute.

You cannot help noticing that the romantic image has ended commercially, with a hint of sexual waste. Orsino expressed it gracefully, but the fact is that he is paying a price for his passionate surrender: expense of spirit, disappointment, a bankruptcy in which even sweet music sounds like the rattling of tin cans.

A second voice offers to help. Curio might be one of the musicians, a courtier or a friend. Sturdily he suggests a bit of exercise, as one might a cold shower; but, poor man, he is subjected to a lordly quibble:

> CURIO: Will you go hunt, my lord?
> ORSINO: What, Curio?
> CURIO: The hart.
> ORSINO: Why so I do, the noblest that I have.
>   O when mine eyes did see Olivia first,
>   Methought she purged the air of pestilence . . .

It seems that not only does Orsino do most of the talking here, but he is able to turn everything to self-pitying advantage. However, the reason for his storminess has at least been named: Olivia. It is a relief – perhaps this is to be a love story between real people after all. But Orsino has not finished with his contraries: this woman is benevolent enough to destroy disease in the air we breathe,[1] but she also provokes a chase to the death – in fact violence within oneself, because at the sight of her he was divided into two, his own hunter and quarry:

> That instant was I turned into a hart;
> And my desires, like fell and cruel hounds,
> E'er since pursue me.[2]

Abashed, Curio withdraws into the shadows and will barely speak again.

Silence once more, and perhaps some embarrassment. Is Orsino always like this, speaking in a style that nobody can find the right way to respond to? Perhaps he wildly overstates his mood for poetic purposes, perhaps his torment is real. Fortunately, there is a new arrival, Valentine, as deferential to him as Curio was, but hiding who knows what thoughts of his own:

> ORSINO: How now, what news from her?
> VALENTINE: So please my lord, I might not be admitted;
>   But from her handmaid do return this answer . . .

His practicality freshens the air, as if the sun was rising and the windows being opened a little. He sounds like a civil servant mortified by a foolish mission but taking it on the chin: at least he is trying to reorganise the disarray. Although he speaks poetically, as a compliment to Orsino, it is in a much simpler style; and again, there is an acting choice to be made, between irony and romance. What Valentine says may be a tactful dressing-up of a blunter message he has been given at Olivia's house – to go away – or a direct quotation carefully memorised. If the second, we seem to be in a world in which everyone sings in the same key, a handmaid offstage sounding as good as Shakespeare; if the first, the euphemistic spin is quite comic:

---

1   London was afflicted with plague almost cyclically: in 1582, 1592 and – the year after *Twelfth Night*'s premiere – in 1603, when 30,000 lives were lost. For any adult at this moment, it was a living fear; for the actor of Orsino himself, more than a fancy idea.

2   This sidelong reference is to the (then) well-known story in Ovid's *Metamorphoses* in which Actaeon, having accidentally seen the goddess Diana naked, was punished by being turned into a 'hart' (a stag) and devoured by his own dogs. The Elizabethans took this sort of allusion in their stride and would have admired its application to Orsino (it is after all a definitive image of the arbitrary and merciless female) – we, less well-trained but erotically alert, get the general idea.

> The element itself, till seven years' heat,
> Shall not behold her face at ample view;
> But like a cloistress she will veiled walk,
> And water once a day her chamber round
> With eye-offending brine . . .

Imagining Valentine and the handmaid in a little huddle, whispering at Olivia's front door, we get a distant glimpse of the woman Orsino confusedly celebrates, and she seems as self-conscious as he is. Explaining her seclusion, Valentine is incredulous, and can't help adding a discreet comment of his own:

> . . . *all this* to season
> A brother's dead love, which she would keep fresh
> And lasting in her sad remembrance.

The stupendous use Orsino makes of the bad news is a tribute to his abandon and resourcefulness. He is not at all interested in the dead brother, but it strikes him that if Olivia will sequester herself like this for him, how passionately will she commit herself to her man when finally ravished by the 'rich golden shaft' of his love – an event now somehow taken for granted. Perhaps he needed the flat rejection to animate him, for his confidence is suddenly as great as was his wallowing despair. Now his love will kill

> the flock of all affections else
> That live in her . . .

– and he will be king by violent conquest of her every function, 'liver, brain and heart'. It is a lover's magnificent ace, breathtaking for his companions, who are ordered to run off ahead of him to lie down on beds of flowers. Or is it just a metaphor? All this poetic one-upmanship could try the patience of a footsore courtier.

As they go, questions hang in the air: it is not so much that we want to know what will happen next as to get some purchase on what we have seen, since Orsino's lofty form of speech has provided few bearings. *Twelfth Night* has certainly announced itself: one way and another, music and love will dominate the proceedings. But there is hardly any plot information (as there is in *King Lear* or *A Midsummer Night's Dream*), few brooding atmospherics (*Hamlet*), and certainly no Chorus – nothing that offers a glimpse of some real world beyond the words. This short opening scene has left us as suspended as the musicians.

Already I have declared a preference, I suppose. Orsino's para-doxical style is certainly typical of a particular kind of Elizabethan wit and poet, but it also seems neurotically self-regarding. For all its lyrical swing, the language works in uncomfortable opposites – love, food and music immediately get mixed up with nausea, surfeit and death; and the images – violets, perfume and melody – are rather promiscuous. In the end, he tetchily rejects the whole clutter. How seriously should he be taken? He seems to have found a kindred spirit in Olivia: to seclude herself for seven years is to push sorrow past the point where it might properly die, just as Orsino is forcing himself beyond the human need for rest.

For the actor, the first of his (only) four scenes contains a large ambush. Probably cast for his rhapsodic abilities, he needs to add to them the flashy skills of the quibbler, and to handle a heave of feelings wholeheartedly. Most trickily, the neurosis has only tunefulness with which to express itself – it comes out not with the jaggedness of Stravinsky but with the opulence of Rachmaninov. Around him is a series of apparently thankless parts; but, although he has absorbed most of the oxygen, this is, in a limited way, an ensemble piece. Curio's entire role was hostage to a poetic conceit and Valentine was just the fretful messenger, but we will have watched them keenly for orientation – and we specially tried to see Orsino through the eyes of his patient musicians.[3] It is a truism in the theatre that we believe someone is a king, and what kind of a king, not from his own behaviour but from the attitude of those around him – so their precise reactions will count for a lot. Even so, we don't quite know where we are or how to take anything: powerful emotions are in the air, but for some reason we want to laugh. The first line of the next scene is like a discreet joke.

1.2.

'What country, friends, is this?'

The stage seems to widen and deepen. A woman with the remnants of her belongings, and some sailors – and a gravity in them, as if

---

3   Shakespeare's working musicians remain stoic or opportunistic in the face of all life's caprices. In *Othello* a wind ensemble is asked only to play music that 'may not be heard' and is then paid to go away altogether; then there is the band in *Romeo and Juliet* who come to play for Juliet's wedding, find her apparently dead and the household hysterical, but decide to hang on for dinner. Sometimes a tiresome Clown is left behind for them to parley with; but it may be no easier to put up with Orsino. In practice, of course, the opening of *Twelfth Night* is not about put-upon minstrels risking expulsion; but they do need to have some character. For a director, it is better to hire actors who can play a bit rather than musicians too embarrassed to act.

being here brought them no ease but they are undaunted. The man's answer is a first moment of summary:

> This is Illyria, lady.

The woman called them 'friends', and to this Captain she is 'lady': these are the first people to pay each other proper attention.

The new landscape is hardly conceivable beside Orsino's – wind scurrying along a beach in front of an infinity, the suspended, baleful light that follows a storm, these tiny figures.[4] They speak a soft and steady verse – the lines full of light where Orsino's were congested, lucid where his jostled for scale and meaning. The melodiously-named country is counterpointed straight away with the fabulous home of the blessed, but the real name sounds no more substantial than the mythical:

> VIOLA: And what should I do in Illyria?
> My brother he is in Elysium.

If we have settled, it is only on sand. However, there has been a real tragedy, in contrast to the romantic martyrdom of the distraught lord in his court:

> VIOLA: Perchance he is not drowned; what think you, sailors?
> CAPTAIN: It is perchance that you yourself were saved.

Orsino compared the 'spirit of love' to an ocean that reduced its victims to 'abatement': but this is the real thing, an elemental force destroying and restoring at will.[5]

---

4   Shakespeare's occasionally makes the second scene of his story render the first almost unbelievable; *Hamlet* is the outstanding case.

5   A symbol of the subconscious from Euripides to Coleridge, from Conrad to Freud, the sea intensifies its meaning for Shakespeare play by play. Its influence culminates in *The Tempest*; but even in *Pericles*, a play of mixed authorship, you can hear this beautiful obsession in lines he could equally have given to Viola for Sebastian:

> The unfriendly elements
> Forgot thee utterly, nor have I time
> To give thee hallow'd to thy grave, but straight
> Must cast thee, scarcely coffin'd, in the ooze,
> Where, for a monument upon thy bones
> And aye-remaining lamps, the belching whale
> And humming water must o'erwhelm thy corpse,
> Lying with simple shells.

For the first time too, one character adapts to the needs of another: having dismissed the possibility of anyone else surviving the shipwreck, the Captain is touched by Viola's forlorn hope

> O my poor brother! And so perchance may he be

and changes his story for her benefit. The two of them embark on a gentle and respectful game, watched, rather like Orsino's musicians, by a handful of sailors who keep their views to themselves. The Captain borrows Viola's elevated vocabulary:

> I saw your brother,
> Most provident in peril, bind himself . . .
> To a strong mast that lived upon the sea,
> Where like Arion on the dolphin's back,[6]
> I saw him hold acquaintance with the waves
> So long as I could see.

This heroic pictorialism – like an illustration to *Captain Hornblower* – drops a hint: is he telling the truth? Perhaps, like Valentine with Orsino, he is dressing bad news up a bit. Viola sees his glorious simile for what it probably is, rewards the performance:

> For saying so, there's gold

and colludes:

> Mine own escape unfoldeth to my hope,
> Whereto thy speech serves for authority,
> The like of him.

The fragile picture fades away. What more is there to say? He might have survived but most probably not: the dead must bury their dead, even a brother, and Viola lets it be.

To describe *Twelfth Night* as musical is to say nothing very much: but already the key-changes are allowing one group to comment on

---

6   Abstruse classical learning in every mouth is commonplace in Shakespeare (and rather shaming to us). Just as Curio should not miss the reference to Actaeon and Diana in the previous scene, the Captain has no trouble with this simile of the maritime pied piper. At the same time it is probably sentimental to imagine that everybody in the Globe Theatre's pit understood the references – it is striking that Shakespeare chances two of them within the opening ten minutes of this play, but after all *Twelfth Night* was probably not written for the Globe. However, many of his spectators will have got an education of sorts from the theatre. Nowadays, Tom Stoppard's virtuosity sometimes flatters the audience with information just beyond their own while sustaining them with incandescent wit, and the Elizabethans will have been carried along by Shakespeare's energetic story telling and just about followed his erudition.

another. Though Viola and the Captain started a little disjointedly – the opening verse lines each missed two beats – their style has the natural proportion of their characters. Their taste for monosyllables and disyllables again underlines the contrast with Orsino, whose rackety anxiety ('capacity . . . validity . . . abatement . . . fantastical') only loosened in his final moments; and their triple antithesis on 'perchance' has a melancholy sweetness quite beyond him.

In a similar way, the light keeps changing on each action as we watch it, and we may find something harmless soon after taking it seriously. Already, a slight sense of dream is distancing the fact of this shipwreck while preserving the idea of it. Viola re-starts conversationally, trying to get more bearings:

> Know'st thou this country?

This is done in the middle of a blank verse line,[7] and the rapid change is a big hint to her character – she will always be inclined to move on. In fact, nothing stays still for long – so, having seen that some arbitrarily drown while others are flung up on the beach, we swiftly arrive in the land of happy coincidences. The Captain not only knows where they are, but was himself born

> Not three hours' travel from this very place

– which is governed by someone we know – a duke 'noble . . . in nature as in name':

> VIOLA: What is his name?
> CAPTAIN: Orsino.
> VIOLA: Orsino!

Viola dresses him in a blithe light:

> . . . I have heard my father name him.
> He was a bachelor then

and the terms of romantic comedy are declared: her interest in such an important person is for his marital reputation. The Captain, having pocketed his tip, becomes a stock character, no longer the watchful counsellor but a gossipy confidant:

---

7 For the actor, the retarded beat won't wait for long – indeed, iambic fundamentalists among our directors would insist the line must always continue on the same breath. Though the audience is not always conscious of the verse form, they do sense its unobtrusive structure, and become unsettled if they can't tell the beginning of a line from its halfway point.

And so is now, or was so very late;
For but a month ago I went from hence,
And then 'twas fresh in murmur (as, you know,
What great ones do, the less will prattle of)
That he did seek the love of fair Olivia.

This is a bit obsequious – we poor folk tattle while the great ones make the news – and suggests that Illyria is full of tabloid-readers wondering who has caught their Duke's eye. Everything is suddenly, vigorously, two-dimensional. Telling the story of Olivia, the Captain blunders into a parallel family bereavement: she is

the daughter of a count
That died some twelvemonth since; then leaving her
In the protection of his son, her brother,
Who shortly also died . . .

It is an unfortunate coincidence: and as he tries to get off Viola's toes, a sympathetic laugh may hover in the theatre.

Using Viola's mental agility as a feint, Shakespeare has moved into a style as far from real tragedy as tragedy was from romantic agony, and a fairy-tale is arising from desolation. Olivia's melancholy seclusion (less lofty in the Captain's mouth than in Valentine's) strikes a chord in Viola: she immediately wants to 'serve that lady', seeking sweet companionship in her sorrow and time to re-design her life. It is quite picturesque. Persuaded that 'that were hard to compass' since the reclusive Countess would not welcome her, she comes up with a still more audacious plan, consistent with stylised comedy: sexual disguise. She will serve Orsino as a singing feminine boy.[8] This is obviously so reckless that she must prime the Captain, whose help she needs, with compliments and a little bribery:

There is a fair behaviour in thee captain . . .
I prithee (and I'll pay thee bounteously)
Conceal me what I am, and be my aid
For such disguise as haply shall become
The form of my intent. I'll serve this duke;
Thou shalt present me as an eunuch to him.

Money changes hands for a second time – a gentle reminder, in an unlikely setting, of how things stand. Put to him like this, the plan

---

8 Viola doesn't in fact sing (though the nineteenth-century American actress Helen Modjeska performed 'Come Away Death' to a harp accompaniment). Most likely, Shakespeare didn't follow up the idea of Viola's entertaining like a eunuch in an Eastern court because he had a better (and gutsier) idea for the music in the interim: Feste.

sounds good to the gallant Captain: his heroine, able not to dwell on her emotions, is going to confront a melodramatic man who can do little else. He is inspired to a linguistic joke – he will be her servant in the harem – and (a Shakespearian sign of confidence) to a rhyme as well:

> Be you his eunuch, and your mute I'll be;
> When my tongue blabs, then let mine eyes not see.

Echoing Viola's own rhyme, it is their cue for action. Inspired by her, and with rather more sense of purpose than Orsino's courtiers to the flowerbeds, the group sweeps off – half a hundred lines from their collapse on the beach and half a lifetime away from it.

This seems to be the way – we glimpse something and it is immediately spun through another angle. Certainly, the simultaneous weight and lightness of this scene has required a deal of discretion from the players. It was a real, mortal storm, but too much waterlogged flailing and wringing-out of clothes will have prevented it shifting into eery romance. It will also, as it turns out, be our only opportunity to see Viola dressed as a woman; and so we need to get a strong impression of the speed of thought and irresistible optimism of Shakespeare's typical female hero – Portia, Beatrice and Rosalind before her, Imogen and Perdita to come. All these women disarm the sceptics around them and leave men struggling for control – the practical Captain is certainly no match for Viola. As our memory of her becomes remote, her heroic gifts will be suspended for the new fruits of secrecy: dogged patience and the discreetest wit.

She is also still unnamed, though she has identified Orsino, giving him some retrospective glamour. In fact, we will share Viola's life before we learn the lovely real name she left behind. Olivia's name, by contrast, has been compulsively established: when we finally meet her we will want to know how she lives up to her reputation. The musicality of the names is quite subtle, and it extends to the place – the play's key-signature, you might say. Real as it is, Illyria also sounds like a mellifluous invention, and for Shakespeare's dreaming audience, it could be the land of their imaginings, as beguiling as Verona or Messina, as fantastical as Ephesus, Bohemia or Navarre.

The first two scenes of *Twelfth Night* have sometimes been reversed – presumably on the principle of starting with a bang. John Philip Kemble, normally a good editor of Shakespeare, was the first to commit this violence, in 1815. A shipwreck (as in *The Tempest*) certainly attracts attention before the poetry starts, and would have appealed to the scenically-minded producers of the nineteenth century: it could be done before a frontcloth which then calmly rose on a complicated interior set for Orsino. It also makes a literal narrative sense: Viola setting out from the seaside towards him, and then a preview of what she is getting into. But Shakespeare's taste is otherwise: more intriguing (and more disorientating for his audience) to have the stifling self-consciousness of Orsino's world scattered by rolling natural elements – which now lift to reveal the warm domesticity of Olivia's parlour.

1.3.   It is very unusual for Shakespeare to introduce three seemingly unconnected groups of characters in such rapid succession. In *A Midsummer Night's Dream*, the Court, the Mechanicals and the fairy world are brought in within three scenes, but each is given a hundred or two hundred lines to get established. But in *Twelfth Night* the introductions are as frenzied as at some bewildering party – Orsino and Viola take the stage for barely five minutes' playing time each, and after a brief return to Orsino's in 1.4, there is the further novelty of Olivia's inner circle to come in 1.5. We are still gently circling all these characters rather than meeting them. At least the latest arrivals will have a little time to make themselves known, so there is a slight feeling of expansion – and a light link in the narrative as well:

> What a plague means my niece to take the death of her brother
> thus?

This might seem to refer to Viola's bereavement, but we have presumably not moved away from Illyria, so the niece is more probably Olivia, whose grief seems to be the one unifying theme so far. There is no consensus about it – Orsino sanctified her, the Captain gossiped, and the newcomer is shockingly dismissive:

> I am sure care's an enemy to life.

What kind of man can this uncle be? A brother's death, reduced in scale to a 'care', can hardly be over-mourned. Perhaps the convivial tones mask the cold heart of the hedonist. He is identified by his companion, who confirms something of his temperament as well:

> By my troth, Sir Toby, you must come in earlier o' nights. Your
> cousin,[9] my lady, takes great exceptions to your ill hours.

This easy, colloquial prose is reassuring after Orsino's uncertainty
of pitch and Viola's disconcerting gift for turning tragedy into a
high-spirited game: perhaps a conversation between a dissolute
gentleman and some kind of female Good Counsel will steady
things up. Also, a comic flare is being sent up by the musical, tit-
for-tat quality of the dialogue, not to mention Shakespeare's typical
inclination to a pun: the original audience, spotting the prose
pattern and Toby's self-announcement (no doubt with gestures)
would surely have recognised the new mood as swiftly as we might
the clowns in a circus after the ballet acts.

If Shakespearian verse soars out of its time, his prose is far more
evanescent: we can enjoy the sound of the jokes, but their meaning
is often a struggle, especially when delivered at speed. Toby defends
himself from criticism with an evasive quibble:

> Why, let her except, before excepted

– he is mimicking a technical term from legalistic Latin, but all we
will get from it is his insouciance. He then tries another, with
'confine', using the cramped sound of the consonants to reject all
measliness in favour of life's breadth and extravagance:

> . . . these clothes are good enough to drink in and so be these
> boots too; and they be not, let them hang themselves in their
> own straps.

This is promising – coldhearted or not, Sir Toby, like his relative
Falstaff, has a drinker's joviality and a punster's subtlety. Flam-
boyantly immoral, perhaps he is to be our lord of misrule.

Maria betrays her anxiety about him with a tautology:

> That quaffing and drinking will undo you . . .

and to clinch her point, a third character is identified. Maria has
been given a caution by Olivia, who objects not only to Toby's
lack of discipline but to being bothered in her grief with a
'foolish knight' whom he 'brought in one night here to be her

---

9 Just as Orsino's exact rank – a 'duke' when he is authoritative, a mere 'count' when he is
a lover – is uncertain, so is the kinship between Toby and Olivia. Is she his niece or his cousin?
'Cousin' is not precise in Shakespeare, meaning little more than 'relative'. Toby repeatedly
calls her his niece, although he is generally described in return not as her 'uncle' but as her
'kinsman'.

wooer'. Having not met her yet, it is difficult for us to sympathise –
we like Toby now, and when he names the stranger things get even
better:

> Who, Sir Andrew Aguecheek?

This, the first funny name we have heard, is in the manner of Ben
Jonson, whose characters are often identified by their prevailing
'humour' (Diaphanous Silkworm, Sir Politick Would-Be, and so on).
It would have suggested to the Elizabethans not so much sickness as
the thinness that sickness might cause, rather as if a man were called
Mr Skinny. It is hard to see how Toby and he fit in with the Italianate
Orsinos and Olivias and Curios, but for the first time we sense un-
ambiguous good company.

In his stride, Toby equivocates like a saloon-bar Orsino, and
his rally with Maria forms a controversial build-up to Andrew's
entrance. According to Toby, Andrew is 'tall' (brave), according to
Maria a 'fool and a prodigal'; to Toby he is not only rich ('three
thousand ducats a year') but immensely talented, a linguist and a
musician: to Maria he is just quarrelsome and cowardly. They can
agree that he and Toby are 'drunk nightly', whether with drinking
healths to Olivia or not – and in fact Toby is magnificently claiming
that his entire project is for the greater glory of his now marvellous
niece:

> . . . he's a coward and a coistrill that will not drink to my niece
> till his brains turn o' th' toe like a parish top.

The disagreement over Andrew is immediately settled by his arrival
and behaviour. He is announced with the utmost banality:

> . . . here comes Sir Andrew Agueface

– his funny name further distorted, he thus raises a laugh before he
even appears. However, he himself trumps it the next moment by
revealing Toby's splendid surname:

> Sir Toby Belch! How now, Sir Toby Belch!

It seems that Maria (now identified as Olivia's chambermaid) has
been ungenerous in her assessment of Andrew: the first impression
he gives is of bashfulness rather than foolishness. 'Bless you, fair
shrew' is a perfectly good greeting ('shrew' not always having the
overtone it does now and sometimes did then), and it is not inconceivable that Maria's surname might be 'Accost' – it would be no

sillier than Belch or Aguecheek.[10] He is hardly to blame for needing some general tuition in the art of courtship, and he is decently embarrassed by sexual innuendo. Bluntly invited there and then to 'front . . . board . . . woo . . . assail' Maria, his reaction is properly shy:

By my troth, I would not undertake her in this company[11]

– and he can only parrot his master:

TOBY: An thou let part so, Sir Andrew, would thou mightst never draw sword again.
ANDREW: An you part so, mistress, I would I might never draw sword again

before venturing the merest overture of his own:

Fair lady, do you think you have fools in hand?

Polite and likeable (and probably unaware of the mild *double-entendres* in what he has said), Andrew is swiftly outclassed as Maria invites his hand to 'the buttery-bar'. She might as well be speaking a foreign language, and we have some sympathy. However, you can smell the gaminess – a buttery-bar was a shelf above the serving-hatch where a man might place his tankard, and generations of productions have had Maria guide Sir Andrew's 'dry [impotent] hand' to the 'buttery-bar' of her bosom. The business is so hackneyed that a director will do almost anything to avoid it before capitulating. No matter – it graphically establishes Maria's self-confidence and Andrew's lack of it, even if you keep wishing you could think of something better.

The tension in his captured hand seems to take the strength from Andrew's legs. He is reduced to helpless, agonised questions:

Wherefore, sweetheart? What's your metaphor? . . . what's your jest? . . . are you full of them?

– and in a moment she's gone. Unaccustomed to the torment of blatant women, he becomes much more comfortable – verbose, even, in his relief – when he is left alone with Toby, grateful for a seat

---

10   And much less so than Bottom, Froth or Mouldy – let alone the offstage army Shakespeare blessed with names no human should have: Jane Nightwork, Master Tisick the Deputy, and Young Drop-Hair (That Kill'd Lusty Pudding).

11   He could be referring to the audience watching him as much as to Toby – Shakespeare's comics broke down the theatre's 'fourth wall' without hesitation, and it is good for us, trammelled in realism, to be reminded of it.

and a drink. Clearly, Andrew has fallen into the elephant-trap of the unconfident male: inadequate to the rough world around him, he relies on a treacherous form of male camaraderie. We soon come to realise that he is subsidising Toby in return for having his delusions fed about Olivia's favour, and that he is not strong enough to resist. This may be pathetic: but still, the two men's talk comes like balm – sustained interplay, supple and swift, real conversation at last. We might almost be sitting at the same table with the two entertaining knights: intellectually ill-matched, they are nevertheless very easy and natural, and they form a hallowed team – fat man and fool, braggart and wimp. Comforted by his glass of sweet wine[12] and melancholically contemplating his débâcle as a wooer, Andrew shows a taste for the banal non-sequiturs a man only uses when permanently stuck for an answer:

> Methinks sometimes I have no more wit than a Christian or an ordinary man has . . .

The comparison where there is no comparison is typical, and it seems to give him confidence: but every time he achieves a kind of flow, he is assailed by some insinuated doubt. He firmly blames his lack of fizzle on his diet,[13] but at Toby's apparent reassurance (really a dire confirmation) he loses his nerve and contradicts himself:

> ANDREW: . . . I am a great eater of beef, and I believe that does
>   harm to my wit.
> TOBY: No question.
> ANDREW: An I thought that, I'd forswear it.

He even threatens to 'ride home tomorrow' – a rare bad moment for Toby, ever alert to the loss of Andrew's open purse; but, like a child, he is easily distracted by the use of a foreign word, which makes him intrigued and insecure all over again. Any idea that Toby was telling the truth to Maria is exploded – Andrew was to be a man with 'three or four languages without book', but he doesn't understand the simple French word for 'why':

> What is *pourquoi*? Do, or not do?

12   A fortified wine, like sherry, originally from the Canary Islands, sweet where Falstaff's sherris-sack, for instance, was dry (the word 'sack' comes from the French 'sec'). A sulphurous hangover in both cases I should say.

13   It was sincerely believed that beef was bad for the intellect. To the French in *Henry V*, it is the reason the English are stupid; to Thersites in *Troilus*, the cause of Ajax's folly.

But Toby doesn't answer questions: his forte is to distract his victim this way and that, like a farmer depriving a pig of truffles. Faced with that impermeably encouraging smile, Andrew is bafflingly thrown back on himself:

> I would I had bestowed that time in the tongues that I have in fencing, dancing and bear-baiting. O, had I but followed the arts!

Swordsmanship was a normal aristocratic accomplishment at this time, but in this context, combined with bear-baiting and opposed to the arts, it could suggest some insecure aggression.[14] Arrestingly, Toby (using the Elizabethan pronunciation that made 'tongues' identical to 'tongs') attributes the straightness of Andrew's uncurled hair to his illiteracy, even making his scathing comment sound like a compliment:

> Then hadst thou had an excellent head of hair . . . it hangs like flax on a distaff; and I hope to see a huswife take thee between her legs and spin it off.

For once, this isn't perfectly judged – a 'huswife' was also a hussy, and venereal disease was thought to cause hair loss. Stung by the compound vulgarity, the chaste Andrew achieves a rare flash of realism – this thin hair of his, dead as fibre, and his general lack of class, mean he has no chance with Olivia, especially as Orsino is after her as well. No question, he should go home before he bankrupts himself, home to where people say what they mean, where they don't encourage you with their eyes while tying you up in verbal knots. As it turns out, this second alarm presents Toby with no more trouble than the first: he dismisses the distinguished rival Orsino as too old and superior – whereupon Andrew, mildly flattered as the younger wooer, changes his mind again, an opulent vision of premarital dancing and drinking flooding his brain. He will 'stay a month longer' – which is not a matter of irresolution, but of his own fascinating eccentricity:

> I am a fellow o' th' strangest mind i' th' world. I delight in masques and revels sometimes altogether.

The truth is he will do anything for a good time – it would of course be far better for him to call it a day, but his moments of resolve are

---

14   One of the confirmations attending the discovery of the Rose Theatre in London's South-wark a few years ago was that it had been used for bear- and armadillo-baiting as well as for the playing of Marlowe and Shakespeare. Obviously Andrew never stayed on for the play.

easily dismissed. But then he is dealing with a master – throughout the muddled confessional, Toby has been the perfect provocateur, encouraging bottle to hand to distract him at inconvenient moments of self-knowledge.

Wound up like a doll to some 'kickshawses' (a French word – *quelquechoses* – but this time not mortifying for him) Andrew claims to be a good dancer as long as he is not compared 'with an old man' – he cuts a higher and higher caper, ventures a more and more risky 'back-trick'. Toby is there for him, satanically supportive, his language rippling with more sensation than logic:

> Wherefore have these gifts a curtain before 'em? Are they like to take dust, like Mistress Mall's picture? Why dost thou not go to church in a galliard, and come home in a coranto?

The general prodigality is irresistible to Andrew, who in any case has difficulty concentrating on details. Keeping him giddy, Toby suggests (and perhaps demonstrates) four separate dances, all of them lively and potentially silly, and throws in a couple of verbal cartwheels to get the two of them off – to another day of revels that celebrate nothing much.

The lights of *Twelfth Night* always seem to come up when Aguecheek arrives: the part is a gift for an inventive performer, and liable to attract a director's best attentions as well. His anxiety about his appearance, his no doubt miscalculated clothes, his slowness on the uptake and his embarrassment, are just the start of it; and even if he leads the dance now, he will spend most of the play struggling to keep up. Ahead of him is a woeful pursuit of Olivia as, progressively fleeced, he becomes entangled in frustrated gestures, an absurd duel and, finally, physical injury. Maria was a good witness after all – this is a fooled fool and a quarreller, with an ominous mixture of obtuseness and pugnacity – but at heart he is also decent, human and accessible, and his 'weakness' of character vividly projects our own feelings of inadequacy. Against him, Toby is coarse, exploitative and cynical, but good company: his specious existential energy is to be avoided in life but enjoyed in the theatre. Deadly fun, completely without morals, articulate, witty and full-blooded, he knows all the weaknesses of his prey: he would never quite steal from Andrew, but his pockets will always be oddly empty until Andrew's are as well.[15]

---

15   The ride Andrew is being taken on is a large one, two-thirds of his annual allowance. Toby has said his victim is worth 'three thousand ducats a year'; and by 3.2.52 he will have had 'two thousand strong' off him.

In practice, certain dangers intrude: as Toby is so quickly identified as a toper, you can imagine how coarse it can all get as the actor establishes this. With both Toby and Maria, in fact, the spectre of stereotype looms – call it the loveable rogue and the buxom barmaid. For the first, Franz Hals' *Laughing Cavalier* gives you the remorselessly bibulous man in his boots, and words like 'substractors' can be fallen on for rubber-tongued drunken acting – not to mention the temptation of his surname. In any player, trying to hit a role's keynote from the start is a form of nerves: but you don't have to achieve everything in the first five minutes – better to let the action reveal you in its own good time. There is something to be said for a hangover here for Toby, seen off by the hair of the dog and finally forgotten as Andrew arrives to make sense of the day – it is logical enough, establishes the alcoholism, and may give an anxious actor something precise to do.

Meanwhile Maria, about whom we have learned the least, risks becoming the good conscience who can't help but adore Toby – another archetype. But of course this is a real situation in a real house on a real morning (there could be a breakfast tray) and her advice was tactical as much as moral. Clearly, she is embedded in the household, near enough to Olivia to hear her views and so act as something of a double agent: she should be listened to. Her sexual merriment with Andrew was interesting next to her censoriousness of him: probably done largely to please Toby, it was well done, and diluted the early impression of her as a scold. In fact she is largely responsible for the warm domesticity, practicality and nurture, the whiff of kitchen and laundry-room, that is creeping into the play. From her point of view, as she tries to balance one thing against another, at least the two men are getting off her hands and out of the house. Buoyant again on their cup or two of canary, they go galliarding away, having set in train a third story-line and a first-class double-act.

1.4. Though the action returns abruptly to Orsino, the introductions are not complete: there is another new character to meet, Cesario. The audience needs a moment to absorb that this is Viola, and so matters begin with an unimportant bustle, in a workaday prose held over from Toby's and Andrew's scene:

VALENTINE: If the duke continue these favours towards you, Cesario, you are like to be much advanced; he hath known you but three days, and already you are no stranger.

Just as we were fooled for a moment, Viola's stunning disguise has succeeded with her new master and his court.

This provision of new facts while we are looking elsewhere – at how exactly she has done it – is an old Shakespearian trick. The scene feels like a direct continuation of the previous three, themselves so rapid and various that they might have taken place simultaneously in their different locations. To sneak in a narrative gap now – that Viola has been with Orsino for three days – gives the characters a more spacious history: we seem to have lived with them that bit longer, even as the action rockets along.[16]

From now on, there is Viola and there is Cesario: Viola speaks to the audience and Cesario to the others in the play, but sometimes, as now, they are as one. The reply to Valentine sounds sharper than you might expect from Cesario, as if Viola was retaliating to some teasing edge:

You either fear his humour, or my negligence, that you call in question the continuance of his love.

To her it is not a matter of 'favours' and being 'advanced', but of personal loyalty. She may also have spotted that Valentine is camouflaging a small professional pique – Orsino has a new favourite. However, from his point of view, once he has weighed it against the indignity (in a moment Orsino will instruct him to 'stand . . . apart', before dismissing him as 'a nuncio . . . of more grave aspect'), the benefit could be that this new junior will run the more absurd errands in future, allowing senior officers to stand down. For her part, Viola is, definitively, on edge, very wary of scrutiny: she probably looks a little diminutive among men who lead confidently with chest and abdomen, and she needs all the fight she can muster. We don't yet know what it is, but her slightly weak finish

Is he inconstant, sir, in his favours?

has another question hidden within it – but to Valentine that is like asking if there are elephants in the sea:

16   The play requires three months of 'real' time but only two days of 'theatre' time. Part of the interest of the sequence of plays beginning here will be how Shakespeare starts to abandon his covert 'double time' technique and moves on chorically to announce large blatant intervals – three months in *Pericles*, sixteen years in *The Winter's Tale*. In the latter case he brings in the figure of Time himself to announce it.

> No, believe me.

He does speak from the most trying experience.

Orsino suddenly interrupts, bringing on the poetry – the rapturous Orsino we know, but with a new practical energy:

> Who saw Cesario, ho?

Everyone comes to a sort of attention. But there is no small talk with Orsino – and his surrender to his new confidant immediately has something of the ravishment of Olivia's imagined surrender to him:

> Thou know'st no less but all; I have unclasped
> To thee the book even of my secret soul.

In fact Cesario is already so deeply trusted that (to Viola's dismay) he must go straight to Olivia to plead Orsino's suit. The count's fantastical instincts paint a dramatic picture around the simple situation:

> stand at her doors,
> And tell them, there thy fixed foot shall grow
> Till thou have audience . . .
> Be clamorous, and leap all civil bounds,
> Rather than make unprofited return . . .

Clamorous himself, he sweeps all reasonable objections aside – Olivia won't receive Cesario, what is Cesario to say, he may not be up to the job. Over his crass vision of breaking and entering, his fancy blooms, and he imagines the page heroically acting his 'woes':

> O then unfold the passion of my love;
> Surprise her with discourse of my dear faith . . .

He is sure that Cesario's youth stands a better chance than Valentine's solemnity, and not only that: though it hasn't struck him before, the oddly feminine sympathy of the page may be effective in gaining Olivia's trust. It is very interesting to him, the contradictory hormone in the boy, and he closes in, elaborating more intimately:

> For they shall yet belie thy happy years
> That say thou art a man; Diana's lip
> Is not more smooth and rubious . . .

Viola stands her ground: we and she hold our breath. It is not what anyone would expect: Orsino normally treats other people more or less as accompaniment, but now he is paying attention, as if his baulked celebration of Olivia has been alarmingly deflected to a new object:

> thy small pipe
> Is as the maiden's organ, shrill and sound,
> And all is semblative a woman's part.

He is so hot, so in the vein, in such a state of overflow, that the scene sways for a giddy moment. However, he breaks off, oblivious to the effect he has had. After a formal commendation:

> I know thy constellation is right apt
> For this affair . . .

and a standard promise of future favour, the whirling dervish is gone, with a final Garbo-like sentiment:

> I myself am best
> When least in company.

True enough – alone, he can stay fixed, contemplating himself in reassuring stasis. He leaves Viola electrified, though we only know half of the reason.

Orsino's constancy is the constancy of Narcissus: if he was attracted to Cesario for a moment, it will have made him still more fascinating to himself – like Aguecheek, he has 'the strangest mind i' the world'. Guilt is not part of it, and he didn't break off shame-facedly, straightening his clothes: rather, he will have accepted his complex feelings with enthusiasm. What he doesn't know is that the warmth he feels for Cesario will lead to something he needs more than the fulfilment of his desires. Half of his scenes are now played, though there is much more substance to come: and though the hardly-breathed actor may feel he is building bricks with only a little straw, at least he has had *carte blanche* to startle, moving through all his moods with imperious abandon.

At the centre of the brief exchange is, of course, the enormity of what Viola has done and where it is leading her – everything else is a pretext for looking at her dilemma. As ominous as any practical danger[17] is the fact that she has fallen among obsessives: Orsino and Olivia are set to share her in an erotic *huis clos*. Her disguise is a staple of romantic comedy, but it is also her danger and intermittently her liberation – just as the fact that Orsino sends messengers to do his wooing is both a convention of romance and a psychological point (the evasion of her reality). And there is some-thing else: so that the whole episode does not depend on one exemplary joke, Shakespeare has prepared a tremendous flip to its tail, which Viola just has time to execute before she is swept up by the 'four or five' appointed to attend her:

> VIOLA: Yet, a barful strife!
>   Whoe'er I woo, myself would be his wife.

This brilliant twist makes us scan what has been said for new meanings: delivered as a merry rhyme, it is also funny. But there is an odd little shock. Viola has been with Orsino, gagged by her disguise, for three days, and would now spend her life with him. Why? He is not, on the face of it, a good bet, being temperamentally preoccupied with himself and practically spoken for – as if that mattered in the world we are beginning to enter. Having swiftly disposed of her dead brother's memory, Viola now seems ready to throw herself away too. This is in fact the first of two *coup de foudres* in the play arising from the erotic overspill of bereavement – wayward, arbitrary and only in the very end creative. Few are spared, it seems; and just as the play is gathering momentum and we are prepared to depend on Viola's grace, sense and good humour as our guide, our anchor may be coming adrift.

1.5.   Every time the play starts to move forward, it seems to pause and spread like water. Back at Olivia's, Maria is scolding another newcomer, as she berated Toby. With this one, it is not a matter of being

---

17   Writing at around the same time John Donne advised his mistress not to follow him on his travels abroad disguised as a page:

> Thou shalt not love by ways so dangerous . . .
>   . . . all will spy in thy face
> A blushing womanly discovering grace . . .

– going on into a half-humorous xenophobic frenzy over what an Elizabethan audience might fear Viola too is risking:

> Men of France, changeable chameleons . . .
> Love's fuellers, and the rightest company
> Of players, which upon the world's stage be,
> Will quickly know thee, and no less, alas !
> Th' indifferent Italian, as we pass
> His warm land, well content to think thee page,
> Will hunt thee with such lust and hideous rage
> As Lot's fair guests were vexed.

Better to have nothing to do with these versatile mediterraneans, and stay in England, where only the 'spongy hydroptic Dutch' will bother her.

out late and drunk, but of complete absenteeism: and again her concern is not so much moral as practical. This household depends on a
degree of order – imagine the impact of his disrespect at this moment
on Olivia, who is now credited with the power of life and death:

> Nay, either tell me where thou hast been, or I will not open my
> lips so wide as a bristle may enter in way of thy excuse: my lady
> will hang thee for thy absence.

The new renegade, with every reason for fear but apparently feeling
none, deflects in a style as careless as Toby's – the same defiant
credo, and in it the same hint of a pun:

> Let her hang me! He that is well-hanged in this world needs to
> fear no colours.

Maria is intrigued enough by this riddle to ask for its application:

> Make that good

but the answer is banal:

> He shall see none to fear

– in other words, because he will be dead. However, she did spot the
source of the joke – the old military meaning of 'colour' as an
enemy's flag. So the connection with 'collars' is logical enough to
please the two of them; but it is barely glimpsed by us, as is the
reason why such an answer was 'lenten'. Fortunately, the next
exchange starts more freshly:

> God give them wisdom that have it; and those that are fools, let
> them use their talents

and it ends with a really good paradox:

> Many a good hanging prevents a bad marriage.

In fact the linguistic thicket could be pruned a little in performance,
without damaging the stony fact inside it – that the malingerer really
is in danger of execution, or an expulsion 'as good as a hanging'. The
exchange's other value is for character. Maria can riddle too, and
likes the contest, but this newcomer has the edge – so that, to compete, her humour has to become broad:

> FESTE: . . . I am resolved on two points.
> MARIA: That, if one break, the other will hold, or if both break,
>   your gaskins [fool's breeches] fall.

Perhaps she suits the sabotaging action to the word. For all the clever jokes in this scene and in the earlier one with Toby, the groundling inside the audience of smart young lawyers is not being neglected: Toby also moved in a reassuring world of boot-straps, quaffing and old clothes, and the new comic's riddles might result in his braces ('points') being released from his trousers.

Maria's retaliation is 'apt' enough to provoke him to a hint – that she has a love-life, and that it has something to do with Toby:

> . . . if Sir Toby would leave drinking, thou wert as witty a piece of Eve's flesh as any in Illyria.

The innuendo is a little below the belt, and it certainly affects Maria:

> Peace, you rogue, no more o' that. Here comes my lady.

Her urgent hushing may be defensive, simply embarrassed, or perhaps even flattered: it is certainly more than a bridge into the next part of the scene. This is an intriguing secret, one better kept in the subdued and discreet household: and in these confidential moments before Olivia arrives, we have again sensed the covert warmth and shared history among her people.

The *flâneur*'s name is Feste, though it will rarely be used – he will almost always be described simply as 'Fool' (Curio calls him 'a jester'). His privilege seems to date back to Olivia's father, who 'much delighted' in him, and this probably puts him at something like a generation's remove from Olivia herself, still young where he could be more or less middle-aged.[18] The Fool is an archetypal figure throughout Shakespeare, first performed by one of his company's specialists – William Kempe and later Robert Armin are the ones we know. He has been Touchstone in *As You Like It*; and will be Lear's Fool later (also singing of the wind and the rain, also threatened with hanging and perhaps hanged), Hamlet's Grave-digger, Lavache in *All's Well*, and (most unsung of all) the Fool who makes a brief sour appearance in *Timon of Athens*.[19] He is a walking

---

18 It's a running debate, all the same. When Harley Granville Barker cast as Feste 'an actor no longer young' (Hayden Coffin), in his ground-breaking Shakespeare season in London in 1912, it caused quite a stir. For some reason, a conspicuously young Olivia still raises critical eyebrows too.

19 There is also a hapless Clown in the early *Titus Andronicus*, who, apart from being signally unfunny, has the bad luck to be sent by the crazed Titus with a letter to his enemy the Emperor. Having read it, the Emperor summarily orders the Clown to be hanged, rather as if he were tipping him.

paradox: negligible in the world's eyes, he is nevertheless looked to for special wisdom (like an 'idiot' in Russian[20]), and the fact of not wearing 'motley in [his] brain' determines his character, his *métier*, his personal defence. It sounds simple enough: but although we are used to adapting most Shakespearian prototypes – the warrior, the poet, the princess – to some equivalent of our own, our imagination may grind to a halt in front of a Fool – largely because of the received image, awesomely dead to us, of baggy breeches, cap and bells. This outfit only works in an Elizabethan production, and is so irritating that it is itself, I would say, a good reason for not doing the play in that setting.

In modern life many people – in schools, offices, theatre companies, families – develop an unofficial role as funny man: it can be the salvation of the socially uncertain. But it is not their job, and they don't get tipped. The idea of a king's jester is an old one, going back to Saxon times – both Edmund Ironside and William the Conqueror had one, as did Henry VIII; but Shakespeare's innovation may have been to extend his function: the more reproachful his uneasy riffs, and the more he threatens to make foolish leaders wise, the greater the risk he takes with his life but the more rewarded he is. In production, Feste appears to be a sort of floating familiar in Olivia's house, protected by special dispensation, coming into his own whenever formal systems break down. Whimsically called upon to sing and make his masters laugh and think, he is then as casually dropped by them, and they don't even remember his name: this indignity he defies by coming and going exactly as he pleases, even disappearing entirely – vulnerable, independent, never explaining.

Sure of his ground, Feste may have been lolling about, getting under Maria's feet as she tidied the room: still, he knows his traditional skills are about to be tested. It is the kind of extremity he looks forward to, and which she hopes he will survive, since she seems to care for him in some way as she cares for Toby.

The First Folio edition of *Twelfth Night* simply reads 'Enter Olivia', but subsequent editors say she is 'attended' – by enough 'fellows', in fact, for Feste to play off. Like Orsino's musicians, they

---

20 The *yurodivy*, or holy fool, wanders through Russian literature, and the word may come from the same root as 'deformed'. Shakespeare's fools are not 'holy' in quite that apocalyptic, itinerant sense, but on a more domestic scale they too tell the truth no-one wants to hear.

are probably not anonymous, but other members of her household we have yet to meet – a significant steward, a Waiting Gentlewoman or two, Fabian, perhaps the Priest – and Maria will soon efface herself among them. At Shakespeare's Globe, new characters might have arrived by chance, solely for the sake of making a new scene, but a modern audience needs a reasonable pretext – perhaps the regular morning meeting of the household staff – and since the scene's main operation will be to debunk, the more formality it starts with the better. The play's most heralded character is here, the famous doubly-bereaved woman who 'purg'd the air of pestilence' for Orsino, the modest recluse fresh from watering her chamber with eye-offending brine. How will she be?

Peremptory and authoritative:

> Take the fool away.

It is quite funny. Elevated by other people's poetry, perhaps she is a blunt and practical person after all.

In need of inspiration – he is supposed to be in peril of his life – Feste has blessed himself meanwhile:

> Wit, an't be thy will, put me into good fooling!

– and has warmed himself up with a simple enough maxim about the wit of fools and the foolishness of wits. Reacting swiftly to Olivia's order, he straight away claims her as one of his own:

> Do you not hear, fellows? Take away the lady.

The company is aghast; but she doesn't seem to mind, although she is not at all interested in the proof:

> Go to, y'are a dry fool; I'll no more of you.

The calm implacability is tough for him – he needs something like Maria's invitation to 'make that good', and if he can't force a chink of attention his act will break down. He riffles through some serviceable antitheses between drink and dryness, mending and patching, but they have more rhythm than meaning, as if he were anxiously treading water – and they bring him round to a QED he has barely justified:

> The lady bade take away the fool; therefore I say again, take her away.

So far, so not so good. Olivia hasn't budged: the noose still awaits.

Her interest begins to flicker at the old Latin tag about the clothes not making the man:

> FESTE: . . . Cucullus non facit monachum . . . Good madonna,
> give me leave to prove you a fool.
> OLIVIA: Can you do it?

An opening at last: the effrontery paid off. Feste pushes his luck further:

> FESTE: Good madonna, why mourn'st thou?
> OLIVIA: Good fool, for my brother's death.
> FESTE: I think his soul is in hell, madonna.
> OLIVIA: I know his soul is in heaven, fool.

Even for an 'allow'd fool', that is quite some licence, though it serves Olivia right for co-operating in his patter. Anything is possible now, and Feste's punchline is very classy:

> The more fool, madonna, to mourn for your brother's soul, being in heaven.

A silence falls, thick with suppressed laughter. Olivia looks at him and he at her: this is his *moment juste*. She unexpectedly turns to an observer, Malvolio, for his opinion, which, confident of being on the right side of the argument, he swingeingly gives:

> OLIVIA: What think you of this fool, Malvolio, doth he not mend?
> MALVOLIO: Yes, and shall do, till the pangs of death shake him.

Malvolio has assumed that Olivia used the word 'mend' sarcastically, as he would have done: but he may have miscalculated. Feste and Olivia conspire for a moment to draw him into their game:

> FESTE: God send you, sir, a speedy infirmity, for the better
> increasing your folly . . .
> OLIVIA: How say you to that, Malvolio?

– but he will have none of it:

> I marvel your ladyship takes delight in such a barren rascal. I saw
> him put down the other day with an ordinary fool that has no
> more brain than a stone[21] . . . I protest I take these wise men that
> crow so at these set kind of fools no better than the fools' zanies.

Well, it is candid, its one virtue a chill intellectuality; and we, enjoying the entertainment, realise that this man doesn't approve of us

---

21   Stone, by the way, was the name of a well-known tavern fool; he is mentioned in Ben Jonson's *Volpone* and elsewhere.

either. Fortunately, it turns out he is in the minority, like a solitary critic in the stalls:

> OLIVIA: O you are sick of self-love, Malvolio . . . There is no slander in an allowed fool though he do nothing but rail; nor no railing in a known discreet man though he do nothing but reprove.

Malvolio didn't entirely deserve this scathing analysis of his *amour propre* – and certainly to face him down in public is the surest way to hurt such a man. It makes him feel he has been lured into a trap. In fact, Olivia's instinctive judgment is reanimating the warmer values of the play – for all her propriety, she belongs in a kinder world than his. Exonerated, Feste can hardly believe his luck:

> Now Mercury endue thee with leasing,[22] for thou speak'st well of fools.

Clearly, Olivia's childhood affection for him, and her father's approval, count for more than the new loyalties forced on her by her inheritance. To one of her rank, if you have the prime virtue of being 'generous, guiltless and of free disposition', it is easy to shrug off the 'birdbolts'. Her limited egalitarianism, part of an older humanity than Malvolio's, protects an eccentric like Feste from the humiliations of his bitter profession.

With Maria's entry, the revealing episode closes. The figure of Olivia, at once rebellious and wise, has been the most ambiguous. Why did she banish the unruly Fool and then champion him because of a good joke? Did she bring Malvolio into the discussion simply to exemplify her own values? Malvolio, who expects people to live up to their positions in life, must find her extremely wayward, though he can hardly show it. His own entry into the play has been, unlike hers, completely unheralded: nobody outside the household seems to know anything about him, and nobody in it has mentioned him before. Boding and solitary, he has stepped out of the shadows and witheringly lived up to his daunting name (the converse of Benvolio in *Romeo*), nicking Feste, quite unnecessarily, on the jugular. Meanwhile, what Olivia has done for us, as we try to catch the play's moral register, is to broadcast the basis of his disastrous personality – an unaccommodating, ungenerous self-regard.

---

22   Mercury was, among other things, the god of lying, a word of which 'leasing' is a variant.

Feste and Malvolio have both ended up in positions they didn't expect – and as well as enlarging our sense of relationship, Shakespeare's destabilisation has allowed deep mourning into a comedy. There is nothing like black for subduing an audience, and the absence of colour might have bleached good humour out if we had not sensed a hum of anarchy behind it. The onstage witnesses will have been encouraged too: struggling a bit to keep up appearances, nobody daring to be out of line, they will have noticed that it is possible to make a joke about the dead man and survive.

With Feste through his test, Olivia herself is to be tried. Maria sounds genuinely enthusiastic about the arrival of Orsino's personable new page: he is

> a fair young man and well attended.

'Attended' is probably a compliment to his own graces rather than to his companions (Valentine and Curio?) – in this world the first comment on someone new is invariably on what figure they cut. Since Olivia will receive no men, it is odd that Maria troubles her with the news at all. If all is as it seems, another delegation from Orsino is an irritation she should be spared – as she might have been, were not Sir Toby, who 'speaks nothing but madman' at this time of day, the unfortunate sentry rather than the efficient Maria. Having a shrewd idea of her uncle's state, Olivia knows she will make a better impression on the visitor by dispatching the officious Malvolio: and his departure gives her the chance for a friendly warning to Feste, to smarten up a little and stay on his toes:

> Now you see, sir, how your fooling grows old, and people dislike it

– 'old' in this context meaning stale. Deflecting again, he replies in his elaborate fool's way:

> Thou hast spoke for us, madonna, as if thy eldest son should be
> a fool, whose skull Jove cram with brains . . .

– brains taken perhaps from Toby, who arrives not so much 'half-drunk' as three sheets in the wind and dyspeptic. Olivia's salon now feels like a thoroughfare, with Toby as a runaway wheel. The canary-wine bottle was broached early this morning, as we have seen: now he completely fails to oblige with any information, even mistaking 'lethargy' for 'lechery' (or bloodymindedly pretending to). Committing the nameless visitor to hell and uttering a morose drunkard's *cri de coeur* – 'give me faith, say I' – he weaves away, the air behind him touched with the vapour of pickled herrings. The uncooperativeness stymies Olivia, and for a moment we can see how vulnerable she is. She calls in Feste for a professional insight:

What's a drunken man like, fool?

Identifying the three stages of intoxication – somewhat along the lines of the man drinking the bottle, then the bottle drinking the man – Feste's wit is mature and worldly-wise. Whenever he is at ease in the play, his tone of voice is simple and direct – however sophisticated his thought and however hard the hit. In a hiatus like this, he is the perfect ally for Olivia – psychologist and diplomat as much as Fool – and, who knows, even Toby might become manageable in his hands.

What Toby has achieved is to give Malvolio time to go to the gate, dispute with Cesario and return. Malvolio and Feste perhaps crisscross frostily in the corridor: and, oddly enough, Malvolio himself hits form now – the same coldness of heart as before, but more elegant and consistent to himself. He is here because there is an obvious limit to what he can do: whatever excuses he offered on the doorstep, they became the very reason Cesario 'comes to speak with you', and under such circumstances, he has simply had to refer back. Asked to describe the visitor, he blooms into genuine humour: Cesario is

Not yet old enough for a man, nor young enough for a boy; as a squash is before 'tis a peascod, or a codling when 'tis almost an apple . . .

A leisurely self-love stalks through this to be sure, but even Feste might be proud of it. It also constitutes a small revenge: determined not be put down again, Malvolio feels he has reinstated himself in the company's eyes with an expatiating wit of his own. But once more he is caught out – hardly has he delivered a fine punchline –

One would think his mother's milk were scarce out of him

– than Olivia snubs him again. Contradicting his permanent instruction to protect her, contrary to all her known rules, to the amazement of all and for who knows what capricious reason of her own, she orders

Let him approach.

It has been a bad morning for Malvolio, only trying to do his job. First the ambush of being asked for his opinion only to be denounced for it, then made to run an errand which Maria really ought to have managed, and now his fine and excelling humour met with a curt order to eat humble pie. One could see how he might begin to go about his business muttering under his breath – even, ultimately, conceiving the idea that unreasonable treatment like this was some perverse test of his manhood. Humiliated and spurred on, all at once: a pair of yellow stockings awaits him.

There seems to be no persuasive reason why Olivia should act so contrary – and even if Orsino was right to guess that Cesario would be his best messenger, Olivia hasn't set eyes on him yet. She replaces her mourning veil, which seems to come off and on rather for effect. In the text, Malvolio is given an exit here, as if he deserved a break, but there is no great reason for that either – and some advantage to his staying, swelling with objections to Cesario that he has no chance to vent. The remainder of the company, suddenly cast as chaperones not employees, stay as well, struck by the new perversity.

Olivia's and Viola's first strange and fatal interview[23] immediately shows Viola at her best, entering stylishly into her role, and Olivia increasingly wilful – the more so the more pressure she comes under. She starts by making rather unfunny play out of being or not being 'the honourable lady of the house'; but Cesario, who is in fact an aristocrat and a wit, is a match for her, and having graciously agreed to receive the emissary, Olivia soon finds herself unable to control him. Her own humour is rather haughty and colourless:

> Your will . . . whence came you, sir . . . are you a comedian?

but Viola is firing on all cylinders: if she is enduring a 'barful strife', she covers it with a fine and witty performance. Like most Shakespearian figures who conceal their identity, she finds herself an unnervingly good actor – more than a mere 'comedian' – and her character becomes oddly opposite to itself. Graceful and sensitive as Viola, she is 'saucy' as Cesario; normally patient, she is now alert to the slightest affront. She has an answer for everything, and is swift to blame any rudeness of her own on her treatment by Olivia's staff.

---

23 I have staged the play three times, each time bringing Cesario on with an improvised serenading band (sometimes Valentine and Curio). I wouldn't do it again: I wish I had seen earlier that the fragile figure of Viola unattended is much better. Her solitude increases our sympathy for her and prepares us for the confidential soliloquy coming soon.

She also knows – it is a point of honour in both her and Olivia's training – that a messenger has rights: courtesy from an aristocrat, and absolutely no nonsense from the likes of Malvolio and Maria, who is astonished to be seen off with a flick of the wrist, as Viola might her own servant:

> MARIA: Will you hoist sail, sir? Here lies your way.
> VIOLA: No, good swabber, I am to hull here a little longer.

A page of such high competence, proud and spirited, would be intriguing to anyone: but what she takes to be an undercurrent of mockery increasingly nettles Olivia – it is certainly 'not that time of moon' in her life for courtly unkindness. An initial ravishing compliment:

> Most radiant, exquisite and unmatchable beauty

was immediately withdrawn: sounding like Orsino's style, this was only a 'speech . . . excellently well penned' which Cesario has 'taken great pains to con'. The flirtation is provoking, as if Cesario had publicly caressed her and then insisted the hand was Orsino's.

The introductions jolt argumentatively along, the visitor far more voluble than the host. Cesario shifts from a gentle gallantry – 'good beauties . . . good gentle one' – to plain sexual homily, declaring in front of everyone that Olivia is positively obliged not to

> usurp yourself, for what is yours to bestow is not yours to reserve

– in other words, she has a duty to give her love. Eventually (with the help of the female sensibility controlling him) he waxes quite seductive – he holds 'the olive in [his] hand', and is himself a musky mystery:

> What I am, and what I would, are as secret as maidenhead . . .

Of course Viola is only doing her job,[24] but she instinctively grasps that some part of it must be to attract Olivia: in the event, her male effrontery will be her undoing. The technique works so well that Olivia impulsively clears the room of her astounded entourage to concentrate on the visitor, her veil, perhaps fortunately, still hiding her face:

> . . . we will hear this divinity . . . Now sir, what is your text?

---

24   The boy actor of Viola is, after all, being restored to his young masculinity.

Intrigued by the speaker as much as the speech, she embarks on revenge. Since Cesario only speaks prettily as a professional necessity, she will play the literary critic:

> A comfortable doctrine, and much may be said of it . . . In his bosom? In what chapter of his bosom?

Olivia has the insight to deconstruct the conventional metaphors, and perhaps is entitled to; but to the third person in the room, Viola herself, intently watching the scene, she sounds irritatingly spoilt. Tiring of her measly badinage:

> O, I have read it. It is heresy. Have you no more to say?

Cesario asks to see Olivia unveiled – on such a delegation, it is silly to address someone you can't see, and it will satisfy Viola's private curiosity. The famous beauty turns her compliant gesture into something like a sexual disclosure:

> . . . we will draw the curtain and show you the picture . . . Is't not well done?

But neither Cesario nor Viola has much truck with this vanity: extremely cheekily, Cesario implies it may all have been done in a dressing room:

> Excellently done, if God did all

– but has the sense swiftly to go into lyrical verse, as if apologising for the joke. Behind her mask meanwhile, Viola has made a bittersweet assessment of her rival, and it bleeds into Cesario's language:

> 'Tis beauty truly blent, whose red and white
> Nature's own sweet and cunning hand laid on.

Whenever we hear Viola's thoughts in Cesario's mouth like this, we touch on something fundamental in the play, its raw material perhaps: a sort of silence surrounds these moments, like a briefly-shared meditation.

Cesario repeats the idea that it would be cruel to let beauty die with the bearer (a recurrent Shakespearian concern):

> Lady, you are the cruell'st she alive,
> If you will lead these graces to the grave
> And leave the world no copy.

This is meant as an invitation into Orsino's arms; but something is developing that Viola hasn't noticed. To ward it off, Olivia makes a heavy-handed joke – she will draw up a pedantic list of her features:

> . . . item, two lips, indifferent red; item, two grey eyes, with lids
> to them . . .

However, Viola assumes the prerogative of an equal, and faults her affectation:

> I see you what you are. You are too proud;
> But if you were the devil, you are fair.

The imagery is darkening, and, its emotions cranked up a notch, the dialogue is breaking mutually into verse – with a sense of surrender, the release we feel when we finally start telling the truth. Olivia cannot resist having her praises sung, even by the despised Orsino:

> How does he love me?

– but even the eloquence of

> . . . adorations, fertile tears,
> With groans that thunder love, with sighs of fire

is not good enough or personal enough: her pride is sustained but her heart untouched. Disappointed despite herself, her response:

> Your lord does know my mind; I cannot love him . . .

is reasonably mature, a flash of candid regret; and so probably is her list of Orsino's qualities:

> Yet I suppose him virtuous, know him noble . . .
> In voices well divulged, free, learned and valiant,
> And in dimension, and the shape of nature,
> A gracious person.

It makes no difference – she repeats that unchangeable

> But yet I cannot love him.

She doesn't say why – but then who can ever say why? It is a fact of life, and it causes the deadlocked Viola to take a reckless, self-defining chance. She surprises herself with a beautiful image of the persistent devotion which she can already foresee for her own life – basing it not on Olivia's intransigence but on how she would behave if she, Viola, were Orsino. In fact, it almost reproves Orsino for not working hard enough and relying on messengers. Faced with a denial like Olivia's, what would Viola do?

Make me a willow cabin at your gate
And call upon my soul within the house . . .

The famous and lovely passage draws on the same poignant image of forsaken faith as Desdemona's Willow Song in *Othello* – it is also the posture mocked by Benedick, who offers to make a soppy garland from the tree for Claudio in *Much Ado*.[25] Here it is used quite humbly, as a modest material for a devout lover's hideout. The speech is not quite what it seems: although she is pretending to be Orsino, in her heart Viola is describing what she would do if she were wooing him and being rejected as he is by Olivia – all in a dutiful effort to impress Olivia with Orsino's love. Its virtuosity depends on a pattern of tension and release:

Make me a willow cabin at your gate

is specific and factual, but

. . . call upon my soul within the house

is an open-vowelled call; likewise

Write loyal cantons of contemned love[26]

applies the brakes a little with its mass of consonants, and

. . . sing them loud even in the dead of night

releases the pressure again, preparing for the soaring arc of

Halloo your name to the reverberate hills
And make the babbling gossip of the air
Cry out 'Olivia!'[27]

Having spotted this music, the actor has the subtle problem of controlling it. That may involve doing the whole passage on a breath or

25   By the sixteenth century, the phrase 'to wear the willow' already stood for mourning a sweetheart, and so it remains, in poetry and folk-song. W.H. Auden uses it in this way in *Underneath an Abject Willow*; and at some point the tree has become the source of comfort and protection, as in Joan Armatrading's lovely song *Willow*.

26   'Cantons' is the latest in a series of words in the scene – 'dexteriously', 'foreknowledge', 'comptible' – that Shakespeare only ever used once (as well as a phrase – 'this present' – which he often used but seems to have invented himself). The reason for 'cantons' must be a most subtle musicality, since the more normal 'cantos' would have done. The inventive merriment of Shakespeare's relationship with the language – his sheer ear – is forever astonishing.

27   Peggy Ashcroft, a famous Viola, almost called out 'Orsino !' at the climax of this speech instead of 'Olivia !' Not so good an idea on paper perhaps, but like all great actors she had the ability to turn on a sixpence which I can believe made it thrilling.

two only, since, once started, it can't lose momentum, for all its technical changes and intensification of feeling.

The graded pressure of this central speech is typical of the whole remarkable duologue, which is packed with psychological interest and highly volatile. It alternates concession with assertion: each phrase changes the situation and affects the minute balance between the two women. They are finding what they have in common – intellectual expertise and speed of response – and the odd kinship of their names, the one almost an inversion of the other, now seems more than accidental. They are, in fact, each other's equal, and as in all Shakespearian antagonisms, electric wit unites more than it separates. Through the whole scene, the conscious purpose of Viola's ambiguous beauty, impertinence and lyricism has been survival only, but their unbidden impact on Olivia's tamped-down spirit is leading the Countess into a comic struggle to subdue sexual desire to her self-image. The process will make her far more sympathetic, since we all know something of what she is enduring, and the battle between her pride and her hormones will make the play tenser, funnier and more pitiful. The complexity for Viola, meanwhile, is hair-raising – Olivia's denigration of Orsino should have been music to her ears, but she is more fairminded than that, and she was stung instead to a spirited defence which unexpectedly opened her own heart. Her passage through the play is clearly going to be hard: she will need all her airy talents.

Meanwhile, wooed by Shakespeare's best efforts from the mouth of a lackey, Olivia is a lost thing:

> You might do much.
> What is your parentage?

The question of rank is important, and this messenger has been a big surprise. Could he be other than he seems? Viola, under the pressure of Olivia's petty manoeuvrings – being asked to come back tomorrow to report Orsino's reaction, even being tipped as if she were a 'fee'd post' – partly gives herself away with an outburst beyond her role:

> Love make his heart of flint that you shall love
> And let your fervour, like my master's, be
> Placed in contempt. Farewell, fair cruelty.

That will happen – but when it does, Olivia will be kindlier dealt with than Orsino is by her.

If Viola has touched on love's abandon, Olivia, tasting self-forbidden fruit, is the mouthpiece of its embarrassment – going over the words Cesario said after he's gone, picking over meticulous details of his behaviour, assembling a singing fantasy of the whole man:

> Thy tongue, thy face, thy limbs, actions and spirit
> Do give thee five-fold blazon.

She tries to rein the feeling in:

> Not too fast! Soft, soft!

– since, all said and done, a lady should fall in love with a 'master', not a 'man' – and she decides to play a teenager's trick. She will send a ring after Cesario, pretending it was somehow left behind. To the discomforted Malvolio, perhaps waiting to be summoned only a few inches out of sight, this is reasonable, even if the instruction to 'run' is not so welcome: it will be a new opportunity to put the tiresome young man down. He is not acute enough to smell a rat in Olivia's cobbled-up invitation:

> If that the youth will come this way tomorrow,
> I'll give him reasons for't

and he doesn't notice her exaggerated dignity, since he listens only to himself.

His departure, all his lordly manner applied to a disguised *billet doux*, is for Olivia like the irrevocable moment when a fateful letter is finally let drop into the mouth of the post-box. She immediately feels giddy panic:

> I do I know not what, and fear to find
> Mine eye too great a flatterer for my mind.

To her, unlike Viola, love is both a game and 'the plague', a fearful thing and a secret mischief: unable to resolve things, she lazily throws the whole thing off as predetermined:

> Fate, show thy force; ourselves we do not owe;
> What is decreed must be, and be this so.

Her future is in the hands not of a good God, but of some capricious Pan dressed up as destiny. Perhaps there's nothing else she can do; but returning to her devotions, she has the devil inside her.

★

The play is beginning to pull away, like a train mastering its load – Viola's and Olivia's argument was, at last, unrestricted, poetic and fiercely human. But it has taken some time. Three of the first Act's five scenes have been daringly short, there have been four locations, and we have briefly met a variety of characters, vignettes with tenuous links. How to ensure a flow? This is the part of the play where a director will be most tempted to invent some context – Feste as the MC, a sustained view of Olivia's mourning – to make it all seem a whole.

But it is not a need that would have been felt originally. We don't know if this play was ever performed outdoors at the Globe Theatre: but if you visit the Middle Temple Hall, where the audience would also have been on three sides, you can imagine Orsino and his lords sweeping into the thirty-metre chamber like Francis Drake and his retinue, sending the play's opening lines bouncing back from the spectacular roof and demanding our attention, in spades. They would then have been quite brutally supplanted, as each new arrival – Viola, Toby and Maria, inevitable extroverts – clamoured to establish themselves. Similarly, in unlit public theatres like the Globe, entrances and exits would have been taken at quite a lick: apart from the rare occasions when a scene was to be 'discovered' on the inner stage by the drawing of curtains, it was brought onto the platform by actors coming boldly from extreme right and left upstage entrances. With traffic from one side simultaneous with that moving towards the other, the flood of language would have been uninterrupted: physical energy would have kept the stage alive and few questions been asked. The flow, in other words, took care of itself.

Shakespeare made a virtue of this practicality with some wonderful counterpoints between one manner of speech and another, and these certainly evaporate in the modern theatre's long scene changes, which give an audience too much time to reflect on too little. But to some extent we are stuck with these delays, and they can certainly cut this Act, *Twelfth Night*'s most fragile, adrift.[28] However, we have an advantage. The Elizabethan style must have given everything rather a public clamour, the actors having to pull

---

28   The Victorians got so bogged down in decor that (as a variant on reversing 1.1 and 1.2) a typical reordering of the first half had all the scenes in Olivia's house (1.3, 1.5, 2.3) played through first; then an interval, followed by Orsino's (1.4, 2.4). In this version 1.1 and 1.2, and 2.1. and 2.2, were in their right place, but either played before a frontcloth or 'described . . . by the characters or in a prologue' (Horace Furness, 1901).

the attention from one side to the other across a span of more than a hundred and eighty degrees. We have more various means of capturing our audience, and consequently a new liberty of mood. For one thing, the cinema has affected our expectations with its variety of conventions, especially in its ability to move from the spectacular to the unbearably private. Some of this freedom has fed back into the theatre, where we also have the technology to make an audience, controlled by our light in their darkness, feel they are moving in to look at something small or laying back for something big, as we please. We too zoom in and out, snap-cue our lights, mix and jump-cut. In the famous opening of *Hamlet*, you might be almost physically drawn into Francisco's eery solitude for a tense few moments before 'Who's there?' makes him jump, or we might ignore his feelings and start right in with the line, in a sort of master-shot. *Twelfth Night* could begin with Orsino listening to a large group of musicians, in which case he is unashamed of his love and announces its symptoms to all: or he might confide his secret to one player alone, while we lean forward, becoming what the Elizabethans couldn't have imagined, eavesdroppers. It depends on what we want of the characters. To make Orsino less windily exhibitionist is an attractive option – introversion sometimes seems like the badge of 'truth' – and the principle can be applied to every scene, so that Toby becomes more ruminative and less coarse, and Viola arrives stunned into silence by the shipwreck. Shakespeare, on his one lifelong set lit by candles or God, might find it all very odd: but it is easy for us to alternate introspection and barn storming, rhetoric and self-analysis. We balance our personal tastes with what we dimly perceive might have been his intentions – far from a precise code of course, more a sense which you gradually grasp with experience of what he tended most often to do. And it is sometimes very satisfying to take a liberty – he did, often.

At the least, the company needs to know what kind of a musical relay they are in. Every time I have worked on the play, the actors have commonly warmed up before a performance by running this Act alone – the job, of course, being less to draw attention to their own debuts, more to listen to what surrounds them and help the forward movement. In many ways, the evening will depend on generous teamwork.

Whatever the segues into it, the closing scene of *Twelfth Night*'s first Act has exemplified its blend of lyricism and satire. This has even been hinted at in the contrasting music of the people's names: romantic figures jostle for splendour but are haunted by Belch and Aguecheek. Throughout this play, euphony and mockery go side by side, unabashed – as they do in the otherwise much different *Troilus and Cressida*, written at about the same time, which brilliantly presents images of deserved and undeserved glory, depending on which way you brush its nap. Like the mythical heroes of that play, but with more sense of fun, everyone in *Twelfth Night* has a contradictory birthright: self-absorption but lightheadedness, vanity and vulnerability, their own particular wit and beauty of speech – they are both banal and marvellous. In a sense, Viola stands alone, her sorrow buried deep within her. Her only foible has been her unlikely infatuation with Orsino, but now she has justified it with a lovely utterance: the sense that she alone survives criticism is giving us our only confident sense of order.

ACT TWO

Act 2 Scene 1–Act 2 Scene 5

2.1.   Having scorned the Victorians' transposition of the first two scenes of *Twelfth Night*, I had better own up. I have myself always switched 2.1 and 2.2, so that Malvolio, dispatched after Viola in 1.5 with Olivia's ring, is then seen breathlessly catching up with her – and also so that after Viola's soliloquy that follows this, Sebastian can, with a little legerdemain, instantly take her place on the same spot. Since we have had no warning that Viola's brother is to be a twin, this seems to me an agreeable kind of showmanship. Having recorded my own preference,[1] I now return tolerantly to Shakespeare.

Whenever it comes, the sight of Sebastian is a fine moment: we believed him dead and forgotten, and never expected to revisit the beach, in calm weather now, to see such an elegant double step into his sister's space.[2] An audience will immediately skin its eyes, grateful for the production's best efforts on their physical likeness, and then be struck by some deeper similarities. The two of them seem to have the same humour and modesty: and when Sebastian, some way into the scene, refers to his sister, it is with her own unaffected charm:

> A lady, sir, though it was said she much resembled me, was yet
> of many accounted beautiful . . .

Like her, he handles strong feelings with a certain buoyancy. And just as Viola's grief was soon overtaken by plans for the future, Sebastian's more explicit sorrow at having lost her – 'mine eyes will

---

1   It is certainly no worse than Augustin Daly's 1894 production, which started with 2.1, followed by 1.2, then 1.1.

2   The location of Shakespeare's scenes given in most editions is not his own – to him all things took place in the Wooden O – but the work of the eighteenth-century editor Edward Capell; the author would have thought his efforts pointless, but the reminders are quite helpful.

tell tales of me' – is tempered by concern for the feelings of his new friend Antonio:

> I shall crave of you your leave that I may bear my evils alone. It were a bad recompense for your love to lay any of them on you.

His sensitivity here is like his sister's later sympathy for Olivia when she realises the Countess has fallen in love with her disguise. The one difference is that the strong Sebastian weeps; Viola, a woman with full cause, never.

Since the first printed cast-list of the play (Nicholas Rowe's edition, 1709), Antonio has been described as 'a Captain'; but he is still a bit of a mystery. The end of the play will show him to have been a formidable sailor – in Orsino's prejudice a pirate, tormenting Illyria's fleet in some unimaginable conflict. He has rescued Sebastian from the wreck within an hour, Sebastian believes, of his sister's drowning – but whether that means that Antonio was on the boat, or that he saw it all from his own vessel or from the beach (and why is he, Orsino's enemy, still in Illyria at all?), is left open. To me, he has the air of a beachcomber, outside the law, and, most important, a man hitherto sufficient to himself: but now he has developed the most powerful protective feelings for the young man he has saved, and has perhaps fed him for a day or two from his fishing catch and dried out his clothes.

On one level, then, he is becoming Horatio to his friend's Hamlet. It is interesting, too, that Shakespeare has already used the name of Antonio as a protector in *The Merchant of Venice*, where Bassanio's usage of the older man's friendship to court Portia exploited his feelings for him. Like both of those outsiders, and like Don Pedro in *Much Ado*, *Twelfth Night*'s Antonio is important to the story, but somehow on its edge; like Aguecheek, he will make an odd number at the final marriage feast. He starts by speaking with an attractive balance of competence and vulnerability, and the directness of Shakespeare's working man:

> Will you stay no longer? Nor will you not that I go with you? . . .
> Let me know of you whither you are bound . . .

while Sebastian's diction – easy, antithetical, graceful – establishes his aristocratic credentials:

> My stars shine darkly over me; the malignancy of my fate might perhaps distemper yours . . . my determinate voyage is mere extravagancy.

He has noticed Antonio's 'excellent touch of modesty' in not pressing him for details about himself: so he deserves a decent explanation, which Sebastian supplies, including the oddity that he has been using an alias, Rodrigo. He and his sister come from a famous foreign family Antonio has surely heard of, just as Viola had heard of Orsino: they were 'both born in an hour', and at the thought of her, his formality slews:

> . . . would we had so ended. But you, sir, altered that, for some hour before you took me from the breach of the sea was my sister drowned.

This accusation is a morose figure of speech of course, but Sebastian's suppressed grief should make it sound as if he really blames Antonio. He tests himself further with a lovely description of Viola:

> She bore a mind that envy could not but call fair

– and the memory of her gifts (which we have seen as well) breaks him:

> She is drowned already, sir, with salt water, though I seem to drown her remembrance again with more.

The balance between the two is evident again: just as Viola can pass for a young man, there is a delicacy in her brother that supports rather than qualifies his masculinity. The part needs to be played by a young actor with an unusually open heart.

Antonio fears that he may have made matters worse – but his being so hard on himself again brings out Sebastian's generosity:

> ANTONIO: Pardon me, sir, your bad entertainment.
> SEBASTIAN: O good Antonio, forgive me your trouble.
> ANTONIO: If you will not murder me for my love, let me be your servant.
> SEBASTIAN: If you will not undo what you have done, that is, kill him whom you have recovered, desire it not.

These are lovely antithetical cadences, but some of the words ('murder', 'kill') are extreme: the men's courteous argument is passionate, as if, after Sebastian's breakdown, the barriers between them had fallen. His recovery has given Sebastian energy, impetuosity even:

> I am yet so near the manners of my mother that, upon the least occasion more, mine eyes will tell tales of me. I am bound to the Count Orsino's court. Farewell.

Like his sister, he is taking charge of himself and moving forward towards the geographical centre of things – partly to subdue the power of his female element and partly to create a rich expectation for us, since anyone who arrives there stays in the play. Like those of 1.2, 1.4 and 1.5, this ending swells with promise.

Antonio is, very suddenly, alone with his old life. He moves into benevolent verse, almost like a requiem:

> The gentleness of all the gods go with thee.

But life is for living, and the more he realises that it would be insane to follow, the more he knows he will: he adores Sebastian (the word was just as strong then) even more than he did before their talk. It is terribly ill-advised for him but absolutely necessary.

The whole scene gently reverberates with one of the play's main themes. Under unlikely circumstances, an intense friendship has grown between the two, who at first sight could have been mistaken for Viola and the Sea Captain. It is also a repeated version of the passionate reaction to loss that took erotic form with both Viola and Olivia. Each man's 'bosom is full of kindness' – the eyes of each 'will tell tales' of him. On the face of it, Sebastian was volubly in charge throughout, while Antonio was plain and subservient: but Sebastian's control was only apparent, and in many ways the poor and self-invented man, virile but yielding, held the power – until he was betrayed by his own overwhelming sympathy. As between Olivia and Viola, the emotions move like mercury, but the difference is that these two show each other unfeigned goodwill and sensitivity: Antonio continually apologetic for intruding, Sebastian seeking to save him from being jinxed by the friendship.

The passionate attachment of two men is a regular theme in Shakespeare, especially in the Sonnets, where the characters are an older poet and a younger protégé or patron – the poet sounds so like Shakespeare himself, and sometimes so like Antonio, that this may have obliquely contributed to the unsubstantiated idea that he himself played this part in *Twelfth Night*. Of course, to define Antonio's relationship with Sebastian as homosexual is to use a cramping definition Shakespeare would not have understood – even now, the word clunks onto the page.[3] There is a whole range of

---

3   I did hear of a production which began with Antonio and Sebastian taking a shower together – it was done by an English director in Japan, trying out some ideas before asserting them in a later staging in England.

homoerotic possibilities in these plays, both lyrical and predatory –
Aufidius and Coriolanus circle each other hungrily, and so do
Hector and Achilles in *Troilus*, under the pretext of gladiatorial
warfare – but whether through cowardice or restraint, Shakespeare
never (with the single exception of Achilles and Patroclus, a story
that comes direct from Homer), explicitly treats male-to-male
sexuality. In this, as in other things, he was far less direct than
Christopher Marlowe.[4]

One temptation for the actors in this scene is simply to play a
mood – prevailing sadness for Sebastian, and from Antonio a sort of
fierce kindness – but the trick is continual variation: while their
combined strength remains constant, its mass continuously fluc-
tuates as if they were at two ends of a rope. The other risk is to make
too much of it all – these are the last on of the main cast, their debut
is frustratingly brief and followed by another long wait before they
return. But the scene's nature is rather quick, and self-indulgence
will seriously inhibit the play's movement. The performers have to
be as noble as their characters: move mercurially through it all, get
off, and trudge upstairs for another hour.

2.2.   Unless the excellent precaution has been taken of advancing
this scene to before 2.1, Malvolio has only now caught up with
Cesario in the street. With cheery Elizabethan logic, the stage direction says they enter 'at several doors': but we surely expect them one
after the other, not as a converging double-act. Irritatingly for
Malvolio, Viola asserts that she has arrived at this spot 'on a
moderate pace': is the boy implying he has been slow to catch up,
being out of condition? As he discharges his office, Malvolio speaks
as much 'in starts, distractedly' as Olivia did – his sentences are
shortened by breathlessness and linked up by afterthoughts: 'She
adds, moreover . . . And one thing more . . . ' It is not quite the fine

4   The question of Shakespeare's own orientation has of course arisen. Some gay people are
offended that Stoppard and Madden's whimsical *Shakespeare in Love* insists on his
heterosexuality: meanwhile some heterosexuals have trouble with the homoerotic content of
the Sonnets, and cling rather anxiously to the dubious theory that in them Shakespeare was
simply following a literary convention with no emotional investment of his own. In fact, all
special sexual pleading for Shakespeare is as thankless as for most dead artists, and in his case
probably as useful as arguing that Bacon wrote the plays. Alan Bennett once remarked that
identifying a person's sexual tastes is a bit like establishing which brand of mineral water they
prefer in the middle of a desert: and the truth is, we each want Shakespeare to be like us.

speech he would have liked to make, and as a result perhaps, he can't resist a petulant nudge about the ring:

> You might have saved me my pains to have taken it away yourself.

He slightly rephrases Olivia's invitation to 'come this way tomorrow' – not to misrepresent it exactly, but to add a little discouragement of his own:

> . . . that you be never so hardy to come again in his affairs, unless it be to report your lord's taking of this.

It is his own small interference in the course of events, but its impact is small compared with the shock Viola has just had. She has immediately seen Olivia's ploy for what, alarmingly, it must be: but this is someone who can put a brave face even on a brother's drowning, and she gallantly saves Olivia's with a swift fib:

> She took the ring of me. I'll none of it.

Malvolio is thus stuck with the thing, and called a liar: it is very provoking. His eagerness to discredit the bumptious boy leads him into a wild invention, delivered with complete conviction:

> Come, sir, you peevishly threw it to her.

The fun of this is that they both know it never happened, though it is what Malvolio would like to do now. Goaded all morning beyond his rather small limits, and now unable to get Cesario even to proffer his hand, he lets the ring end up on the ground:

> If it be worth stooping for, there it lies, in your eye . . .

This is a Malvolio Moment, recorded in stage history in two main versions. In one, the lofty hand, with the pinkie cocked, drops the ring from a great height. The trouble with this, as I know from experience, is that it rolls away down the rake of the stage or between the floorboards, whereas Viola will want to retrieve it in a moment without scurrying around. So that is the selfish variation. Teamwork is better served by the second, whereby Malvolio places it over the shaft of his staff of office and lets it slide more governably to the ground. Or, as with all Malvolio Moments, you can simply disregard the opportunity – and in fact, I don't know why Malvolio should go to so much trouble. It may be better to concentrate on the comic possibilities of his departure, as, obscurely humiliated once more, he breathes deeply and trudges all the way home, trying to reassert a stately tempo. As he moves more and more slowly, he will no doubt be thinking of the more stunning things he might have said.

There is a sense in which the play is simply enjoying itself. With the plot still relatively loose, Shakespeare has allowed himself to experiment with promising character duologues – Andrew with Maria, Toby drunk with Olivia, Olivia with Cesario – only some of which advance the story. This face-off between the codling and the crab-apple, their friendship hardly made in heaven, certainly makes up for not having seen their first meeting at Olivia's gate. But now it is time for a summary, by means of a theatre device that hinges the past to the future.

The soliloquy that follows is the play's first, and – if you exclude Malvolio's meditation in the garden – its central one. It is Viola and *Twelfth Night* in their essence. Only she (and her twin later on) has the friendliness to speak directly to us at length, as if we were as important to her as she to us. There have been hints of this before – her swift declaration of love for Orsino, and a complicit nudge in the scene with Olivia:

> . . . by the very fangs of malice, I swear, I am not that I play

– and they were preparations for what is always a thrilling thing in Shakespeare, an extended confidence. The placing is consummately done. In *Hamlet*, with a sort of sublime mischief, Shakespeare has his hero, recently tested by a great variety of visitors, start a major soliloquy with a profound paradox:

> Now I am alone

– whereupon he discusses his position with hundreds of us. With Viola too, the moment has been prepared for by a massive inner solitude. She has no friends on the stage (or none who see her clearly), and, like Hamlet's, her isolation touches us: it is urgent to collude with her. I am sure actresses of the part can report a most welcome thing at this moment – an audience like children, forward in their seats and ready to join in.

She asks us questions we could easily answer, five in the twenty-five lines of the speech, starting with:

> I left no ring with her; what means this lady?

– and she reasons exactly as we would if we didn't know the facts, step by step: *I believe she liked me, and, yes, she did keep looking at me, her speech was broken up – yes, oh God, she loves me.* Like many of Shakespeare's reports on the past, it has changed a bit in the recalling: it isn't really true that Olivia

> did speak in starts, distractedly

– at least the actress will have strained at the quite regular verse if she did. And the idea of Olivia's breath being taken away:

> . . . methought her eyes had lost her tongue

is a charming untruth – the Countess is never short of something to say. At the time, Viola lost patience with her tricksiness; but now she generously interprets what has happened not so much as it affects herself but the 'poor lady', and the final dropping of the penny is, for emphasis, almost completely monosyllabic:[5]

> None of my lord's ring? Why, he sent her none;
> I am the man; if it be so, as 'tis,
> Poor lady, she were better love a dream.

It makes her hate the insincerity she has been forced into:

> Disguise, I see thou art a wickedness
> Wherein the pregnant enemy does much.
> How easy is it for the proper-false
> In women's waxen hearts to set their forms!

In its contempt for 'seeming', and the apparent weight of the images, this could be *Hamlet* or *Measure for Measure*, but the voice is lighter, both rueful and confident, essentially not introspective; and the thought resolves itself in a rhyme, which in English generally makes things a little humorous:

> Alas, our frailty is the cause, not we;
> For such as we are made of, such we be.

Her sisterly solidarity with Olivia is affectionate and rather home-spun – you can hardly imagine a tragic heroine looking into the future with:

---

5   Hamlet again. At the critical point of 'How All Occasions Do Inform Against Me', he is given

> I do not know
> Why yet I live to say 'This thing's to do',
> Sith I have cause, and will, and strength, and means
> To do't.

> How will this fadge?

or describing herself, being both man and woman, as a 'poor monster'.

More than anyone else in the play, Viola speaks simply, with classic Shakespearian diction, fresh and springy – her talent always being to experience painful ideas with an essential lightness of spirit. Resigned like Olivia but without Olivia's narcissism, believing with Toby that care's an enemy to life but without Toby's spiritual decay, this is a tolerant voice in an increasingly barmy world, and it softens a situation alarming for the speaker and apparently hopeless for all of them. Orsino cannot have Olivia, Viola's own state is 'desperate' because she cannot have Orsino, and Olivia's life will fill with 'thriftless sighs' because she cannot have Cesario – but still it will be all right. Viola's fatalistic conclusion:

> O Time, thou must untangle this, not I;
> It is too hard a knot for me to untie

is a much sweeter version of Olivia's melodramatic couplet earlier:

> Fate, show thy force; ourselves we do not owe.
> What is decreed must be; and be this so.

We want to help her, but know she will somehow manage on her own.

For the actress beginning to work her way through the part, this is obviously a big milestone, and it completely depends on her willingness to meet the audience in her own person, candidly – not as easy as it sounds, except that there will be great good will in the air. The technical rests in the speech are easy and logical, and each time it is as if she had finished – 'She loves me, sure . . . I am the man'; but these light markers, built towards enthusiastically, need to be moved unselfconsciously past. Some Shakespearian monologues are mountainous; this one is gentler, as long as you are watchful and receptive – start simply, don't get too excited too soon, breathe and keep going. Above all, never draw back from us. There are giddy moments: but the air at the top is clean and fresh.

2.3.

'Approach, Sir Andrew . . . '

After Viola's marvellous clarity, speech wobbles and slurs – and this is one benefit of keeping the scenes in their original order. It is the wrong end of the evening for Toby and Andrew. Olivia's mansion being quite uncongenial for their form of recreation, they have been out all day and are returning with some relics – nowadays it might be a pint mug or beer-mats stolen from the pub, then, I suppose, an empty flagon or feathers stuck in their hats. Whatever fun was to be had has certainly been had. Everyone has gone to bed, and the furniture forms vague shapes to be negotiated in the dark. Their clothes will not be of the freshest either.

Remembering Toby's disruption of Olivia's scene earlier, it is easy to guess his condition by now, and it is difficult to imagine Andrew holding his drink well at any time. The laborious tone in which they discuss the rights and wrongs of staying up late certainly suggests alcoholic fatigue rather than its inspiration:

> TOBY: Not to be abed after midnight is to be up betimes, and *diluculo surgere*, thou know'st –
> ANDREW: Nay, by my troth, I know not; but I know to be up late is to be up late.

Their stubborn hedonism has not so much made them reel as interfered with their sense of consequence: Toby's reasoning is truly, dully, confusing. If it is after midnight and you are not in bed, then you could be said to be up early; but if you then go to bed you are retiring in good time as well. In fact, the Latin tag that supports his argument recommends rising at the break of day, not being still awake then; but Andrew would hardly spot it, and just now Toby can't tell the difference either. This is what gives you their drunkenness: the banal momentousness, the nose-tapping gesture towards learning, the feeble begging-to-differ. It is as if something of actual meaning has been said.[6]

The effect of these deliberations on Andrew's cerebral cortex may be imagined: they hurt. Being rather sensitive about foreign languages, he is alert to an affront, and certainly not to be patronised

---

6 A recent (1999) production of the play in Regents Park in London by Rachel Kavanaugh offered something I have never seen before in this scene: a thoroughly dyspeptic Andrew, ill-humouredly tolerating the attenuated revelry. In fact, he need hardly be drunk at all, and he has certainly had a long day.

with Latin. For him, commonsense is enough, to be up late is to be up late, and life is all about food and drink. Toby, like a bar-room philosopher spotting the touch of genius in a plain talker, congratulates him on this worldly wisdom as upper-class drinkers still do: one must salute the other as 'a gentleman and a scholar', and call for another round.

In fact, whatever else they have arrived with, they have nothing to drink; and so the sleeping house is disturbed by an anguished call:

Let us therefore eat and drink. Marian, I say, a stoup of wine![7]

– whereupon Feste, always a surprise, appears instead. It transpires later that he has been singing at Orsino's tonight, so perhaps he is on his way there, or just returned: as Toby immediately calls for a song, it will be as well if he has his instrument with him. His immediate joke:

Did you never see the picture of 'We Three'?

actually refers to a sign-board on which two asses are joined by a spectator, but for us the more familiar Hear no evil/See no evil/Speak no evil is easier. To the tired knights, this is suddenly the best of jokes, and Feste is a hero. Andrew, wistful as ever about the accomplishments of others (and no longer boastful about his 'back-trick'), deeply envies his skill at song and dance as well:

I had rather than forty shillings I had such a leg, and so sweet a breath to sing, as the Fool has.

His mind seems to be a little on money – no doubt he has lost more than forty shillings to Toby, and he still dances like a clodpoll – and he goes on impertinently to ask Feste if he received a gift of sixpence for his 'leman' – an old word for a sweetheart which unfortunately makes her sound like a working girl. Why would Andrew be giving money to Feste's girl friend? Perhaps he just regards wealth as a passport, like a man who suddenly pays everyone's bills in a restaurant. However, Feste's private life is not for Andrew to poke about in: he acknowledges the gift, which presumably went into his own pocket, with a dazzling routine of verbal nonsense, pleasantly bewildering

---

7   Toby is always inventing nicknames for Maria, either out of affection or idle playfulness; a 'Maid Marian' was the leader of morris dances. He enjoys fictionalising Maria, but has scant respect for her office, which protects him.

A 'stoup' is an unusually large vessel – Claudius calls for two of them for the duel in *Hamlet*.

everyone. It comprises an impenetrable elaboration of the words 'pocket' and 'gratuity', obscure reassurance about the limits of Malvolio's powers, and a celebration of Olivia's beauty – and it is capped by the surreal appearance of Achilles' private army from the *Iliad* in a public bar:

> I did impeticos thy gratillity; for Malvolio's nose is no whipstock, my lady has a white hand, and the Myrmidons are no bottle-ale houses.

Captivating Andrew, this needs to be delivered without compromise, as if it were the most sensible thing in the world. Feste uses this surreal technique – somewhat like Lewis Carroll's – quite often, and here it helps him avoid unwelcome intimacy with an ingratiating customer.

There is still no drink being taken: and the business of keeping their spirits high is becoming an uphill battle for the two gentlemen. After the fun with words, perhaps a song will do it. You have to pay, of course. Feste is doing well – sixpence yesterday for his girl, sixpence more now from Toby, and sixpence (a 'testril') from Andrew. But would Toby ever part with cash? He may find he has empty pockets, and be obliged to use Andrew as his banker again, in which case Andrew has spent eighteen pence on Feste alone in the last twenty-four hours.

However, although you can hire Feste's services, you can't buy his flattery: he gives them a love song, 'O Mistress Mine', whose first verse woos and whose second ambushes. 'Journeys end in lovers meeting' – so Andrew will have his Olivia ('excellent good, i' faith'); but happiness only lasts a moment and life continues to decay ('youth's a stuff will not endure'). The trailing emotional fuse lit by the first verse starts to race in the second (perhaps with a change of tune[8] or key): the effect will surely be to bring matters to a standstill, since the blankness of their future is not precisely what two maudlin drunks want to hear. The pitiless Fool always judges his audience carefully as he takes their money, in the light of his own undeceived nature – soon his 'dulcet contagion' will seriously discompose Orsino, and in the last moments of the play he will turn his quizzical skills on us as well.

---

8   The traditional tune, a pretty waltz in G, was used by both Thomas Morley and William Byrd – it is possible that Morley collaborated with Shakespeare on this version.

In the quiet house, some time after midnight, energy is flagging and hangovers loom – the party seems doomed. Toby, who must be used to treacherous shoals like this, is quickest off the mark:

> But shall we make the welkin dance indeed? Shall we rouse the night owl in a catch that will draw three souls out of one weaver . . . ?

London's weavers were often Calvinist refugees at the time, and vigorous singing relieved the boredom of their sedentary work – though they sang psalms rather than 'catches'. So perhaps the loudness of 'a song of good life' will subdue the black dog sitting inside Toby. The idea takes hold, as almost any new idea would now, and it is a particularly good plan since Andrew remembers that this sort of thing is a speciality of his:

> And you love me, let's do't: I am dog at a catch.

He hardly needs encouragement, but Feste, interrupting his preparations with three snappy one-liners, makes him ever more excited:

> . . . some dogs will catch well . . . I shall be constrain'd in't to call thee knave, knight . . . I shall never begin if I hold my peace.

In a 'round', each singer comes in with the same phrase but at a different starting-point, and then proceeds through the verse and begins again: it is a perfectly honourable canonical form, but its secular version is by definition silly. And will they be good at it? Apart from the difficulties of getting started (and whatever he says, timing his entry may not come easily to Andrew), the song's complete inability to develop far beyond the initial phrase means that interest will have to be augmented in other ways. Rhythmic dancing is almost inevitable, together and apart, and every available prop – tablecloths, curtains, hats – will be called into service: the 'caterwauling' is specially horrifying to Maria, who probably arrives in time to get forcibly caught up in it herself.

The spell of Feste's delicate, troubling tune has certainly been broken. The few exchanges between Maria's attempts to contain matters and Malvolio's famous entrance are essentially improvisational: the lines are fragmented and difficult to grasp, and at least three contemporary songs are dipped in and out of. Although the pace and volume mustn't slacken, there is one important moment that should not be lost. As Feste admires Toby's performance:

> Beshrew me, the knight's in admirable fooling

Andrew suddenly asserts himself; he won't have it – he is just as funny himself, and actually a bit more human as well:

> Ay, he does well enough if he be disposed, and so do I too; he does it with a better grace, but I do it more natural.

If only his choice of words didn't once again undermine his strong intentions. The rest is a matter of the house being rattled into wakefulness, for any number of lights to go on, for any amount of scuttling through corridors and for many attempts to restrain Toby to fail, so that mounting confusion gives Malvolio an ideal cue – in fact it has gone on almost long, and we are quite relieved to see him.

Malvolio's arrival from his bed is another of his Moments, of course.[9] This inspired character, historically the play's special attraction, promises much at every entrance; but the obligation to make an impact each time places a certain burlesque burden on the actor. Experimenting with candle (complete with dripping wax), silly nightcap, curlers in the hair, hairy legs and beauty pack makes for happy rehearsals – but, because of the different perspective, what is good in the rehearsal room is not always successful on the stage, and there is a danger of strain. Malvolio should be played with as much integrity as funny nightclothes, and he should look possible: one good joke is worth half a dozen old chestnuts.

And his moral position is quite correct. He has gone to bed and been roused by sudden intolerable noise: and he is now doing just what the steward of a great house should do. This responsibility was defined for his own establishment by the young Viscount Montague in 1595: the steward's job was to correct 'negligent and disordered persons . . . frequenters of tabling, carding and dicing in corners and at untimely hours and seasons'. Malvolio is so diligent that, rather admirably, he has forgotten about his own appearance. As well as outrage, he may feel some amazement at what he sees, even a little morbid curiosity at how the rest of the world is capable of behaving – it is quite outside his experience. I feel quite sorry for him – his is a desolate spirit, with no talent for pleasure, even if such loneliness is the consequence of his self-regarding habits: and although his private rituals and his dreams, his night attire and his solitary practices, are an easy laugh throughout the play, such things are, after all, a man's own business. Certainly, to object to being kept

---

9   Beerbohm Tree was the first to wear a nightgown: it is hard now to imagine a Malvolio who doesn't.

awake by careening stupidity – for a house in mourning to be kept awake by it – is reasonable enough. The revellers pride themselves on drawing 'three souls out of one weaver', but he is more accurate – they are gabbling 'coziers' [cobblers'] catches': they are making 'an ale-house of my lady's house', and they do indeed have 'no respect of place, persons nor time'. Drunkards confronted with the dull moral force of sobriety, they can only counter him with silly puns and rudeness, fuelled in Toby's case by a swelling biliousness:

> We did keep time, sir, in our catches. Sneck up!

or by singing daft duets:

> SIR TOBY: 'Farewell, dear heart, since I must needs be gone.'
> FESTE: 'His eyes do show his days are almost done.'

Even Toby's best argument, irresistible to an audience:

> Dost thou think, because thou art virtuous, there shall be no more cakes and ale?

ignores the selfish time and place of consuming them.

Morality has a funny way of skewing on the stage. The devil has the best tunes, and, delighted by the inspired childishness of Toby's party, we too are ready to denigrate Olivia's regime and all who serve it – especially now we have seen her fallibility. In this mocking world, Malvolio is never going to win a round; but there are worse things to be than a killjoy. Unfortunately he is that too, and more, inclined to abuse his position like some dreadful commissar. He warns Toby that Olivia is thinking of sending him packing, implies that he strongly supports the idea, and threatens Maria that he will be making a report on her as well:

> She shall know of it, by this hand.

This is what is pernicious about him – his ability to manoeuvre into a position which Olivia doesn't like but seems to need. From it, he can unsettle not only her loyal staff (Maria), but her relatives (Toby) and her old friend (Feste): except that the Fool is too clever for him and quietly disappears before the searchlight can catch him.

As he stalks away, invited to rub his chain with crumbs and shake his ass's ears, the thermometer drops a bit. It was his manipulative-ness rather than his reasonable protest that soured the air. Andrew and Toby may shout after him, but it is with the energy of noise rather than of good partying. Children deprived of their toys, they both feel a blood-lust swelling – comically in the case of Andrew, who reminds us of his warlike disposition. He imagines himself inviting Malvolio to a duel and not turning up – that would be as good an idea, he thinks, as to have a drink when you're starving. To Andrew, when Maria comes to mention it, Malvolio's great crime is that he is 'a Puritan', for which he, Andrew, plans to 'beat him like a dog'; but his vehemence brings down on him what an intellectual chancer fears most – everyone stops and asks him what he means:

> TOBY: What, for being a Puritan? Thy exquisite reason, dear knight?

But you can't pin down someone with 'th' strangest mind i' th' world', and with a small flick of bravado he goes back into his shell:

> I have no exquisite reason for't; but I have reason good enough.

Toby, too, can imagine the comic possibilities of a duel; but in the more longsighted Maria, able to gauge the state of things in the house (including Olivia's strange interest in Orsino's page), the affair has provoked an inspired idea. To have Malvolio act upon hints that Olivia, already discomposed, might be in love with him, would be a punishment fitting his rather complex crimes. She believes that being

> the best persuaded of himself . . . it is his grounds of faith that all that look on him love him

he will easily be convinced by a decoy in the form of a forged letter. Whether she is right about his character or not (and I suspect Malvolio knows he is very unloved), it will be 'sport royal' and righteous revenge: after all, Maria herself was trying to quell tonight's riot, and she got the reverse of thanks for it. In fact, the whole troublesome evening has brought to the boil the long frustrations of holding her job, her relations with Toby and the upheavals in the house in some kind of balance. Still, her vitality is like a warm fire the knights can huddle around as she cooks up her plan – the retaliation of a hard-working professional,[10] but sweetened by the most human imagery:

---

10   Maria's description of how it will all work isn't in fact what happens; in the event the prudent Fool will not 'make a third'. It is possible that the Garden Scene was revised for the first published version of the play, in the 1623 Folio, and this earlier line not adjusted. Maria's description of what the letter will contain is not borne out either.

> Sweet Sir Toby . . . If I do not . . . make him a common recreation, do not think I have wit enough to lie straight in my bed. I know I can do it . . . for this night, to bed, and dream on the event.

As Maria takes life's domestic hopefulness away with her, Andrew's and Toby's balloon continues to lose air: they can keep going only with a sort of sentimental euphoria, all sighs and inspection of the carpet, the last two in the pub when the women have left and the lights go out. They are back where they started, two men with, in truth, not that much to talk about – and a certain sweetness in the scene's unhurried diminuendo barely masks its harsh realities. Toby, with male complacency, boasts of Maria's devotion to him, visualising her as both enormous (Penthesilea, Queen of the Amazons) and minute (a beagle was a small hunting-dog much despised at the time); and Andrew, mistaking his friend's smugness for confidentiality, delivers his most touching line:

> I was adored once, too.

It is the moment everyone remembers, exactly logical within the conversation but completely unexpected. We will never know whether it was Andrew's mother, a girl, or indeed anyone at all who loved him so much that he can speak of it so simply. It makes no difference: Toby brutally ignores the confidence, telling him only to go to bed and, more important, to acquire more spending money. Andrew dimly hears the cruelty, and tries to be clear and strong – if Toby does not succeed in securing Olivia for him, he will not only be 'a foul way out' but very angry.

> . . . never trust me; take it how you will.

His threat of the terrors of the earth is no match for Toby's lazy bonhomie, and Andrew folds up again. They will go and heat up some sherry and spices ('burn some sack'), because, as they were saying at the outset, it's too late to go to bed now, and this way, as the sun rises, they will finally get a drink.

A vein of driving unkindness has been exposed in Toby, probably originating in his depression at Feste's song – it was marvellously explicit with Malvolio and then petty with Andrew. It begins to look as if his energy and disruptiveness has a direct relationship to his despair: he will soon become the play's motor, giving no quarter to anyone, and as he multiplies the farce he will become a darker and darker figure. The foolish knight meanwhile has had a run of bad luck: no-one has listened to him except when he had rather they didn't. First he was ungratefully interrupted by Feste in the very process of paying him:

> ANDREW: . . . If one knight give a -
> FESTE: Would you have a love song or a song of good life?

Then, far worse than being insulted, he was completely ignored by Malvolio. The matter of the 'Puritan' was awkward; and when, still trying to earn Maria's respect, he made a good joke:

> . . . your horse now would make him an ass

nobody reacted very much. His two manly initiatives – that he 'fooled' as well as Toby, and then his financial defiance at the end – were mistimed: his pugnacity must await another outlet and meanwhile he is face to face again with his slim prospects. It will be as well for him not to go to bed and dwell on it all. After an evening as hard on the heart as the purse, he capitulates again to the embrace of his questionable friend, all stale wine and glassy-eyed friendship: it is hard to know whether his liver or his pocket will be the final casualty of his great adventure.

2.4. The critical distance Shakespeare maintains from each group of characters keeps us unusually open to the others. One of the techniques he applies to writing a comedy in which ugly behaviour is never shirked is to avoid exposing us to any variety of it for too long. As the sour contract between Toby and Andrew begins to curdle our enjoyment of them, we return to Orsino, as he explores his obsession with Olivia further. His energies, self-conscious as they are, are at least centrifugal, in some way even admirable: he wastes them generously, and knowing what we do of Olivia, we would, in all humanity, wish them redirected.

In the next subtle and extraordinary episode with him, between two scenes of broad comedy, lurks much of the surprisingly troubled heart of the play. Typically, it appears to be a matter of light entertainment only. Recapitulating the play's opening, Orsino calls for music to echo his passion – but this time his mood seems clearer, less closed-in: he even greets his court as 'friends'. Today, he wants not a repeated 'strain', but a whole song – he heard it last night, and its effect has proved more than he bargained for. The 'old and antique' tune must again be performed by Feste, who for some reason is now in his house, as he was last night, rather than Olivia's: in transit when he sang to Toby and Andrew, he obviously moonlights like any self-respecting musician. The fact that Feste was

> a fool that the Lady Olivia's father took much delight in

probably recommends him particularly to Orsino: it makes him feel closer to his goddess. It might also mildly emphasise his age, which could be somewhere between Olivia's and the dead man's: he was a bachelor (1.2) when Viola's father used to talk about him, and he is about to recommend, perhaps in his own interests, that younger women should take older men. This is a speculation: but certainly Feste is a perennial – he connects past and present as well as contiguous worlds. He might have sung this song, rather less old-fashioned then, as a young man when Olivia was a child and Orsino was, so to speak, in school.

As usual, the event is self-consciously set up: Orsino calls for the instrumental to be played by his musicians while Feste is found, and instructs Cesario to stay close to him. As before, the music affects the rhythm and tone of his speech: his moods sway with the seductive cadences, and there is a slight sense of posture in all of them. Intoxicated, he sees himself as the model of a legendary lover which Cesario can emulate in time to come:

> if ever thou shalt love,
> In the sweet pangs of it remember me

– and his self-portrait:

> Unstaid and skittish in all motions else
> Save in the constant image of the creature
> That is beloved

is comfortingly devotional. Suddenly asked her opinion of the tune, Viola produces an image off the cuff that leaves his self-consciousness standing naked:

> VIOLA: It gives a very echo to the seat
>   Where love is throned.
> ORSINO: Thou dost speak masterly . . .

Yes indeed – but this breath of real sensibility, like her androgyny in the earlier scene, has the unwelcome effect of drawing attention to her. Orsino's headlights swivel again:

> My life upon't, young though thou art, thine eye
> Hath stayed upon some favour that it loves.
> Hath it not, boy?

Viola's nerve is steady as she takes a small risk: yes, there is for Cesario, somewhere, a woman who is

> Of your complexion . . .
> About your years, my lord.

As flattered by the comparison as we are startled by her gall, Orsino sweetly deprecates himself ('she is not worth thee, then . . . too old, by heaven'). This is his amiable side – on show only briefly, for Viola's intrepid quibbling soon provokes a more pompous reply:

> Let still the woman take
> An elder than herself; so wears she to him . . .

His reasoning, which he delivers with the confidence of the expert, is at once elaborate (Cesario's woman should take an older man, not Cesario, just as Olivia should take an older man like Orsino); generous (seeming, in denigrating men, to have the woman's interests at heart); and tactless (indifferent to Cesario's presumed feelings). It is also astonishingly erratic – having declared a few lines earlier that his lover's constancy was the one sure thing about him, he now characterises himself, Cesario, the entire male of the species, as 'giddy and unfirm', all too liable to break a good woman's heart.

From Orsino's point of view, this may all be talk for refined talk's sake; but, knowing more than he does, it is a little nerve-wracking for us. By now we care very much for Viola's feelings, and see how easily bruised they will be by this man. If it brought any comfort to her to tell him in code of her love for him, that is swiftly killed as Orsino declares

> For women are as roses, whose fair flower
> Being once displayed, doth fall that very hour.

He is confiding in a woman who herself may be blighted – a bud made blind by his blindness – and we wish he would stop. Bravely echoing his manner, Viola masks her feelings with male generosity:

> And so they are; alas, that they are so;
> To die, even when they to perfection grow.

Confirmation from the horse's mouth, if he only knew it.

Viola's 'even when' is not a lyrical formality. It is balanced with Orsino's 'that very hour' – they have both had the same troublesome thought. A woman's bloom fades at the very instant it is disclosed – not with a night of grace between, like a day-lily, but there and then: so to fulfil your desires is a sort of death. It is a starker version of the commonplace that consummation is followed by collapse, which the Elizabethans understood so well that 'die' was a regular, quite mild *double-entendre* on sexual climax (as it still is in some languages).[11] Viola's use of the word makes this subliminal connection: it is a shock to hear her despair like this. However the closeness of delight to revulsion is certainly part of Orsino's sexual dynamic, together with his masochism and his sense of surfeit.

The two of them sit and listen to the song, close at hand but worlds apart. Orsino introduces it at length (Cesario seems not to have been with him last night), making it sound like a piece of artless nostalgia: he claims that in the old days

>   The spinsters and the knitters in the sun

and the young lacemakers with their bone bobbins used to sing it, and blithely promises that

>   it is silly sooth,
> And dallies with the innocence of love
> Like the old age.

In fact it will turn out to be a man's song, the ballad of a lover 'slain by a fair cruel maid':[12] and far from being silly, it has the desperate tone of the bluesiest field-holler. Meanwhile Orsino's rather fancy explanation is lengthy enough for Feste to enquire gently (it is worth half a laugh):

>   Are you ready, sir?

– and he starts.

'Come Away Death' has the direct, stark imagery of the best folk music.[13] Its simple, powerful rhymes – 'breath' and 'death', 'save'

---

11   In Oscar Wilde's *Happy Prince*, the Prince and the Swallow die at the moment of union. But it is a children's story, and they are transfigured and borne away to God – no such comfort in Shakespeare.

12   In popular music, the gender of a song can often be changed if necessary; but here 'laid' is an unavoidable rhyme with 'maid'.

13   The original tune is not known, but it could indeed be very old, or brought to London by the same Huguenot weavers, cobblers and tinkers mentioned in 2.3. It is possible that Shakespeare had lodgings at one time with a Huguenot hatmaker.

and 'grave', 'strewn' and 'thrown' – are monosyllables with open vowels ideal for the voice; and the repetitions of 'fly away', 'come away', 'not a flower', 'not a friend', and the hyperbole of 'a thousand thousand sighs', have great force. The scattered images – the cypress and the yew for mourning, the flowerless black coffin that perishes, the bleached bones of the singer's 'poor body' tossed sightless and windblown over the landscape – conjure up a valley of death way beyond melancholy convention. If the song is to reflect a production's chosen culture, it calls for its most native musical form: and to me it sounds far more southern than northern.

The last note decays, the savage picture dissolves. There is silence – it may last some time, as music like this plays on and on in the ears. Finally Orsino pays Feste off without comment:

> There's for thy pains

– and Feste points out that 'pleasure will be paid', a painful truth he has already implied in the music. His habit is always to hang on a moment after he is dismissed, as if to have a last comprehensive word; and here – the man able to tell a mourning countess that her brother is in hell – he ventures another perfectly-measured impertinence:

> Now the melancholy god protect thee, and the tailor make thy doublet of changeable taffeta, for thy mind is a very opal. I would have men of such constancy put to sea, that their business might be everything and their intent everywhere, for that's it that always makes a good voyage of nothing. Farewell.

His insight is unnerving. Orsino is the opal exactly, the precious milky stone that flashes yellow, green and red, at its harlequin best radiating every prismatic colour from invisible fissures. Feste has seen that, suspended over a moral void, this man might voyage round the world to justify purposeless busyness. He hardly knows Orsino (who himself was unaware who Feste was when he called for the song), but he has certainly tagged his romantic imbalance and wasted intelligence. And he gets away with it: the vignette is obscure enough – just – not to cause serious offence.

The musicians pack up, but the echo of the music keeps Orsino's nerves taut as he starts again with Cesario. It seems that he has been considering a new approach to Olivia even as he was being impaled by the song. Its theme is a little surprising – Cesario must explain to her that Orsino's love is not a matter of money. No, it is 'more noble than the world', and it is the 'queen of gems' in her nature, not in her nurture, that calls to him. As he is richer than Olivia, it is quite a measure of his desperation that he thinks he could be accused of gold-digging.[14] For her part, Viola has heard Olivia's rejection, devastatingly casual, from her own mouth: she knows that Orsino's sincerity leaves her cold and the case is hopeless. Viola's own pain, too, has been deepened by the song, which, like the best art, reminds one to live in the present. What has she to lose?

> VIOLA: But if she cannot love you, sir?
> ORSINO: I cannot be so answered.
> VIOLA: Sooth, but you must.

She knows that Orsino has to accept defeat, as she is accepting it every day by his side, with a 'pang of heart' as great as his. His romantic fascism – he will *will* success – aggravates her terribly: if his better nature was showing before the song, it has been displaced by perhaps his worst.

Where is the centre of this weathervane of a man? Having declared earlier that women must be careful because of the giddiness of men, Orsino now thunders that:

> There is no woman's sides
> Can bide the beating of so strong a passion
> As love doth give my heart; no woman's heart
> So big, to hold so much; they lack retention.

This will always get an aghast laugh – how can Viola love such a man? Contradicted on a sacred point of honour, an ugly misogyny is pouring out of him: women are animals driven by their 'palate' to get hungry, stuff themselves and be sickened. Well, he himself is the play's prime bulimic, listening to the same cadence of music over and over till it became as unpleasant as an endlessly repeated word. He thinks again of the ocean that reduces everything to 'abatement and low price' but misses his own irony:

> But mine is all as hungry as the sea,
> And can digest as much. Make no compare
> Between that love a woman can bear me,
> And that I owe Olivia.

The monosyllabic force of Viola's reply, interrupting on a half-line:

> Ay, but I know –

---

14   Toby has already implied to Andrew in 1.3 that Orsino is the wealthier: Olivia will not 'match above her degree . . . in estate'.

stops this rant. She steps out onto a narrow ledge, improvising. She
needs a swift proof that women are 'as true of heart as we', and finds it:

> My father had a daughter loved a man . . .

Will she dare this? Yes:

> As it might be perhaps, were I a woman,
> I should your lordship.

Her father is dead, her brother likewise thought to be, and her own
hopes too, perhaps – the sad music of her life can be heard in her
careful phrasing. She is probably looking Orsino in the face, more
frankly than in the more playful moments before the song. The story
of this sister interests him, he who is so little interested in others,
and he wants to hear its tragic outcome:

> And what's her history?

Viola chooses the perfect word:

> A blank, my lord

as if she herself has been cancelled out: panic begins to form, and a
sense of meaninglessness. Where will she go now?

> She never told her love,
> But let concealment, like a worm i' th' bud,
> Feed on her damask cheek.

Her earlier image of wasted flowers has become still more mortal –
she is being cancerously eaten from within – and the very beautiful
lines are tinged with decay: the yellow of disease, the green of
mildew. To smile like a stone Patience at grief is a sign of real, fatal
love, not male protestation. Orsino is drawn closer – Viola must
dream of these intent but unseeing eyes of his, looking at her
tremendous fraud. He thinks there may be a splendid ending to the
story:

> But died thy sister of her love, my boy?

She could easily say yes; instead she disposes of the invented sister
and looks over her own precipice:

> I am all the daughters of my father's house,
> And all the brothers, too . . .

It is a Freudian slip – Sebastian means more here as her brother
than as her father's son – and, giddy, she pulls back:

> – and yet I know not.

It is true – there is much she doesn't know as yet of Sebastian. She must get off this. Back to business:

> Sir, shall I to this lady?

– and Orsino wakes up too:

> Ay, that's the theme

– how can they have strayed so far from such an important thing?

There have been times in all this when we seemed to be looking deep into water – the images bent, the perspective foreshortened. Now the two of them are back on firm ground – a jewel, a mission – but something more important has happened: Viola has made Orsino listen. As with many intimate rows, they are left in a state of renewed dependence, lovers in all but fact. Most critics have said sooner or later that Orsino is 'in love with love', whatever that means; but the fact is he is able to change. Feeding till now on his over-rich diet of rejection, he has been a dead loss for any woman – but he could be altered by Viola, especially while her maleness forestalls any Pavlovian sexual reactions.

Unless this remarkable scene is played as attentively as this, as an exemplary stage in the two characters' development, it seems to me perfunctory and bland. We are about to leave Orsino till the last act of the play, when he must become a sort of adequate hero, and this episode begins the long span towards that. We should let him go with a hint of change, his self-regard exposed a little to himself; while Viola, her head down, her secret just kept, her pain unabated and her heroic virtues stretched to the limit, trudges off to Olivia on another fool's errand.

2.5. Back to a world in which nothing is taken that seriously, and one more character to meet. It may well be the case, as some editors have thought, that Fabian was carefully brought in by Shakespeare to replace Feste for the duping of Malvolio, but it is hard to know why that would be. Maria promised that Toby, Andrew and Feste would be the eavesdroppers; to abandon the latter without explanation does sharpen our sense of him as the great absentee, but it also feels as if he has been replaced by an understudy. However, any wise Fool will keep out of Malvolio's sights if he can: and Feste is biding his time for the greatest revenge of all.

In fact, this scene is notable as much for those who are not in it as for those who are. Why is not Maria herself, sole begetter of the trick, part of the eavesdropping team? Is this for some reason man's work? As the play moves forward, she is more and more the one bringing bulletins across the lines from the house: and perhaps she can't take a whole afternoon off to enjoy the fruits of her scheming. At any rate here is Fabian, completing the magic figure of three that the best jokes call for; and, like everyone else, he announces himself with an attitude:

> SIR TOBY: Wouldst thou not be glad to have the niggardly rascally sheep-biter come by some notable shame?
> FABIAN: I would exult, man. You know he brought me out o' favour with my lady about a bear-baiting here.

So Malvolio is maintaining his meretricious power, and Fabian has been discredited too. The matter of the bear-baiting plunges us straight into the feculent heart of London in 1600 and far away from Illyria and any other period – but that is a regular Shakespearian event, intended in this case to remind us that new Puritans like Malvolio objected to this popular but cruel sport. That at least is in their favour, even if the objection is to the fun of it rather than the cruelty.

Beyond this sense of grievance, Fabian hasn't much provenance. On the one hand, Rowe's 1709 cast-list makes him 'a gentleman of Olivia's household', which dolls him up a bit; on the other, he feels like a junior, perhaps from the stables or the kitchen, and he may arrive wiping his hands on an apron.[15] At first, he is not, on the whole, witty, and in his emulation of Toby he lags a little behind his hero, though not as far as Andrew does. Neither a natural gentleman nor a natural comic, he is one of the very important local people we depend on for perspective, like the townspeople of Messina in *Much Ado About Nothing*, or the stewards' wives and small-town doctors on a Chekhov estate – a rootstock from which the more dazzling characters blossom. Now that Fabian speaks, Toby and Andrew must give him the stage so that we can have a good look at him, before he disappears behind the box-tree and the even more impenetrable jokes that the three of them will crack from there.

It feels like a sunny day, and we are at last, definitively, outside, where secrets cannot be hidden – it is the perfect place and time for

---

15   He can also get started as a silent witness in 1.5 – the scene can use the extra numbers.

a comic nemesis. Maria arrives in a flurry and drops her letter where we will most appreciate it being found later:

> Malvolio's coming down this walk. He has been yonder i' the
> sun practising behaviour to his own shadow this half hour.

Like all letter ambushes in Shakespeare, the device is irresistible, especially if we also get a tantalising picture of the approaching victim.[16] Maria leaves, the conspirators dive for cover: after the rush and scurry, there is a still beat of suspense.

> MALVOLIO: 'Tis but fortune. All is fortune . . .

He is funny already. The *legato* dreaminess of the line sounds not like an announcement but the middle of some habitual musing: and straight away a decision needs taking. Malvolio is embarking on a false soliloquy, to be overheard onstage as a soliloquy never is, and so he has unusual latitude. A Shakespeare monologue is, with very few exceptions, a discussion with the audience rather than overheard thought (this is a pragmatic point, not doctrine – try it the other way, and see how quickly it collapses inwards and loses its form). But Malvolio will by turns speak and not speak to us: in this set-up he can go into himself, exclude us and still be heard by his tormentors – it is very useful, specially at the start. If he arrives excited, wanting to share some new idea, it will force him into an expostulatory relationship with the audience, and with the eavesdroppers hissing furiously as well, the music will be raucous and stagey. But if he eases his way in in a self-important reverie, and the listeners, even Toby, bottle up their joy, the long scene will have a chance to develop its range.

So this is what Malvolio does in his hour off: strolls in the garden and fantasises. It is his relief from the multiple stresses and obscure indignities of keeping up appearances. The sun beats pleasantly down on his pale face, and he can stretch out, in body and mind. After his splendid opening, the banality of

> Maria once told me she [Olivia] did affect me, and I have heard
> herself come thus near, that should she fancy, it should be one
> of my complexion

16 Compare, in *Much Ado*:

> HERO: For look where Beatrice, like a lapwing, runs
>   Close by the ground, to hear our conference.

shows the pettiness underneath his overweening manners: having just seen himself as a portrait by Velasquez, he now wants a good gossip. Can what he says be true? One can imagine Maria, in some rare chatty moment, mischievously saying such a thing (a seed for her great inspiration); but Olivia's 'confession' must be pure fancy. He has either invented it or worked hard to misinterpret a chance remark: and the commonplace words – 'fancy . . . my complexion' – certainly don't sound like her choice. An odd process is beginning – this remote and frosty figure is confiding in us as Viola did, and we are drawn into an intimacy we were unprepared for. Like the plotters, we are fascinated; unlike them, we may find ourselves – a little – on his side, knowing that he is in great danger of embarrassment.

He has certainly shaken off the real world for the time being: if we remember Olivia's treatment of him over Feste and then the business of the ring, the idea that she treats him

> with a more exalted respect than any one else that follows her

shows how a desperate hope can turn black into white. It is of course Malvolio who treats Malvolio with an exalted respect. Rat-a-tat-tat from behind the tree. The two knights would beat Malvolio for his sad dream, but they are reined in by Fabian – it will be more fun to watch. Now the steward begins to open out, revealing something ignoble: his dreamy longing for Olivia is tied up with his desire for power. The hottest part of his fantasy is to see himself as 'Count Malvolio' – such a stroke of luck happened to 'the yeoman of the wardrobe', after all[17] – and it takes him 'deeply in', engorged with 'imagination'. He will,

> having been three months married to her, sitting in my state

not only be level with Olivia, but, as he feels a man should be, over her – swathed in velvet, he has returned to the house's business with the easy satisfied ache of sexual repletion, while Olivia, completely spent, catches a nap in 'some day-bed' until such time as he disturbs her again. The inequality of the union has its own sexual charge – for Olivia and the Lady of the Strachy, read Lady Chatterley or Miss Julie, for Malvolio and the 'yeoman of the wardrobe' Mellors or Jean the valet. Malvolio is not exactly the pathological Angelo of *Measure*

---

17   No-one has been able to explain 'the Lady of the Strachy' – no doubt she is imaginary. It sounds good, though, and the chattiness shows the original, 'unimproved' Malvolio – you can for a moment see him scandal-mongering at the scullery table.

for Measure, preparing his designs on the devout Isabella;[18] but the vengeful elements in his libido – domineering resentment, frustrated authoritarianism – are unshirked. The mixture is kept airy only because there is more light in Illyria than in the stews of Vienna, and in *Twelfth Night* those qualities are mixed with their more sympathetic opposites.

However, like that distant cousin, Malvolio can, 'dressed in a little brief authority', play 'fantastic tricks before high heaven'. The picture is very explicit: it is almost a throne he will sit in, his great gown, probably custom-tailored, will have a leafy pattern perhaps based on this very garden where he spends so much time; and his 'demure travel of regard', an admonitory panning across the company, will capriciously strike fear in his little court. The main purpose of it all is to get at Toby, whose irritating title has been dropped (he is now merely a 'kinsman'); and that interview is scrupulously rehearsed – no fewer than seven attendants sent for the wretched man, and an ominous silence as Count Malvolio waits, frowning to himself at the gravity of it all and doodling abstractedly with his jewellery. Unfortunately he is so used to wearing a steward's chain that he can't immediately think of a splendid enough necklace to replace it with:

> I . . . perchance wind up my watch, or play with my – some rich jewel.

In this dream, Toby 'curtsies' (a wonderful picture for us, but in fact it only means a bow), and the magnificent carpeting begins. Normally amiable and forgiving in spite of all, Malvolio must quench his 'familiar smile', because the business hurts him, as teachers used to say, more than it does Toby; however the fact is that, since he has been – well-chosen phrase – 'cast' on Olivia, it is only his duty to point out (and that more firmly than she might) that Toby must change his boozy ways. In Malvolio's comprehensive vision of things, even the 'foolish knight', Andrew, whom he has never acknowledged before, is suddenly glimpsed: and the only really good joke to come from behind the box-tree, Andrew's humble

> I knew 'twas I, for many do call me fool

sweetly concludes the sequence as Malvolio, incandescent, spots the letter.

18   Angelo compares them to building a lavatory on hallowed ground, and sees himself as a piece of rotting meat next to her purity. Some degree of guilty self-victimisation is quite common in Shakespeare's writing about sexual love. It is only a question of degree between Orsino or Malvolio and this truly self-hating character.

Where – on the ground, the garden bench, or tucked into the undergrowth? Obviously or subtly hidden, we know that somehow Malvolio will find it, and surely believe in it – once he is caught, logic will be no match for his self-delusion. But for the plotters it is the moment of truth – will he see it at all, let alone have the presumption to read it?

> MALVOLIO: What employment have we here?
> FABIAN: Now is the woodcock near the gin.
> TOBY: O peace, and the spirit of humours intimate reading aloud to him.[19]

The bait is, after all, the weakest part of their plot – the handwriting being only a replica of one he knows very well, and its message ambiguous:

> 'To the Unknown Beloved . . . '

If the forgery is not good enough, he may leave it where it is or tidy it up as litter. Luckily, he has no doubts about the dear handwriting:

> By my life, this is my lady's hand: these be her very C's, her U's, and her T's, and thus makes she her great P's.

Even in our candid days, editors have trouble with Shakespeare: blushes still arise on the scholarly cheek at these identifications. There has been much talk of 'coarse and vulgar appellations', and there's no getting away from it: it is very rude. 'Cut' is the old English for the female genitalia (the word originally meant a narrow passage for water), and Toby has already used it in its abusive sense to reassure Andrew – ('if you do not, call me cut') – just as he might do today. 'Pee' is equally historic.[20] The worst of it is, only two of the four letters actually appear on the envelope:

> 'To the Unknown Beloved, this, and my good wishes . . . '

so the schoolboy joke has been completely manufactured.

There might be a moment of indecision, to the eavesdroppers' horror and our secure amusement, as Malvolio battles with his better nature. But Maria's gamble was shrewd: his prurient curiosity

---

19   A small theatrical joke – reading it in silence would spoil everything.

20   According to most editors at least. The OED dates the word's first appearance as 1788, but that is surely conservative: what else, after all, can it mean here ? As always, Shakespeare is a sucker for a pun – like Mozart's foul-mouthedness and Chekhov's obsession with water-closets, it comes with the territory, and this one scrapes the barrel rather.

(and sense of rivalry – who is this 'Beloved'?) masters him, and he is deluded enough to imagine that the provocative style is in some way typical of Olivia – 'her very phrases'. Carefully, so that it could be re-sealed later, with much mistaken checking that he is not being observed, most delicately – 'by your leave, wax. Soft!' – he eases the letter open and his deep dream begins to come true, with a dream's easy coincidence.

Displacing the conspirators at the front of the frame, Malvolio begins his great fall not so much like an elephant crashing into a pit as a man sliding relentlessly down a muddy bank. He carefully reads the first verse of the letter, observes the change of metre in the second, returns intrigued to the first ('No man must know'). His fastidious habits protect him from racing ahead (and the scene from developing hysterics): checking and rechecking, he is a perfectionist trying to resist an ungovernable hope:

If this should be thee, Malvolio!

He struggles with the details as if wrestling with a crossword puzzle:

'M.O.A.I. doth sway my life'

– all the letters are in his name, but sufficiently cooked up that he cannot make anything of it (indeed he fails to remember that M is his initial). While the plotters pun desperately, he takes still more time:

Let me see, let me see, let me see . . .

then almost loosens the reins on:

'I may command where I adore'. Why, she may command me: I serve her; she is my lady.

Then he reconsiders the four letters with anxious pedantry:

What should that alphabetical position portend?

before expressing a modest hope:

If I could make that resemble something in me . . .

It is wonderful that it takes so long: Fabian believes that 'the cur is excellent at faults' (that is, at picking up a lost scent) but how can he keep missing the big clue?

'M' – Malvolio. 'M' – why, that begins my name!

A jolt of adrenalin – but then disappointment brings back his per-nickety tone:

> . . . but then there is no consonancy in the sequel: that suffers
> under probation. 'A' should follow, but 'O' does.

As he reads the full text – a passage which takes him right through to his exit without interruption – we are to all intents and purposes alone with him. Like Macbeth's dagger, the letter marshals him the way that he was going, the words like Olivia's whispered voice in his ear: don't be afraid, cast off the past, follow your star and climb the ladder – you will find not only celebrity but your sighing mistress languishing for you at its top. By all means patronise your relatives, especially a certain 'kinsman', and give the servants hell: and in fact, the best outfit to do it in would be – yellow stockings and cross-garters. Clothes are important to Malvolio – he started his afternoon organising the line of his own shadow, then imagined himself in a 'branched velvet gown'; but in this unlikely combination he will surpass himself.[21] If it seems incongruous at first, that is only a momentary shadow on his rising conviction that he is the chosen one, one of those remarkable men who have it in them to fashion their own destiny. His long dog-days are over – the 'Fortunate-Unhappy' will bestow happiness on the unfortunate, and if he funks it, well, he will deserve to be forever the 'fellow of servants'.

Maria's psychology has been dead on, and the development of her argument impeccable. Having tickled her 'trout' with the portentous appeal of 'greatness', she was careful to satisfy his specific need to humiliate Toby; he was then lubricated by a sexual invitation:

> She thus advises thee that sighs for thee

so that, at the unmistakeable disclosure

> if not, let me see thee a *steward* still . . .

his mercury shattered its glass. It was a perfect orchestration.

Malvolio is, in fact, completely transformed – he looks out on a future as long as it is wide, an open horizon in which all his dreams, so laboriously sustained, have turned out to be prophetic. It is a recompense for all the nights when he saw his ambition for what it was, for all the weary disgust (known also to Aguecheek) when

---

21   In 1597, Queen Elizabeth passed a Proclamation Against Inordinate Apparel, demand-ing that her subjects dress according to their social position. Malvolio is chosen (gently!) to satirise it.

inadequacy stared him in the face. In this new life, his profound reckoning with Toby will be settled, and the echo of mockery will die in his ears, replaced by the murmured sounds of deference. He will dispatch others on the embarrassing missions that used to be his, he will be consulted about current political thinking, and the unmistakeable charisma of sexual success – he is the man who won the queen – will draw the world to him and take every effort out of his life. He will, in short, be 'the very man' – and though Jove is to be thanked for the chance that this letter found him where he always sits of an afternoon, it was his own minute analysis of its codes that forced it to yield its meaning. Only one small key must be turned in the lock, and it is a charming prospect – he must let his discreet mistress know that he knows, which he easily can by means of his new ensemble.[22]

Who can blame him? Who hasn't thought they were loved when they weren't?

By a stroke of genius, there is a postscript, such as an anxious lover might add, eagerly making a phone call as well as writing a letter. There is to be an extra intimate code, and it will be unmistakeable: while he cannot

> choose but know who I am

she will be looking out for a sign even more explicit than his legwear. He must smile.

This is where the actor needs to take care, where all sorts of ambushes lurk to deflect him from Malvolio's own point of view. He presumably rehearses his smile now, just as he started by 'practising behaviour to his own shadow': and the result may indeed be hideous for us, as if long-unused muscles were cracking his face open. But all the character himself feels is innocent optimism, a faith that can move mountains. What if the smile were unexpectedly sweet? And then, what if apparent climaxes such as

---

22   A small difficulty: it is hard to know why Malvolio says: 'She did commend my yellow stockings of late, she did praise my leg being cross-gartered; and in this she manifests herself to my love' – for surely he has never worn them before. The text is odd; but the line reads well enough if it refers to what he has just read in the letter, as in 'she did commend yellow stockings, etc. to me, here.'

   The image itself now seems burlesque and fanciful: but cross-garters were in fact the sign of a hopeful lover, and yellow stockings symbolised marriage. In other words, it was a recognised code – which might explain why John Manningham doesn't mention these details in his Diary comments on the premiere, even though to us they are the outstanding features of the trick.

> I thank my stars, I am happy

were not absurdly wild, or hammered out like Henry V at Agincourt, but the humble statement of a new truth? And supposing

> I will be proud, I will read politic authors, I will baffle Sir Toby . . .

had, more than vindictiveness, the innocent exuberance of Puck promising to put a girdle round the earth in forty minutes?

Because then it won't be funny enough, the actor may say. Most Malvolios worry, some frantically, about this; to start humanly and let the laughs come in this scene may feel like a dubious option. Stage history books are opened: Laurence Olivier's backward fall off his bench, the possibility of slowly rotating in obedience to

> If this fall into thy hand, revolve . . .

– or the novelty introduced by Donald Sinden at Stratford in 1969, who in winding up his watch adjusted the sundial to match it. But the structure of this exuberant sequence is reliable, and funny business may be irrelevant next to its human architecture – there is certainly a danger of making Malvolio the wrong kind of fool. A child's garden of harmless delights is blooming in him, and reciprocated love liberates him in his own way: he has joined the Orsinos, Antonios and even Violas.

Unaware that he was not alone, Malvolio has been talking for nearly a quarter of an hour. No small order – every mental link has had to be tight and logical, but nearly half of his text has had, every few lines, to leave space for the punctuations of the eavesdroppers and the laughs that they aroused. Which is itself an open question: there are times when Toby and Fabian have become extremely archaic. What can

> Sowter will cry upon't for all this, though it be as rank as a fox

or

> . . . with what wing the staniel checks at it

possibly mean? The Arden or New Cambridge edition will certainly tell you, but it can't help the actor share his knowledge. Cutting will upset the sophisticated structure, and the only option beyond that is the rather questionable one of rephrasing. The alien material just has to be delivered jubilantly, with the merciless slickness of farce. To compensate, the rest of the asides are comprehensible enough:

> O for a stone-bow to hit him in the eye!

if not particularly funny:

> MALVOLIO: 'A' should follow, but 'O' does.
> FABIAN: And O shall end, I hope.
> TOBY: Ay, or I'll cudgel him and make him cry 'O'!

Fabian has been master of ceremonies throughout, controlling Andrew's mild belligerence, his own glee, and Toby's dangerous rage. So he has already developed some stature. Toby has borne the brunt of Malvolio's fantasy – there is a small lifetime of hatred between them – and he might easily have broken cover were it not for Fabian's peacekeeping. The childishness of their reactions is part of the fun – and so too is the scene's artificiality, for all that we touch our hats to verismo. For instance, what seems like a technical problem – where should the three of them hide? – in practice boils down to quite little. Whether they are huddled behind a single box tree, or scattered around the set, popping their heads out to do their lines, what matters is that we neither forget they're there nor have to look at them all the time – often it is better to imagine their reactions. They are always likely to be further away than Malvolio himself, since the audience needs to have its most direct contact with him, not them: if they whisper to each other they will still have to be as loud as him, who of course hears nothing. And actually, because we understand the convention, it is just as funny if they stand immediately behind him and shout.

There is a deeper reason why we sometimes want them out of the way: we too have been begging for Malvolio to step on his banana skin, but now that he is enraptured by his Great Idea, their vengeful binge seems rather unfair, as if they were watching a private fantasy through a keyhole. In other words, the rules of the Practical Joke apply – the victim seems victimised and the jokers callous. What begins to make Malvolio attractive to us is not his virtue, certainly, but his heroically abandoned energy, which compares rather favourably with the raucous celebration that follows his exit.

The silence is as tense and full as just before Malvolio entered. Perhaps the box-tree shakes while they wait – Malvolio must be well out of hearing before they explode, and is likely to get an exit round from the audience anyway. The last beat of the scene is quite difficult to sustain, the plotters' hysteria being rather drawn-out and its metaphors prodigally obscure:

FABIAN: Here comes my noble gull-catcher.
SIR TOBY (*to Maria*): Wilt thou set thy foot o' my neck?
SIR ANDREW: Or o' mine either?
SIR TOBY: Shall I play my freedom at tray-trip, and become thy
    bond-slave?
SIR ANDREW: I' faith, or I either?

As they roll around in glee, we realise that Andrew hasn't been able to come up with anything – from the start, the intoxicating merriment liberating the others has rendered him inarticulate:

SIR TOBY: I could marry this wench for this device.
SIR ANDREW: So could I, too.
SIR TOBY: And ask no other dowry with her but such another
    jest.
SIR ANDREW: Nor I neither.

The other significance is that Maria (who must have seen some of the fun from a distance) reveals the final effect of the trick on Olivia: silly enough in themselves, yellow stockings and cross-garters are an offence as well – 'a colour she abhors' and 'a fashion she detests'. Not to mention that foolish smiles on the last responsible face in her household will bring Malvolio into as 'notable a contempt' as he would wish on everyone else.

Although the exit is climactic, the scene actually ends with a diminuendo – Andrew has the last word, tagging along still:

SIR TOBY: To the gates of Tartar, thou most excellent devil of wit.
SIR ANDREW: I'll make one, too.

The idea that he might himself be wearing something yellow, something that he hoped would appeal to Olivia and which he now has hurriedly to get rid of, is of course nowhere supported by the text, completely unjustified, and doesn't let Shakespeare 'speak for himself'. Let's say I have the copyright on it.[23]

---

23   As if I could have. I saw Trevor Nunn's 1996 film version recently and he did the same thing. There's no question of a copy, either way; both of us had simply answered the play's advertisements.

ENTR'ACTE

Haiyuza Company, Tokyo, 1993

ENTR'ACTE

Haiyuza Company, Tokyo, 1993

Considering what she is about to tell me, Nanako Kume's voice is surprisingly calm. 'I've just been talking to Haiyuza, and they do have one worry. Your *etiquette*.'

Oh no. It is July of 1993, and I am shortly due in Tokyo to direct *Twelfth Night*, in Japanese, for the Haiyuza Company at the Globe Theatre. After our ESC visit in 1992, Seiya Tamura, the Globe's director, decided to present a local version of the play, again directed by me: he would contribute the venue and Haiyuza, one of Tokyo's longest-standing ensembles, the cast and the means. This triangular arrangement has been a year in the planning: the Globe I know well enough, but I had to spend a busy week last autumn auditioning fifty actors from Haiyuza's enormous stable and trying to establish relationships with a designer, Mitsuru Ishii, and composer, Tohru Ueda; since then sketches and demo tapes have flowed to and fro, and only one of the chosen actors has abandoned ship. There has been a volume of faxes on practical and contractual details from Haiyuza's management, their good intentions interlaced with some exquisite misunderstandings, most of them due to the confusingly high number of zeros in any sum expressed in yen. Meanwhile anybody known to Haiyuza with any English who happened to be going to England (such as Nanako, on her way to a Fine Art Course at the Slade) has been pressed into ad hoc interpreting service, if only to check that I am still on the case. I have diligently studied Haiyuza's history and structure, and tried to assess what they should and shouldn't expect from me. And now, it seems, I have offended somebody.

'What have I done?' I falter.

'Like I say, they're worried,' Nanako continues breezily. 'About your *air ticket*. Would you rather go British Airways or JAL?'

The slip of the ear was easy enough: etiquette and its strategic abandonment is part of the director's typical dance away from home. In such an enterprise, the host company will want both affirmation and agitation: so the visitor must negotiate a daily path between politesse and subversion, any heresies sweetened by deference. In the case of Haiyuza, there is quite a stack of traditions to be acknowledged or ignored. The company was founded in 1944 by Koreya Senda, an iconic figure who in Japanese theatre resembles either the cosmopolitan designer Edward Gordon Craig or the parochial actor-manager Robert Atkins, according to taste. The former because, having studied in Germany in the thirties and been much influenced also by the Russian actor-director Vsevolod Meyerhold, Senda returned late in the War insisting on introducing Gorki, Brecht and other socialist European writers to Japanese audiences at that most chauvinistic moment – he was, indeed, briefly imprisoned for refusing to fight. By the time I met him, he was over ninety, as active as he could be (and determined on one great personal swansong, his own adaptation of *The Brothers Karamazov*[1]); but Haiyuza, an established fact but no longer avant-garde, has got a bit stuck. Lacking the disrespect to appoint a new boss with Senda still alive, they are marking time with a repetitious classical repertoire punctuated by the occasional new Japanese play – which, typically, might mildly reassess the country's nationalist past, a thing more easily attempted through artistic code than public debate. Haiyuza's Shakespeare, to judge from the photographs, smacks of timber beams, ruffs and general cheerfulness.

Senda's other legacy to Haiyuza (this is the Robert Atkins side) is an extremely hierarchical structure and a top-heavy management: the offices are full and the actors a little cowed. There are some hundred of them in the company, if 'in' is the right word: they are not financially retained, and work more or less for love when invited to appear, hoping to subsidise themselves in between from the regular flow (two or three TV channels much of most nights) of soap operas and routine samurai drama. However, the tribalism of Japanese theatre makes it almost unthinkable for them to go off and join another troupe. They are always advertised, accompanied by generally out-of-date photographs (an international silliness, this), according to length of service rather than current casting, so the

---

1   Which he did shortly before his death in 1994.

butler sometimes gets top billing. Rates of pay, such as they are, reflect this too, and so, albeit benevolently, do manners in the rehearsal room: complex respect is accorded, and the right to speak out carefully weighed up. It can all feel like the working of a mysterious closed order – the English public school comes to mind, especially as the running of errands is heavily implied for the juniors – but the good side is that, as in many European state theatres, the older actors are financially comfortable and retain some dignity. This was certainly to be the only *Twelfth Night* I have heard of in which the Viola, more junior than some of the stage management, made the tea for everyone.

Arriving in Tokyo (etiquette by JAL) on August 14th and attentive to the newspapers, I note that we are in the middle of the ancient Shinto Festival of O'bon, when the dead are welcomed back into the world with gifts: celebrants traditionally process with lighted lanterns from the graveyards to their houses to show the spirits their way home. Places are set at table for them and special food pre-pared: for those who died at sea, it is put in candle-lit cradles and cast adrift on the waters. On this day in 1945, truly in the month of the dead, Emperor Hirohito surrendered and the next day announced to the nation the end of the War – withdrawing gracefully to allow Prime Minister Tojo and the rest of 'the Emperor's Shield' to face trial and execution for having followed his orders. This weekend in 1993, Prime Minister Hosakawa has startled the world by acknowledging a measure of Japanese responsibility for the conflict, re-lighting as he does so the long-fused debate on atone-ment for warcrimes: it is to be the first in a sequence of apologies, adequate or otherwise, continued by Prime Minister Murayama on the fiftieth anniversary of VJ Day two years later, and then by Hashimoto to Tony Blair in 1998. To many in the West – at least to those mindful of the equivalent suffering caused to Japanese civilians by Fat Boy – this is a gesture easy to admire; but it is a lot tougher for the million bereaved families always led to believe that their country was the world's sacrificial victim. And already there are demands for reparation from the relatives of two million Korean labourers and 'comfort women' forcibly conscripted by the Japanese during the War. Today, the Mayor of Hiroshima, letting loose the traditional flock of white doves to mark the anniversary of its bombing, has emphatically echoed Hosakawa's message. What a moment this would be to do *Henry V*, and hear the footsoldiers at

Agincourt warning of the King's responsibility 'if the cause be not just'. No such luck: this is a classic comedy, with little political static – except that that is never a safe assumption with this sly writer, whose magnet always picks up whatever filings are in the air.

Since Shakespeare is nobody's little piece of land, there seems to me small point in an Englishman directing the plays abroad without testing his 'universality' as thoroughly as possible. So I am determined to look at *Twelfth Night* through a Japanese lens if I can, to see what it might mean in a culture whose axis extends from the wistful beauty of O'bon to a muddled and guilty tradition of xenophobia and violence. In a real sense this is not going to be Shakespeare's comedy at all but a Japanese play built on its groundplan, using the shared memories of Japanese actors and a prose text approximating only loosely to the original. I am reckoning that the intricate sense of status in Olivia's household might be much like that of an aristocratic family of the early Showa period (roughly the early 1930s), implicitly loyal to the Emperor's repressive rule and religion – even though it may be difficult to reconcile Shinto's fastidious attitude to death with the obsessive grief Olivia inflicts on everyone. Meanwhile the lovesick Orsino could reflect a much older spirit – the romantic self-consciousness (as of *amour courtois* in Europe) of the eleventh-century court at Heian-Kyo (soon to become Kyoto). In the ambience of Shikibu Murasaki's *The Tale of Genji* and Sei Shonagon's *Pillow Book*, 'suffering from leisure' was a major affliction, to be ameliorated by the composition of broken-hearted verses and by dandified chivalry – it was a world in which, as Angela Carter describes it, 'fine handwriting, a nice judgment in silks and the ability to toss off an evocative sixty-syllable *tanka* at the drop of a cherry-blossom were activities that achieved the status of a profound moral imperative for the upper classes'. Orsino all over, I'd say.

There has been quite a deal of musing and air-sucking, a typical Japanese hesitation, as I have tried to convince Mitsuru Ishii of the appositeness of all this, and a blank silence from Tohru Ueda when I suggested that the play's finale might have the feel of a Shinto wedding: gong, flute and *taiko* stick-drum. Naturally – he had been wondering whether I preferred Paul McCartney or Van Morrison. Professionals here have come to dread well-intentioned Western efforts (and there have been some) to do 'Japanese' Shakespeare like a sort of tourist *kabuki*, and I am aware that I could make an ass of myself. I hope (well, wouldn't I) to go a bit deeper; but the touch of shyness in the air makes me feel that if we are to achieve anything, Japanese self-assertion will need to be coaxed out from many who find it shameful – imitating the Westerner will be of no help at all. You can certainly see the paradox: Haiyuza have gone to great trouble to buy in a European eye which is already intent on seeing things from a Japanese point of view. Meanwhile I have a trusted assistant with me, Kate Beales, who will keep my eclectic gaucheries under control, and I am reassured by the fact that the classic plays of Chikamatsu Monzaemon, in Shakespeare's own century, are full of unwitting Shakespearian themes, especially the absurd ungovernability by social arrangements of sexual passion (*ninjo*).[2]

★

There have been devastating floods in Kagoshima in the south of the country this year, and only a few weeks ago on the northern island of Hokkaido also, following a major earthquake. A big typhoon named Vernon (at least by CNN News) is expected within a week or so. Looking on such tempests and quite shaken, Haiyuza's administrators, who meet me at Narita airport and drive me through abandoned farmlands to the city centre,[3] look still more haunted by the precariousness of the yen since the Heisei crash two years ago. Six years later, with the Asian tiger mewing piteously, it is obvious they had reason;[4] and though hissed whispers of recession, a new killer disease hard to name out loud, may have seemed laughable to a European at that moment, this was to be the first time in four visits that I have seen people sleeping in the street in the centre of Tokyo. Before the end of the first day, I would to be asked to reduce my fee.

Haiyuza's rather run-down premises, where we are to rehearse for four weeks before moving out to the Globe in Shinokubo for a week's technical work and the opening, sit opposite Johnny Rocket's

2   The wicked steward, the two pairs of lovers in the wood, and multiple mistaken identities both comic and tragic, are common as well. Chikamatsu also wrote history plays that specifically used the past as a critique of the present.

3   The building of the great new airport in the 1970s, at a hugely inconvenient distance from the city, involved reclaiming land from the area's farmers, and there are still vicious clashes between the security forces and those that remain.

4   At the time of writing (1999), Japanese unemployment is the highest since World War Two; there is no unemployment benefit, and the Chuo subway from the western outskirts of the city has become known as the 'suicide line'.

Authentic Hamburgers under the big expressway that lurches over the Roppongi district – the name literally translates as High Touch Town, and indeed it's damnably expensive, a tatty Mayfair under a fetid sky. The first morning, fizzing with tension, is planned as a party of welcome – beers, sandwiches, speeches, many *campais* – to be followed by the readthrough. I reverse this order, for obvious enough reasons. The result (apart from some offence to Mr Sataki, Haiyuza's stage manager, who is inclined to talk darkly about The Japanese Way) is that everyone arrives at the wrong time: half-interested outsiders there for the party have to sit through the play, and those with scholarly curiosity about the Shakespearian event are forced into wild celebration of my safe arrival. There is much snapping to attention before we start: those with a right to make formal speeches of welcome do so, at length; others leap up spontaneously, issuing excited salvoes of greeting like small claps of thunder; Seiya Tamura rushes in late, describes me as a 'world-wide top-star' (a phrase I have otherwise only heard used of the leading male impersonators of the notorious Takarazuka Company) and warns Haiyuza to treat me with respect. His abrasion is rather welcome, though more respect I don't need. We get on with it at last. The play reads encouragingly: the actors, who have had several preparatory readthroughs before I arrived, are passionate and determined, and last year's casting is still right. However, its fluency snagged in a web of Japanese honorifics and circumlocutions, the text presently takes fifteen per cent longer to get through in translation than it might in its original. Sataki, a gavel-banger of a kind unfamiliar in prompt corners of the West, assures me, without circumlocution, that the text will have to be cut: though the performances will start as early as 6.30, there is no question of a Japanese audience watching Japanese actors for more than two and a half hours, though they will do it out of courtesy to a foreign company. Sensing an antagonist lurking in our welcoming circle, I immediately decide to do the play in full.[5]

The first beer naturally lays everybody out, and eventually the actors wander away with afternoon hangovers and, I'm sure, a feeling of bathos: all that nervous tension and then no disclosures, just a readthrough. But before going any further, there is urgent need for a long production meeting with all the technical departments, whose

5 In the event, played up to speed and with a nice symmetry, the two halves ran for an hour and twenty-four minutes each – much what you would expect.

heads I have hardly met – not least because recession has flapped seriously over our budget. It is to be a ceremony marked by extreme courtesy and deep stubbornness, and I learn to sway gently this way and that, adducing discreet swings of opinion from the widening spaces between words. Alertness is all: such meetings tend to happen when the delegates are all fired up for action but the director is tired after rehearsing all day and his guard low. The designer Mitsuru Ishii and I look at each other to see if either has aged. Him I trust – he trained with Margaret Harris of the legendary Motley team in England, and still embodies their approach. For a year we have debated, confusingly, by fax. His early bulletins on the set referred to the venue as the 'Glove Theatre': haunted by marionettes, I wrote back that knowing the dimensions of the *Globe* Theatre as I did, an abstract geometric design might be the best way forward; he replied that though he agreed in principle, he felt there shouldn't really be any *globes* among the geometric shapes. Now he has drawn a magic carpet of slatted wood, running from high up on the back wall in a forward curve to the floor; there it is broken into by three doorways with platforms projecting forward from them. The floor then develops in a series of shallow waves that flatten into a very wide apron at the front – the forestage at the Globe is about twice the width of the proscenium opening. Combining curving movement with simple verticals and horizontals, it feels discreetly Japanese, elegant, suggestive and spare: in fact it rather resembles some combination from the *katakana* alphabet, a syllabary beautifully based on what you leave out.[6] The undulations on the floor are obviously going to be very good for Viola's shipwreck – they will light at first as waves of the sea and then, as the scene settles, as sand dunes – and I can also see Andrew and Toby negotiating them in their cups, the undulations now being in their minds. In general, as Mitsuru has pointed out, the actors can on this floor 'hop and jump freely'.

Of course it's all too expensive now. A familiar pattern is set: asked for economies, I wait till I have two requests in, give in on one and refuse the other. I accept that the wooden structure, originally planned to fly and furl in sections like slatted blinds, will have to remain permanent, varied only by lighting and careful furnishing.

6   Appropriately, it is used to represent borrowed foreign words. Written Japanese has three separate systems – the others are the complicated *hiragana* and the ideographic Chinese *kanji*. *Katakana* rather resembles Nordic runes.

But the other side of the *quid pro quo* is to spare little expense on the costumes, which are going to be all the more important. After many sad faxes I think we all understand that we are to move to and fro within the twentieth century: 1930s for Olivia's household, their monochromes breaking out into pastels in the second half; for Sebastian and Viola classically-cut ballet shirts, wool waistcoats and flannel trousers, in light browns, greys and mushroom; and for Feste, the look of today's working man without work: vest, red kerchief, broken-down flannel. Some of Mitsuru's early drawings were startling; but Andrew no longer has green stockings with red bows, black enamel 'shooses' and an ear-ring, simply an unfortunate suit – Toby too has lost his unaccountable ear-ring, and is now in tweeds and golfing socks. The very young Viola (Ayako Hirota) is going to have to wear what Mitsuru describes as 'some kind of a Japanese hat' when disguised as a man rather than a short wig, as I would like her to release her beautiful waist-length hair when she returns to womanhood at the end of the play – many eyes brighten at this ravishing prospect. However she and Sebastian have been drawn with thigh-length boots, which I don't like a bit. Mitsuru, who is scornful of the Japanese body, insists that only these boots will make them look okay, and without them we are lost. We dig in for a gentle struggle. After many agreeable musings, the venerable head of wardrobe casts her vote, and they are cut. I have gained a point here: Haiyuza's production manager was dutifully wearing a Whatever-the-Director-Wants face while looking at a £1500 bill. Mitsuru, whose life had seemed to depend on winning the point, gives up with the greatest amiability, perhaps because he senses common cause: we both want to spend a lot of money on Orsino. Mitsuru is proposing a beautiful blue printed material (Hanae Mori – very expensive), whose traditional Japanese feel he will then contradict by cutting it like a European gown, something Garry Essendine might wear in *Present Laughter*. If we then put him on a red samurai cushion at a long, low Japanese table, with a single rose in a vase, east and west will balance nicely. Agreed – all I have to do is to convince the actor.

Seiya Tamura ('how about some small supper?') takes me out to a *yakitori* bar where, for the cost of an advance phone call, the staff will bark out a special greeting to you as you enter, proclaiming your great eminence for the jealous benefit of all. Seiya genuinely despises all this but entertains me, as he always does, with extravagant jubilation (I am blooded in the kamikaze ritual of the *fugu*, Japan's poisonous blow-fish, thanks to Seiya). He now compares the gaping mouth of a mullet sizzling on the barbecue to that of a well-known character actor from the RSC. This is entirely typical. If I need character assassination or English theatre gossip, it is Seiya I should always come to rather than anyone at home. Though sadly now laid off from the Globe by the property company that owns it – not least because of the grandeur of his entertaining – he at this time spent his life buying in world-wide Shakespeare, going through the canon several times in imported productions (all except for *Timon of Athens*, which at a certain point in this evening he urges me to do as a one-man-show): he has more irons in the fire than the *yakitori* chef. But tonight he is troubled, worried about the standard of my cast. Disturbingly, he condemns as old-fashioned several of those I had felt were the freshest; and he has particular contempt for Feste – which at least provokes him to some positive advice: that I should base this character on the *rakugo*, a type of traditional storyteller still popular on television, whose patter depends heavily on puns and surprise endings. He reassures me that he will fix anything I need fixing, and invites me to come and work for his company ('better translations, better pay, better actors') next year – which at least puts his criticisms of Haiyuza into some kind of perspective.

Staring in the small hours at the ceiling of Asahi Homes Room 406 ('your home-from-home in Tokyo'), in the mildly delirious insomnia of the jet-lagged, I realise that Seiya, whose idea all this was, has rattled me. He certainly has a bias, a typical Tokyo producer claiming a 'top-star' as his own man. But he is also cosmopolitan and a good friend, and I suppose he can see something I can't. The heart of an actor may be true, but too idiosyncratic a use of his own language may set off all sorts of unhelpful associations. If Feste sounds too much like Tokyo's Les Dawson, how will I know? And will it matter? If Cesario, instead of embodying the androgyny so beautiful in Japanese culture, adopts the banal inflections of a cross-dresser from the Takarazuka Company, will I catch it? I feel deaf.

More than anything of course, my cloth ear is symbolised by the translation: if I ever undertake such a thing again, I must have two or three versions to hand from the start, carefully re-translated into English for comparison. But this hadn't occurred to me, and Haiyuza didn't offer a choice. For everybody's sake, we should spend most of the first week sitting with the text, translating it to and fro, even if the atmosphere becomes more that of a drafting committee than of the vibrant event everyone is hoping for. And indeed there is politely hidden dismay: the rehearsal room floor has been marked out in the expectation of immediate wonders. It is certainly a bit risky – actors are like dogs who need to bound and bark at regular intervals, and the fatigue that fills a sedentary rehearsal in mid-afternoon, as the collective blood-sugar sinks, can be depressing enough even if you're not peering through a linguistic fog for some pernickety nuance. The haze is hardly dispersed at all by Mr Sataki's electronic translator, which he taps away at for alternatives like some impassive typist, and only moderately by my interpreter Mika, who announces cheerfully at the outset that she is new to the theatre, has a small vocabulary and is particularly bad at numbers. In fact she underestimates herself – though the cast are startled to hear from her initially that the play was written in 1901 rather than 1601. This is a blow – interpreting in the theatre is as specialised, I suppose, as in metallurgy, and Shiomi Watanabe ('remember the name – just think "Show Me What I Wanna Be!" '), hired for the auditions a year ago but no longer available, has spoiled me. Within the next couple of days five versions are hurriedly gathered: the Japanese, which I cannot read; the original Shakespeare ('What relish is in this? How runs the stream?'); a literal translation from the Japanese back into English ('What is this? How am I? My brain become problem? Am I dream?'); another literal, slightly polished up and therefore rather less help; and a live running version by Mika, who grew up in New York ('What's gonna happen? Am I crazy?'). Thus tested, the forty-year-old Japanese text by Isao Mikami proves to have the solid virtues of its age, like a Victorian version of the *Odyssey*: accurate and steady, it renders everything into painstaking prose, occasionally taking a sparky opportunity to substitute a Japanese reference for an arcane Elizabethan one. Thus, when Aguecheek tries to escape his duel with Viola, the horse he offers her as a bribe, 'grey Capilet', has become 'Ao', which is both the Japanese word for blue and the name of a famous horse from the *kabuki*. When Viola finally meets Sebastian he reassures her that he is not a ghost by saying that he has hands and feet, which Japanese ghosts traditionally lack. Most engagingly, when Malvolio condescends to Cesario – 'one would think his mother's milk were scarce out of him' – he now says 'his bottom is still blue', referring to the Mongolian Mark, a temporary blue blemish at the base of

Japanese babies' spines. On the other hand, 'Make me a willow cabin at your gate' has become, disappointingly, 'Build me some kind of a nice wooden hut outside your house'; Sebastian's reaction to seeing his lost sister – 'It isn't possible' – seems a poor substitute for Shakespeare's 'Do I stand there?'; and Orsino's regret for beauty's mortality in 2.4 has become 'Women are like roses: beautiful when they blossom, but soon the petals fall' – which substitutes a rather soppy sense of gradual change for Shakespeare's startling idea of death-in-life. However, when stumped by the most baroque flourishes, Mikami has tended to give up and cut, and so we set about supplying our own versions. After all, when Fabian warns Aguecheek that if he loses amorous courage he will 'hang like an icicle on a Dutchman's beard', the English audience has lost the reference too, but the phrase is so good it should be kept anyway: it is duly translated, to the astonishment of all, while Mr Sataki looks anxiously at his watch.

As we finally test each scene by reading it through, the sound I am hearing is strong, demonstrative and very monotonous: spoken Japanese varies more in pitch than in tone, and as the volume jolts up and down the colour remains much the same. In brief moments, Shakespeare begins to swell and flow, but on the whole both parties remain baffled. What we are missing is the natural rhythm of feeling, what Virginia Woolf once described as a 'wave in the mind', which 'as it breaks and tumbles . . . makes words to fit it'. This is in fact concisely expressed in Japanese, in two words: *honne*, which represents the way things truly are behind the appearances (*tatemae*), and *kokoro*, which implies heart, soul and mind all together. If ever the cast senses the beautiful movement under the problematic words, it is like dance music to them – they want to get up and get going – but, stuck in our chairs, we push cruelly on, driving on the brakes.

All the painstaking editorial work is also an alibi for me, looking for insights into the actors as they struggle – once the staging begins they may become conscious of being watched and put on invisible masks. Some of the cast (not only the young ones) seem bold and febrile, while some are clamped down by polite shyness: Viola is very lacking in confidence, there is a certain sullen resistance beneath Sir Toby's grave courtesy, both Olivia and Maria are a little suburban, and Feste looks as if he might be having a breakdown. Though Hirosi Murakami was recommended for Aguecheek, I cast him as

Orsino just because he has a certain moonstruck daftness about him (exclamations of wonder from Haiyuza at the originality of this). He was surprised himself, and is now bothered by our design – being asked to think like a Heian courtier, or indeed any kind of Japanese, has him simpering with embarrassment, his eyes rolling, his hand covering his mouth like one of those teenage girls. Murakami wants to be an *English* actor – but not as badly as does Seiya Nakano (Malvolio), who has studied reviews of Olivier's 1955 performance and is much exercised about what funny business the great man might have done. I can remember, but decide not to tell him – I don't fancy seeing all that again. He buttonholes me daily: Should he wear a chain of office with his nightgown? Maybe some cold cream? A little hand-mirror to admire himself in? How should he Smile? In short, is the part a real person or simply a rich opportunity for physical jokes? The answer is obvious, but he is becoming so frustrated that we have a special meeting with Mitsuru. The designer, at other times so cosmopolitan, goes into local code: sucking gently on his teeth, smiling almost to a simper, he insinuates himself into his sentences rather than starting them. Cannily he discusses with Nakano his designs for the other characters, which flatters the leading man: I assure him from his other side that the reality with which he's reading the part is already making props and funny business immaterial – rather hoping this speech will have a self-fulfilling effect. Relaxing under the massage, Nakano reveals a sweet nature that will be very good for the steward, an innocent who allows counterfeit flattery to get the better of him. He also has some of the gravitas of a *noh* actor: and as it happens, the translation gives him some old-fashioned samurai phrasing very apt for Malvolio's absurd sense of destiny – the Spanish side of him, you might say elsewhere. Nakano is the best known of the company, a big local favourite and in that way the most vulnerable: he needs cherishing, and perhaps a bit of a shove.

Kate Beales, a terrier by my side with a look of permanent affront, and I spend much of the weekend with Hajime Mori (Fabian) and Ian de Staines, translator, diplomat, broadcaster and bi-lingual man-about-Tokyo. We drive south of the city, down the beautiful Izu Peninsula, beneath Mount Hakone. Hajime's English is good: and he is so loyal, so determined to make everything work, that he already suspects Haiyuza of treating me imperfectly – since he is also popular in the company he will be the perfect mole. Strolling

through a botanical garden, he now confides that though he himself
has optimism, the company are fussed – no business fixed, no moves
to memorise, no firm instructions: what am I up to? It is very much
not Haiyuza's way; and even though some of the actors (unpaid for
rehearsals) are holding down evening jobs to live, Sataki is proposing
to keep them back for secret sessions after I have gone home, to be
led by himself: these he will characterise as line practice, but Hajime
knows better. Struck by the bathos of betrayal in this garden of
flowers, surrounded by kindness and good intentions, I am afflicted
by a sudden, desperate homesickness: it is like an illness, and I feel
completely lost, unredeemable by philosophy or the telephone. It
passes, leaving me sentimental in the extreme: as Typhoon Vernon
comes and goes on Sunday, I think affectionately of Vernon
Dobtcheff, the British actor who is something of a legend within the
profession for being everywhere at the same time (amazingly, he
turned out to be in Tokyo at this moment): he never misses a first
night either in person or by message, and there may be more than
one of him. I feel he is here in this gentle typhoon (which holds up
the trains but hurts nobody), listening sympathetically to my
maundering soliloquies.

★

In a single day, Vernon has scattered with twelve inches of rain the
August humidity which has made even fashionable Roppongi smell
like a garbage heap. But we plunge into the second week with the air
at Haiyuza uncleared and strong evidence that Hajime spoke true.
Fortunately the cast, for all their worries, will have none of Sataki's
manoeuvres, no doubt feeling that importing an English director is
an expensive way of being instructed by their own stage manager.
Endorsed, I decide not to confront him – urbanity will serve better
until he tries something else.

In fact, the actors' panic reflects no more than a jam on first
principles: no foreign director has worked with Haiyuza before, and
the fearful enthusiasm surrounding the event could deadlock it.
Everyone is craning to glimpse what is up the billowing English
sleeve: but myself, I know that any rehearsal process can be as dully
practical as building a wall. The cast are also taken aback at being
treated courteously – I wonder what old Senda was like. We are
to rehearse from eleven to five with one ten-minute break (which I

tend to extend in my own interests – the director's Johnny Rockets opportunity and very much the English Way); and I plan to work with each individual group at first – Olivia's family, Orsino's household and the twins, concentrating on scenes when they don't intermingle – in the hope of making separate little communities. However at Haiyuza the tradition is full-time attendance by all; so the unused cast turn up and listen, and I haven't the heart to exclude them once they are there.[7] Used to being told what to do, even mildly gratified at being barked at, they offer no ideas of their own: discussion is so laborious that, in a provocative fit, I propose an exercise in which the actors observe each other's work and gently comment on it. It is the sort of thing that might build up trust and unite the company, if only against the director. Wrong again – it is very hard to raise a sacrificial volunteer to start, and in the end everyone freezes into mutual respect: Feste, the longest-serving company member, escapes comment entirely. I have a slight sense of being humoured, and Mr Sataki looks a little smug. For several gridlocked days, two nearly-closed books blink at each other: what I am getting from these very polite people is awe slithering towards bewilderment on its way to disillusion.

Stubbornly vamping till ready, I postpone staging of any kind until next week, the third: in a sense any fool can stage a play, but only a fool would do so here before he understands the actors. And gradually seeping out of our painful conversations is an interesting proposition: that Shakespeare's characters might be real people, as diverse and complicated as the group of us in this room. To many Japanese, the Bard of Avon seems as remote as *kabuki* or even *noh* to us, so the actors' delivery sounds artificially high-church; and, used to being bullied for results, they generally side-step ambiguity and go straight to effect. The new ideas are intriguing them: that the play's 'villain' might also be its anti-hero; how sexual desire can possess a woman in grief; how romantic agony is sometimes laughable. It is like life. We must sit tight on these frail eggs and forget the ticking clock – with patience they just might hatch.

And at least we have an Aguecheek who will try anything. He is a romantically lugubrious young actor called Yosio Kato: even sitting and reading, he reminds me of Charles Lamb's description of the

---

7   It took an age for someone to explain gently to me that the only way the actors could get their next rehearsal call was if they were there all the time to hear it announced – very few of them had telephones.

performance of James William Dodd in 1771, 'who in expressing slowness of apprehension . . . surpassed all others. You will see the first dawn of an idea stealing slowly over his countenance, climbing up little by little with a painful process . . . a glimmer of understanding would appear in a corner of his eye, and for lack of fuel go out again.' Cut off by more than the centuries from this description of himself, Kato seems to know that character is defined by opposites – the strengths of a weak man, the occasional courage of a coward – and he is finding a wonderful timid assertiveness. Conversely to Murakami, Kato had offered Orsino at his audition, but his startled doe-eyed look seemed to me better for Andrew: he finally walked away with the part by the cunning use of a country accent (undetectable by me) that reduced the Japanese witnesses to helplessness.[8] Not only that, but he played the violin. Wonderful Aguecheek wooing Olivia with moon-face and fiddle!

Halfway through the week, and partly to get rid of the cramp, we impulsively stand up and do an improvisation. It is Act 2 Scene 3, the midnight party. There is no mistaking the cold sweat that breaks out on Nakano at this prospect – I know, because I have an encouraging hand on his shoulder at the time. But there is nothing like a veteran, and he scuttles away, reappearing moments later stripped down to a hairnet and flimsy dressing-gown, to interrupt Toby's and Andrew's revels. He obviously had it all ready, so that I have the odd feeling of having been second-guessed: and although this is not so much improvising as seizing the chance to display long-dreamed-of effects, it sets an example. At the very idea of the exercise, Sen Yano (Toby) shot me a look thick with panicky resentment (the essence of Toby, rancour and pride beneath a jolly air); but he puts on a *matsuri* carnival mask, comes out to play, and, his worries unjammed, begins to sound like a real drinker for the first time.

Thank God – without two seniors taking the lead like this, I would have been stuck. Playfulness begins to lighten the desperate

8   Oddly, none of them could place it geographically: although many urban Japanese speak in the dialect of their hometown (*furusato*) inside their families, they never do so at work, and they find other regional accents quite difficult to identify. When I asked what Kato was up to, some placed him in Tohoku, an old rural area in the north very suitable for a country-cousin, others in Chugo-ku in the south, where archaic styles of speech have survived; Kato, a crafty trouper, said it was a little invention of his own. In fact, all my earnest attempts to explore regional sounds – Osaka for Feste, even the rash suggestion that Viola and Sebastian, as two foreigners, might be Koreans with perfect Japanese – were to fall swiftly to the ground. Just as well – you do want Viola and Sebastian to be liked.

urge to Get Shakespeare Right, and the play's sinews soften a bit. Imagining the rehearsal room not as a frightening decoy stage but just as one room in a real house, the cast scatter through Haiyuza's building (to the amazement of Accounts but the delight of Wardrobe) and even out onto the street – there are no box-trees, or green of any kind, in Roppongi, but plenty of sidestreets to hide in. The company's canteen kitchen becomes Olivia's beneath-stairs, its dressing-rooms her bedrooms, while in the rehearsal room itself we turn out the lights (there are no windows) to enact the terror of a shipwreck, the black freezing sea and the hostile limbo of the shore. This exercise leaves a deep imprint on Hirota (Viola): from then on her first scene would always be scarred with ugly remembered confusion. As if released from school, the actors cavort around or talk quietly to each other in corners, paraphrasing the half-learned text when they can't improvise, moving according to their instincts, forgetting to impress the director. Left out, I trail them around the room, eavesdropping: they sometimes address their asides to me as if I was a passer-by. I learn something new from this: that Viola often senses her lost twin at her elbow, and admits her feelings for Orsino, her delight over the ring or her longing for a beard, as much to him as to the audience. Sataki, unable to participate or to control, relapses into an acrid tolerance. Good theatre subverts at every level, and you are forever robbing Peter to give confidence to Paul: I am convinced now that Sataki, like a Malvolio observing our Feast of Fools, represents something in Haiyuza that I would like to dismantle. At the end of the week, a prouder company glows athletically, seeing the foreign author as a possible friend, and a war-cry goes up: '*Ordinary* Shakespeare!'. Close to the half-way point of rehearsals, with not a move settled, they feel like shareholders.

Something else too: however wild their inventions, when a degree of formality is needed these actors don't bump into each other. Rather, they fall instinctively into fastidious natural groupings. After all, the Japanese sense of another's territory, the instinct for an unexpressed mood, is as acute as their appreciation of a rock garden or a room for drinking tea in. For a director, always trying to think ahead, the trick is to spot something like this, exploit it and ditch your previous plan: so, late on Friday, we stage off the cuff the scene in which Olivia's household first appears. This, after all, is a formal situation upset by various agents of misrule, and it already seems to appeal to the actors, who are used to the daily overturning of order in a society impossibly dedicated to conformism. A gong sounds: a servant slowly crosses the stage with a broom. Brassware is polished at its gentle daily speed, Maria works meticulously on the household accounts, candles are deliberately trimmed: then Feste wanders on not in a burst of jester's jollity but tinkering on a country guitar. If the stage management, imagining themselves Olivia's staff, will likewise adjust the furniture in a slow and deliberate way, not in the usual flurry directors demand, they will confirm the hypnotic tempo. Into all this Toby will drunkenly reel, followed by the gate-crashing Cesario, complete with musicians (Curio and Valentine), picking out *The Shadow of Your Smile*: we indent for a clarinet, which I know Curio can play, and a kazoo, which anyone can. The whole effect is very pleasing, and the actors have done most of the work themselves. Taking the advantage, I promise to stage the whole play in the first half of next week and outline a practical plan for the two and a half weeks following: reassurance fills the room like a blossom.

A second typhoon, the worst since the War, kills fifty people in Kyushu, at the very moment my son Mark is taking off from London for Tokyo to join me. It is called Yancy. Knowing he is in the air, anxious as hell but with nothing I can do, I go with Kate Beales on Sunday to see the shallow end of the transexuality *Twelfth Night* so interestingly explores: the Takarazuka. The British Sunday supplements have caught up with them now, so you may know something of this élite company, but in 1993 they were a novelty for most Westerners. The idea was conceived eighty years ago by the owner of the Takarazuka-Osaka railway as a modest means of reversing the mainly one-way traffic towards Osaka: the little resort town gave the company its first home, and they later expanded into Tokyo, where they are now a big fact. The other reversal is that whereas in traditional theatre the men play the women, this is an all-female company; and the training of the five hundred carefully selected girls involves a regimen which, to quote one recent observer, makes the Von Trapp family look like disorganised hippies. This can mean a year of cleaning the premises, then a year supervising the cleaners, occasional training in discipline by the Japanese Self Defence Agency (its peacetime army), before being unleashed on the public, hair slicked back and kiss-curled like fifties rock 'n' rollers, to realise not some exquisite aesthetic but brainlessly manipulative spectaculars that would make Barry Manilow blush. The company's stars are everywhere – on phone cards, T-shirts and powder compacts: and if they marry they are required to leave the company. For a repertoire, operetta based on the stories of Tolstoy and Shakespeare, kitsch revue and Copacabana-style extravaganza are bundled up together. Truthfully, this is an enterprise born in banality labouring to bring forth trash – but not sleazy trash: despite the obvious sexual titillation and (because of its hermetic tradition) the hints of backstage passion, Takarazuka dangles an innocent paradise before mature women on the run from 'salary-man' husbands and girls pubescently facing up to them. The Takarazuka 'male' hero – gentle, strong and wise in all situations – is for both groups a much-needed dream: the crush potential for the younger audience of the stars in their tuxedos and painted moustaches is considerable, and for an older group, chronically bruised as wives and mothers, so is the subconscious relief of knowing that these splendid males carry no offensive weapons. Takarazuka's every aspect is a reflection, perhaps, of some bad thing about Japan[9] – but it is worth seeing. Once. It is certainly the only time that a man is likely, in a full house of nearly 3000, to find himself alone in the Gents.

This astonishing experience is Kate's final impression of Japan. Tomorrow, her job done, she flies back to London, her place in Asahi Homes and the rehearsal room taken by Mark, now safely arrived to do a photographic project on the show and to substitute emotional support for professional. I take Kate to dinner and, gripping the meat-grill for emphasis, barbecue my thumb. We have been talking about where the production is heading, agreeing that the company must, having found the play's liberating Fun, get rid of the Charm. As I suck my stupid wound, we agree that *Twelfth Night*, marinaded in cruelty, also mixes absurdity and pain, and should stalemate its audience between laughter and pity, as I have just done to her.

★

Before embarking on the rest of the staging, we start the week with a little more work on the Olivia scene that stood up so interestingly on Friday night – something tells me that it is a crux. On second viewing, the sleepy routine of the introverted old household is fine,

---

9   Militarism funnelled through economic competitiveness into domestic brutality – the famous coarseness of many working Japanese husbands is the product of piteously confused conditioning, but an awkward daily fact.

but there's not enough ominous weight behind it to suggest the suffocating obsequies muffling everyone's lives. The hush needs to be less Turgenev, more Ibsen, you might say. A complete skeleton of the set has appeared in the rehearsal room, swiftly thrown up by invisible hands on Sunday as if in response to Friday's practical work. In Mitsuru's three doorways we set candles and a kneeling tryptych of Olivia, her Waiting Gentlewoman and Maria, one in each, dimly silhouetted. Wary again of the scattered nature of the play's first half hour, I suggest the tableau could be there from its beginning, unifying the action (poor patient actresses: the director goes home after the first night). Even in Japan endurance has its limits, and discreet hassocks appear for them. As this fifth scene begins, the light will rise fully on the women for the first time, accompanied by a shimmering gong and flute, and their grave image will weigh gently on Feste's and Maria's wrangling.

Though nothing quite as interesting as this happens again, the rest of the play gets adequately staged over the next few days: the actors naturally warm to the practicalities, and some performances begin to peek out, their weaknesses as revealing as their strengths. Murakami is still embarrassed as Orsino. Hirota is wonderfully natural (always the justification for casting Viola young), but she doesn't stand up to Orsino, and in the scenes with Olivia (Yeuko Yamasita) she lacks Cesario's impertinence, being inclined to defer both as character and actress. This makes her seem 'feminine' as the page – and in her rehearsal breaks she also has to listen humbly to off-the-cuff advice from the older actors while offering them biscuits. It is difficult too to get from the good-natured Yamasita the imperiousness of a woman born to command: though, interestingly, she plays the shame of her attraction to Cesario – everything in fact that touches on humiliation or regret – with deep feeling. Flinching from the cliché as it looms, I have to notice that both women find it difficult to assert themselves, let alone rejoice in their waywardness. It is a little surprising, for the submissive Japanese woman is only a very partial truth now.[10] In fact some say that the wives control this country by running the men who run it – applying an iron hand to the household, awarding pocket money to their husbands before perhaps dismissing them as *sodai* (big rubbish) and divorcing them.

10   By night I interrogate the invisible sceptic in the ceiling of Asahi Homes – am I making too much of all this? Acting after all is common coin. Yes, but why shouldn't these Japanese actors reflect something in their culture?

It's an exaggeration, of course: women have had the vote for less than fifty years, and they claim their birthright hesitantly; but it is true that feminism generally takes the form of skilful organisation behind an acquiescent pose rather than through public campaigning. Even in the charmed circle of the theatre there is little brazenness – the Americanised Mika covers her face and shuffles into a corner when praised, and she is noticeably prudish in translating Shakespeare's bawdry.[11] Although Yamasita and Hirota have their own status – the former well known and well married with a young son, Hirota glamorous enough for her forthcoming marriage (which may cost her TV-star fiancé his fan club) to be kept secret from the press – their crucial showdowns in the play are still shrinkingly polite.

Observing the actors who have been with the company longest – Sen Yano (in life the father of the Antonio), Nakano and Hajime Syozi (Feste) – I have to admit that the brief liberation they found in last week's improvisations has faltered, and I am now watching their half-baked effects and old-fashioned bluster with diminishing patience. The pulling of 'appropriate' faces and windy vocalising wrecks Shakespeare, whose emotional shifts are too jazzy and volatile for such posturing: their hamminess is obscuring the hard edges from which the comedy bleeds. Toby Belch is a true alcoholic, and Malvolio ends up in a straitjacket mocked by Feste as a vengeful Fury – the belief that it will be funnier that way, as well as truer, flickers only fitfully in these stalwarts. Like all permanent ensembles (look at the German and the Russian), Haiyuza has both protected and borne down on its actors, generating a mixture of anxiety and laziness that does them small justice. The symptoms are immediate – these older actors sound as if they were making announcements, relying heavily on that guttural overemphasis, resonated in the throat in a way that would give Western players laryngitis: whereas the younger ones speak quite clearly. In England, where Shakespeare is our man, directors are often grateful for experienced performers: in Japan, where the territory is new, the kids get the point quicker and the older flail about, scared to break new ground. Perplexed for the moment, I am comforted by Kato's wild fooling as

11 Let alone where the translator has made it still worse. Toby's 'Out, scab !' translates into Japanese as 'you syphilitic' and there has been a great deal of anxiety about it, since, according to Mika, 'sex things' can't be said on the stage – at least on Haiyuza's stage. It is all very prim and tiresome; and Sataki has uncharacteristically quashed the argument in my favour, allowing Haiyuza to take a small step forward towards the millennium.

Aguecheek, already the production's highest card, and by the un-ashamed emotionalism of a new generation – Sebastian and Antonio hug each other with unhesitating passion.

Reflecting these tensions perhaps, it seems that more anxious out-of-hours meetings are being convened, this time to discuss the humourless purposes of the Western director – Sataki is again exhorting the cast to ignore me and go for the laughs in their tradi-tional way. Alternatively, he will change it all when I'm gone – what a thought. Once more, the actors will have none of it, and as if the necessary ritual of airing their anxieties has relieved them again, my stock ends up higher. With a most wonderful willingness, each begins, at his own speed, to step out onto a new catwalk, becoming passionate, unreserved, willing to try anything that is asked for – they are more punctual than I am, and I leave guiltily in the evenings as they continue to fend off Sataki. They are, of course, working as if their lives depended on it, as actors will where conditions are most hard: they are also unremittingly kind. Every morning Fabian brings in the English-language *Japan Times* for me, and the Waiting Gentlewoman a great variety of teas, rice cakes, little lunch boxes, carrot and burdock ('some kind of a special Japanese vegetable!'), pastries and even second-hand kimonos. Then we rehearse, and they all try to behave like shits – interrupting each other, elbowing their way forward, everyone on the make. It's still a little strained: and as the actors become emotional they also become over-excited, in an hysterical spiral. Someone has to hit the jackpot cleanly soon, and, predictably enough, it is Kato: as he realises at last that Olivia will never care for him or his violin, he furiously packs his bags and rockets out of the house, heading for home. Dimly perceiving the mockery underlining Toby's and Fabian's efforts to turn him back, feeling his resolution falter, confusedly furious at his humiliation, he bursts into inconsolable tears – real tears, not funny Aguecheek ones. It is a great Shakespearian moment, an arrow to the heart of the comedy. The rest of the cast watch, upset, uncertain how to react. *Now* we're cooking. We eat more cake.

Weekends working abroad can be daunting. Terror of Sunday in a hotel room drives you to accept the most unlikely invitations – then the strain of communicating with kind hosts forces you back into the room on the pretext of 'work'. In this case the invitation is to turn some pots with the parents of Hajime Mori (Fabian and my mole), retired meteorologists now fully devoted to their hobby: they live in a sort of Japanese Golden Pond with an enviable view of Mount Fuji, which gently changes colour like Cezanne's Mont Saint–Victoire beyond their windows. We sit together for tea on arrival for perhaps two minutes only before Hajime's father slaps his hands and urges us to get to work: in any case hardly a word is possible without Hajime's mediation, and peacefulness, as if spooling from the spinning wheels, quietly engulfs us for two or three hours. The sweetness of the experience – working (incompetently in my case) in the famous Shigaraki clay and admiring (and therefore loaded down with) the couple's work – is not quite dispersed by the five and a half hours it takes to drive the hundred kilometers home in the evening: worse than the M4 into London, but at least there are helpful signs every few moments announcing the exact length of the jam. I still have my pots, and after all they're not so bad, as if the marvellous clay had lent me some of its worth.

★

The fourth week begins with a long-postponed meeting with the composer Tohru Ueda and the sound department to finalise what is to be heard in and around the action. The abstract set inclines the play away from the workaday, and too many natural effects in the interior scenes – Olivia's dogs barking, doors slamming and so on – seem misplaced against it; but for some reason atmospheric sound outdoors is all right. Olivia's garden will benefit from birds of course, but also from *higurashi*, a particular Japanese cicada whose weird tropical hum, as of high-tension wires, fills the late summer air: there is much debate over the appositeness of this.[12] I am confidently told that these doomed creatures live seven months under the ground, then one day above it, and then die as quickly as Viola's blossoms. Tohru has mercifully despaired of getting Feste's songs into the hit parade, and his version of 'Come Away Death' is edging towards folk-blues; while the ancient sound of the gong behind a delicate arpeggio theme for Viola and Sebastian expresses mortality and Shakespeare's bargain with it. The cast has enough musical talent overall to develop Feste's final song into a gentle company

12   It was triumphantly vindicated. At the climax of Malvolio's joy in the Letter Scene, the plotters were shaking with laughter so much behind their wooden screen that Malvolio heard it rattling. But the sound was so like the *higurashi* permanently on the sound track that he assumed that the cicadas were hitting a sympathetic climax, and danced off in rapture.

anthem, which is expedient since Syozi's singing is not really strong enough to sustain it alone: this will involve Olivia's Priest racing round behind the set to shoulder his twelve-string Gibson guitar. As this song dies and the stage light fades, the figure of Malvolio, an indestructible ghost, will quietly pass across the candle-lit tableau. Horses for courses: no satirical Arts Council officer this time – we are in the East, beset with different demons, looking inwards to dark mountains, and fearfully outwards over an oceanic rim.

A newly uncompromising cast seize on random ideas and run with them as if they had been waiting for the chance, and their impetuosity wins back time lost in the debilitating process of translation. The latter just takes so *long* (though it's sometimes been unnerving to hear my two-minute discursions to the company reduced by Mika to a fifteen-second summary); now that we know each other well, mime proves a better shorthand, while Mika begins to sit back and enjoy the show. Suddenly, there is an almost competitive eagerness to introduce Japanese references. Fabian, Maria and Toby enact Shinto exorcism rituals to coax out Malvolio's bad *kami*, provocatively surrounding him with animal bones – these can stay in place and form the outline of his prison later, sharply focused under a fierce white top-light. One problem with these bones: in the interim Andrew and Cesario have to fight their duel, where they will be a nuisance. But of course – at that point they stand for, oh, Olivia's newly-installed rock-pool, complete with carp, which the duellists must be careful not to fall into: the cast are relieved to find that directors have to improvise as well.

My son, with the fastidious instincts of a good photographer, is frustrated by trying to catch the actors' most revealing moments on the hoof in lousy light, but at least he is seeing Japan, and everyone is extremely hospitable to him. Kato continues on his way, a pained, hopeless giant with a rubber body and some of the reflexes of Buster Keaton. At the sight of Malvolio in his night-gown, he collapses into the space of half a tatami mat, like a conjuror's handkerchief from which the supporting stick has vanished; moved to drunken tears by Feste's singing, he sits like a Buddha on the crest of one of the waves on the stage floor and very slowly slides to its base without noticing or changing his attitude – I may never forget it. Since he hardly ever repeats himself, the task is to nail down moments like these before they disappear forever. Malvolio gets his looking-glass, but, more important, in his belief that Olivia loves him, turns from a moody samurai into a grateful human being: dancing in his yellow stockings, his jacket (with yellow buttonhole) and tie still intact, he looks like a stricken fairy. Sen Yano, fed by his own turbulence, begins to dismantle the acting habits of a lifetime to achieve a grainy bloody-mindededness as Toby, Maria's big baby and a fractious drunk. A comfier Orsino, absurdly doomed, and Olivia, forthright now if not haughty, make parallel journeys. The bespectacled Maria (Maumi Amano), a tight-lipped governess in public, is as addicted to a tipple as Sir Toby; Feste's Sir Topas haunts Malvolio like some black-winged vampire – Syozi, though nervous, generates the cruelty the Elizabethans loved, jarring and overstated as it is to us. Hirota as Viola hints at the greatest growth of all, an apprentice beginning to carry the play on the lightest of shoulders. How has all this happened? As always, by the accumulation of small turning-points largely unsensed at the time; unjammed, the barrels in the lock have begun to slide.

Having postponed a first runthrough as late as I could, fearing its artificial pressure on all the fragile details we have found, we eventually do it, and the relief that follows is like that after an opening night. The company, who are mostly broke, insist on taking Mark and me out to dinner, and with all the ingenuity in the world I am unable to part with any money. This is like a long-awaited moment of disclosure, and at last I learn something about their lives – the Waiting Gentlewoman's gruelling chemotherapies, and, most poignantly, the leukaemia of Mr Sataki's daughter. What a cruel profession this is: its loyalties and animosities so determined by the job in hand that, as a freelance, you may learn little of the tough lives left at the door. In a permanent company the actors come to know everything about each other, a visiting director (perhaps rightly) just a little and that only eventually. Mark and I are inordinately touched by the evening's confidences, as if a barrier had been judiciously raised. In the steam and noise of the *sukiyaki* bar, Katsuro Yano (Antonio) and Rikiya Koyama (Sebastian), children of a new prosperity and standing nearly a foot higher than their parents, yell fluent and eager English. Meanwhile Katsuro's father Sen quietly acknowledges to me what his difficulty has been all along, and it is obvious enough: he did military service for the final two years of the War and still has an emotional, more than a technical, difficulty in learning English – or even using the imported Western words that prevail in contemporary Japanese life. Immediately after being demobbed, he saw *A Midsummer Night's Dream* and decided to become an actor, joining Haiyuza almost on its first day; now his longing to play Toby Belch has overcome a remnant of prejudice against me. I toast his candour, and we agree that although there are many things in the world beyond our control, this moment with Shakespeare is ours.

Mitsuru turns up to rehearsals at the end of this week, as designers will, and I'm glad he didn't earlier when we were running up and down the stairs giggling. We confront him with a worry. The undulations on the floor are a bit steep, requiring the actors to stand on hazardous slopes and risk knees, ankles and balance. Could they be a degree flatter? No: Mitsuru has carefully considered it all and would rather abandon the whole set than change his undulations. Since he feels so strongly I concede, more in studied sorrow than anger – we must keep them as they are and, well, just take a chance with the actors' safety. A little surprised to find me on their side now, Mitsuru beams his beam and agrees to flatten the gradient a degree or two.

★

As we move into the theatre, some journalists and observers are, selectively, let in. Haiyuza's management have been amazed at my long postponement of this: but the actors needed privacy, not inspection by querulous visitors. An interviewer asks me indignantly why Andrew and Viola are duelling with samurai swords – this is an *English* play, after all. At a dance rehearsal the stamping stops but the ground keeps moving. The Japanese laugh at this commonplace event, while Mark and I hold our breaths – for us, rather than the normal ten-second tremor, it could be a repeat of the Kanto earthquake of 1923 that left a hundred thousand dead and flattened half of Tokyo.

We refine the staging on the set in the confident knowledge that the actors will by now take trifling instructions – one step to the left, turn at a sharp right angle – without irritation or carelessness. If the earlier ESC production hovered between relaxed naturalism and a lightweight epic style, here, in more intimate surroundings (and though rehearsals have been conducted more experimentally) the play is emerging cleaner, more choreographed, quite concentrated. Seiya Tamura bustles in to a runthrough: he believes this will be the best thing Haiyuza has done, a real turning-point and the first time they have been an ensemble – how about some small supper? Even Sataki seems to be persuaded. Most importantly, the deep groundswell of Shakespeare's music – his astounding sense of counterpoint and the absolute authority of his spirit – is filling a room in which what he actually wrote remains unheard. What, outside of more typhoons, can go wrong?

The lighting, of course. Initially, the plywood of the set shows bright white, a glare banging up from the floor like noon in the Sahara – fine perhaps for the brief scenes on the beach, but no good at all for Orsino and Olivia, or for the audience's optic nerves. Cursing false economies, we re-angle all the lamps away from the floor, but the actors now look as if they are flood-lit in IKEA. A row develops with Yasunori Ito, the lighting designer: after all, he promised me he could isolate with individual lamps seventy different locations on the stage, and this undifferentiated white light (fashionable at London's Royal Court about twenty years ago) was never the deal. I turn on Mitsuru, who as a designer should have known the wood was too cheap to look good under any light – but he shrugs infuriatingly and bides his time. Ito gracefully apologises, I reassure him that there are, after all, many schools of lighting and that we've misunderstood each other – oh, language, language – but please can I have much more from the front of house and the side, warmer colours overall, some sense of sculpture. At his bark, eight drama students leap onto the stage to re-angle again and apply colour gels which produce a nauseous vermilion and blinding emerald greens. I take a long walk, and then begin to behave badly, which has the effect of making the Japanese deeply concerned, as if for my health, and at the same time strangely unperturbed. Worse, I start using Mika as a battering-ram ('Ask him *what* he thinks he's *talking* about') – but she is used to quick linguistic filletting, and gives no offence. Late at night, I confide in Mark, as we stare at the tracks of a desolate subway stop, that I think I've blown it: not foreseeing the problems of the set (Mitsuru has now repainted it twice, 'some kind of grey'), weighing the whole boat down with cross-cultural speculations, aiming Napoleonically to change Haiyuza's traditional style. He is annoyed with me for despairing, sensing both nerves and a streak of affectation.

For a director every show resembles a departing railway train – best to change platforms as quickly as possible and not wave for too long. I see it coming, and, like a dog trying to leave its scent behind, I ask for a chunk to be taken off my fee for a company party half-way through the post-Tokyo tour, and I leave a private number in England for the actors to fax to if they have a problem. Wishful thinking. By the time I get home, sliding screens will have quietly closed around the show, and I will never know if the cast, having perhaps discovered something important, have the self-confidence to hold onto it – or at least to be less easily intimidated. Conversely, I hope, if they're a success, that they don't become smug. The thin-nest film of self-satisfaction can steal over any well-received comedy: its precious naiveté evaporates, it becomes a little less shared, a little more take-it-or-leave-it-folks, than on that apprehensive night when its first audience, travelling at the same rate, collaborated in raising it to its feet. It almost always happens; but this time, instead of returning, as we say, to 'take out the improvements', the director can only promise weakly to 'stay in touch'. I also feel bad about Ito and his lighting team. And I wish we'd put a black carpet across the back of the set.

Meanwhile, Sataki begins the final dress rehearsal before I have time to get from backstage to the auditorium: his parting shot. The last moments fly by. Wigs are dumped, especially Aguecheek's (a Japanese face under hair that hangs like flax from a distaff has proved a cultural incompatibility, and he looked like an extra-terrestrial): and a silk patch has to be stitched into the seat of his costume since, wearing tweed on the cheap wood, he can no longer execute his famous Buddha slide without splinters. The simulated plastic 'bones' for Malvolio's prison are no good: the Waiting Gentlewoman secretly goes to the butchers, buys some real ones, watchfully boils them all night in her tiny flat, and brings them in – to the embarrassment of the stage management. Longeurs are sliced out, favourite moments sacrificed to the broad movement: with a simultaneous feeling of panic and spaciousness, I think often about going home. On the first night, I sit with Glen Walford, veteran of a dozen Japanese productions of her own and riotously unsentimental about the whole process: we both guess that, from this point on, recession will make it almost impossible for Japan to import European directors, or for them to make pleasant time and money in return. On the stage, as if by devout resolve, the actors draw together everything we have done and said: their nervous energy, instead of scattering the performance to the four winds, narrows to a fierce concentration suggesting ease and time to spare. They bring the play in quite beautifully: I am very touched, as I know their intent was all for my delight, a response to my half-understood promptings as much as for themselves. The British Ambassador, recovering from a recent visit by John Major, weeps as Viola and Sebastian are reunited. At the party later, two great *sake* barrels are hammered open, as is the custom, drenching everyone, and there are wild speeches about life and the theatre, about hands across the oceans. The strangely suburban sidestreets of Shinokubo (like many newly-fashionable parts of Tokyo, it goes to bed early) slumber as we stumble away, euphorically self-justified, aiming for cool sheets with spinning heads.

The rain pours down next morning: a cord is cut and there is suddenly nothing to do except some listless shopping and packing before an evening flight to London. Mark and I, subdued in the limbo preceding departure, go in and have a brief meeting with the company before their matinee. Delirium flares up again: there are tears and more passionate speeches, and a specially generous one from Mr Sataki, who presents me with a pearl necklace for my imagined wife. Why don't you stay a few days, people say, but I couldn't do it to Haiyuza's budget nor embarrass them with the request. We are driving ourselves mad with these valedictions. It is nearly the half-hour call, and, suddenly sobered, the actors wander off to check their props and run a few bits for themselves. Best for us to disappear, quite superfluous, for fear we all shrink shyly back into the awful courtesies of the first day; by the time the company finish their second show we shall be over Siberia, and by their third I shall be driving through Warwickshire lanes.

As it turned out, the press regarded the production as 'a challenge to renew Haiyuza's activity', as 'an incentive' for them, and so on. Much of the drift, in other words, was what it all meant in the company's history and doubtful future. It was only now that it was explained to me that the name Haiyuza means 'the actors' company', and I was able to reflect on what a misnomer this was. This was an institution that pushed its players towards the quick fix, insulting their own gifts in the scramble to please impatient directors. Whatever kind of quantum jump might have been taken on *Twelfth Night*, I certainly wouldn't overestimate the new empowerment – the sad likelihood was that job insecurity would make old acting habits reassert themselves and all would be forgotten. Still, you never know.

I had learned more about the play's infinite variety: but in very fact, I made some mistakes as well. I dragged Mika through a hedge backwards while she diligently tried to do a job that was really too specialised for her; I should have seen that I needed – particular rarity – a bilingual assistant director, and asked for the money to work on the translation with them before starting. Although I saw through the obstructions of a stage manager who clearly wanted to direct the production himself, elsewhere I accepted received wisdom too readily: you must challenge *everything*. Mikami's translation really was a little old-fashioned, accepting the truism that Japanese cannot render English lyrical verse without sounding archaic, whereas it isn't really so – the 5-7-5 syllable shape of the *haiku* and the 5-7-5-7-7 of the *waka* are malleable verse forms that carry lyrical grace, but only recent translators have ventured to use them. It may be that while urging the company to think Japanese, I ended up annoyed they were not more like subtle Brits; and I got Orsino a little wrong for the second time, not because the actors weren't good, but because I slightly miscast them in each case, overstating the daft psychopathology and neglecting legitimate romanticism. I should have asked the set and lighting designers to work hand in glove from the start rather than accepting that that wasn't the Japanese Way. I should have insisted that I would return to see the show later: after its Tokyo run it was to go on a national tour, into civic barns, where whatever delicacy we achieved would be sorely threatened, and technical precision surely lost in the most reckless get-in schedule I have heard of for a show of this size – into the theatre at 1pm, set up, light and be ready to go at 6pm (Viola furiously ironing the costumes). Although Japanese stage labour is plentiful and non-unionised, I couldn't see how it was to be done, and was fearful of what the burghers of Utsonomiyashi, or the guests at the Salad Hotel Wakayama (ominous-sounding venue) would get. So in a way, I am glad that the last I saw of Haiyuza was a sort of self-subversion – the *Twelfth Night* band warming up that wet afternoon for the up-tempo version of 'Come Away Death' that formed an overture to the second half. The joint was jumping: I don't think the chance to play the blues was what these actors expected of their Shakespeare, but it may have been as good a heresy as any to leave them with.

PART TWO

ACT THREE

Act 3 Scene 1–Act 3 Scene 4

1.1.

> VIOLA: Save thee, friend, and thy music! Dost thou live by thy
>   tabor?
> FESTE: No, sir, I live by the church.

The crackle of vaudeville, the paradiddle on the drum, a groan at the
pun. Shakespeare's one-liners are fine, but then he will pull the
stuffing out of them:

> VIOLA: Art thou a churchman?
> FESTE: No such matter, sir. I do live by the church; for I do
>   live at my house, and my house doth stand by the church.

It was a perfectly good joke, then we have to wait while it's spelled
out. Why does he do this? It's the same with the Gravedigger in
Hamlet over-explaining his quip about all the men in England being
mad, and with Cleopatra's asp-seller. Is it possible that Shakespeare's audience enjoyed the laboured QED as much as the gag?

  Twelfth Night is gathering itself for a tremendous *corrida*, though
you would hardly know it. This oddly weightless sequence between
Viola and Feste has the air of a conversation at a bus stop, of two
paths only casually crossing: and surely Feste doesn't live in a house
by a church. However, it does yield some character – the slightly
jovial, hail-fellow-well-met air of Viola's greeting lanced by Feste's
sour monosyllables. Fluent as she is, Viola is no match for his
professional speed, and she can only counter him by going through
the whole joke again, shaping it into a reproachful truism about the
use of language:

> So thou mayst say the king lies by a beggar, if a beggar dwell
> near him; or the church stands by thy tabor if thy tabor stand by
> the church.

Sure, and Feste's unenthusiastic compliment

> You have said, sir . . .

is heavy with our fatigue too. He winds the routine up:

> To see this age! A sentence is but a cheveril glove to a good wit –
> how quickly the wrong side may be turned outward!

Well, not that quickly.

It is quite interesting to see these two square up, vamping till the next bit of plot is ready: they have barely met before, and I'm not sure how much Feste likes Cesario, or whether he is mocking him or flattering him. You never quite know with this Fool – for instance, is he a critic of the time or a creature of it? Does he regret the corruption of language or thrive by it? Words, his and Shakespeare's livelihood, are, he says, too wanton to form the name of a man's sister, debased by being used for promises ('very rascals, since bonds disgraced them'), and unreliable for expressing 'reason'. Words, words, words – the word itself is compulsively repeated till its meaning drains.[1] But of course he is only joking (or is he?), this Fool who cares 'for nothing' (or does he?). Turning the cheveril glove outwards again, he reduces Viola likewise to empty air:

> . . . I do not care for you: if that be to care for nothing, I would
> it would make you invisible.

It is rather tough. Viola would hardly have forgotten 'Come Away Death' so soon, so her enquiry:

> Art not thou the lady Olivia's fool?

is really a means of stopping all this. But Feste has three fine jokes in hand – on Olivia's lack of folly, on the husbands and the pilchards, and a definitive description of himself:

> I am indeed not her fool but her corrupter of words

– they somersault out of one brief speech, their vitality lightening the atmosphere. No doubt Viola appreciates them; but for her to remind Feste where they last met:

> I saw thee late at the Count Orsino's

is perhaps a mistake. Now he is off-duty he can take a good look at her:

---

1 The cancellation of language is a startling, occasional effect in Shakespeare. The loquacious Hamlet dies with 'the rest is silence'; the excoriating Timon with 'let four words go by and language end'.

> I think I saw your wisdom there

and it is as uncomfortable as Orsino's scrutinies – of all people's, it could be the trained eye of the Fool that sees through her disguise. Overreacting a little (Feste has not exactly 'passed' on – that is, thrust a sword at – her), she resorts to giving him money, the one thing that always distracts him, and Pavlov-like, he sets about doubling it:

> Would not a pair of these have bred, sir?

This time it is he who hardly knows when to stop, and his wit begins to fall off as he tries to wring winning lines out of the old story of Pandarus and Cressida. But in some ways this has been his best fooling, when all is done, no doubt because he was under no pressure; and he even let himself be known a little as he didn't earlier with Aguecheek:

> VIOLA: I warrant thou art a merry fellow, and car'st for nothing.
> FESTE: Not so, sir; I do care for something . . .

It's a good moment as long as the actor is not sentimental about it.

Viola has been reduced to a feed, apart from one good joke about her longing for a beard not her own, which she can't share with Feste anyway.[2] But he has caused her to reflect on his methods. What she now tells us has rather more euphony than insight – and her emphasis on Feste's strategy underestimates his triumphant recklessness. That Feste is a 'wise' fool, that he observes

> their mood on whom he jests,
> The quality of persons and the time

is the most elementary thing about him – and as she is only a page, he didn't bother much with her anyway. In fact, we know him better than she does – and remembering him on the subject of Olivia's brother and, best of all, on the character of Orsino, we also know that it is not a matter of 'labour', of 'check[ing] at every feather': his judgment is very fine and daring. No amount of natty antithesis:

> For folly that he wisely shows is fit;
> But wise men, folly-fall'n, quite taint their wit

can conceal a slight sense of patronage in her perfunctory speech.

---

2   These Shakespearian beards. Hamlet claims to have one that is plucked off and blown in his face; most Hamlets don't though, nor Orsinos. Live with it.

Still, Viola is back at centre stage, even if a little less effective and characterful than when she held Olivia's ring. The narrative reins are sharply taken up by Toby and Andrew, arriving in a mock-official deputation – Olivia is asking Cesario inside. Now we can see where we are. This is the new mission that Orsino ordered at the end of 2.4: Viola has been waiting at the gate as she did before, and this time it has swung open. She might have gone through the loose-limbed sequence with Feste with a touch of anxiety about this meeting – though in truth this sort of subtext is not very typical of Shakespeare, for whom the meaning is generally all in the thing said, as it's said.

Toby is rather polite (he has seen Viola only once before but may not remember it), and Andrew gives himself airs, even managing a French greeting which is the exact translation of Toby's:

> TOBY: Save you, gentleman . . .
> ANDREW: Dieu vous garde, monsieur.

French is important to Andrew: it is of course the wooer's right arm, and as he is about to meet Olivia for the first time, any number of small efforts are to be expected. Things are certainly a bit better than when he was flattened by *pourquoi* – however, the greeting is as far as he has thought, and he finds that it is one thing to initiate a conversation in a foreign language, quite another to keep it going. He understands Viola's courtly reply

> Et vous aussi; votre serviteur

but can only respond lamely in English:

> I hope, sir, you are; and I am yours.

Let's hope Olivia is not a linguist.

Viola's rally with Feste seems to have left her with facetiousness to spare. She mimics Toby's affectation that she is here on some commercial mission:

> TOBY: . . . My niece is desirous you should enter, if your trade
>   be to her.
> VIOLA: I am bound to your niece, sir; I mean, she is the list of
>   my voyage.

She then makes fun of his invitation to 'taste' her legs. In this mood she could get up Toby's nose as badly as she does Malvolio's – and as for her pun on 'gait' and 'gate', that sort of thing is better left to Feste.

The sense of a changed, somewhat unburdened world, continues. We are still, pretty clearly, outside, and less restrained: there has already been a fool playing a tabor, and some verbal affectations from normally unaffected people. And this time Olivia is – more than – willing to meet with Cesario, knowing she can always retreat behind her veil if things don't go well. Viola's unusual frivolity now extends to her:

> Most excellent accomplished lady, the heavens rain odours on
> you.

Just as in 1.5 ('Most radiant, exquisite and unmatchable beauty'), she seems to be starting her task by guying it. However, this debased poetry has a great effect on Andrew, who is eager to compete and presumably resentful – at the very moment he faces Olivia at last, he is being upstaged:

> 'Odours', 'pregnant' and 'vouchsafed' – I'll get 'em all three all
> ready.

Perhaps these novelties will serve him better than the French; but Olivia's only response is to tell them all to make themselves scarce:

> Let the garden door be shut, and leave me to my hearing

– and his buttonhole wilts.

Olivia's and Viola's second private duologue, conducted this time in midsummer sunshine, is an intricate study in comic tension. Olivia's volatility (as distinct from her prickly pride before) and Viola's improvisations in dealing with it, make it extremely mobile, and the mood is distinctly less sunny than the weather. After a beat of silence (Toby, Maria and Andrew have to leave, as briskly as they can be persuaded to) matters begin quite gently:

> OLIVIA: Give me your hand, sir.

Is this a formal handshake (by means of the 'sir') or an endearment (because of the touch)? It is equivocal, and, unsure what to do with the invitation, Viola plays for time:

> My duty, madam, and most humble service.

But this is too conventional for Olivia. She comes back bluntly:

> What is your name?

– and it only repeats Viola's problem: is this politeness or intrusion? As with Feste, she is no more than a feed: and just as there was an edginess beneath his banter, it is clear that Olivia's insouciance is only skin-deep. So she retreats still more vaguely into her servant's role, throwing in the bland compliment 'fair princess'. However, Olivia is intelligent as well as proud:

> My servant, sir? 'Twas never merry world,
> Since lowly feigning was called compliment.

Already the scene has reversed the terms of their earlier one: Olivia drives now, mercilessly, while Viola, with the same job to do, waits for a chance to do it. Viola also has some awkward new knowledge, and Olivia knows she has it, and this makes the Countess's bright, ambiguous scrutiny particularly hard to deal with – especially as it seems to be being used as a punishment.

Viola's stonewalling puts Olivia in a strong position: she can now be the ruler tired of flattery, who would feel better respected, not less, if everyone would call a spade a spade – as she herself does now, making Cesario a mere 'youth'. Viola is reduced to her most defensive, equivocating that Orsino's man must also be Olivia's:

> And he is yours, and his must needs be yours;
> Your servant's servant is your servant, madam.

How has the irritating Orsino become their subject? Away with him:

> OLIVIA: For him, I think not on him; for his thoughts,
> Would they were blanks, rather than filled with me.

The cloudlessness of the setting is giving their tight wrangling an hypnotic feel. As the verse loosens, Viola's back comes away from the wall – she spells out her ABC again:

> Madam, I come to whet your gentle thoughts
> On his behalf

and a proper argument begins, in place of all the tense jockeying. In the first broken verse line so far, Olivia brusquely interrupts her:

> O by your leave, I pray you!

– using a command:

> I bade [ordered] you never speak again of him

rather than a request. She is always inclined to pull rank, but of course it is illusory: Viola is as well-equipped as she is, so she keeps getting the unnerving feeling that she is dealing not with a subordinate but an equal in subordinate's clothing. However, she feels

confident enough to approach the main point with an unmistakeable hint:

> But would you undertake another suit,
> I had rather hear you to solicit that
> Than music from the spheres.

This hems Viola in: she knows by now that Olivia's tactic is often to
seek a fresh position from which to talk down, and that she is not
above using her status to make an advance:

> VIOLA: Dear lady –

Olivia overrides, superior and formal:

> Give me leave, beseech you.

Her new grievance is that she has been the victim of a flirt. Granted,
it was a 'shameful cunning' in her to send Malvolio with the ring and
ensure Cesario's return, but that was Cesario's fault – the boy clearly
intended to lead her on, to ruin her even, tormenting her like a bear
at the stake with his 'tyrannous heart'. She must remind him that

>   to one of your receiving
> Enough is shown

and she paints herself into a self-consciously pretty portrait: her hurt
feelings are not hidden as they should be by the muscle and bone of
her chest, but exposed behind the lightest of lacy materials (not to
be confused with the tree of Feste's song):

> . . . a cypress, not a bosom,
> Hides my heart . . .

She is pleased with the speech, and cannot resist asking Cesario
what he thinks of it:

> . . . so let me hear you speak.

But Viola has seen behind it: and she may be touched to watch any
'poor lady' flailing about between hauteur, vulnerability and
artfulness. However, her sympathy:

> I pity you

is not what Olivia wants to hear from a servant, least of all after such
a speech. She is quick to capitalise, jumping in as the shared line
requires:

> That's a degree to love.

But from Viola's point of view this is a little cheap, and her riposte is untypically harsh:

> No, not a grize; for 'tis a vulgar proof
> That very oft we pity enemies.

'Grize', which literally means step, is quite a strong word, so the phrase becomes something like 'not in the slightest'. These moments of sharpness in Viola are worth treasuring, like Aguecheek's rebellions – they tend to happen when her insights are under-estimated, her sympathies taken advantage of, or if she has to face verbal equivocations, which she distrusts even though she needs them herself. For her part, Olivia dislikes being philosophised at by an inferior – stung, she is frankly sarcastic:

> Why then, methinks 'tis time to smile again.
> O world, how apt the poor are to be proud.

You have to admire her combative style, even if she is not as likeable as Viola – she was so sure of her place in the world and now she has to fight for it. In fact, there is a mutual irritation between the women; Olivia has not asked for this interview, so doesn't have to be lectured and feels she can say what she likes – but then Viola has not asked for it either.

The gamey exchange has turned the gas up. To Olivia, it would be better to be prey to 'the lion', king of beasts, than this marauding wolf in page's clothing. Rather awkwardly, a clock strikes (if the action is to finish before nightfall, it will be early afternoon now): but at least it provokes plain speaking and gives Olivia a workaday cue – she is a woman too busy to waste time, and with new effrontery she claims to have no designs on the apprehensive page, no, not at all:

> Be not afraid, good youth; I will not have you.

It is her retaliation for being pitied, and, feeling on top again, she can afford quite a gracious compliment before leaving:

> And yet, when wit and youth is come to harvest,
> Your wife is like to reap a proper man.

Viola's relief is palpable, and she doesn't even mind the condescension: she responds jauntily with the cry in fact used by Thames rivermen outside the Globe Theatre to announce they were leaving for Westminster:

> Then westward ho!

In view of all Olivia's fractiousness, her valediction might have an ironic stab:

> Grace and *good disposition* attend your ladyship

and she is on her way.

Not so fast. Olivia can't quite let go:

> Stay!
> I prithee tell me what thou think'st of me.

This wonderful small feebleness – like 'so let me hear you speak' earlier – is a human opening between bouts of imperiousness. How to meet it? Viola is used to walking on tiptoe on eggshells by now, and she speaks so gnomically that, though she is obviously referring to self-deception, it is hard to catch a single meaning:

> That you do think you are not what you are.

The puzzling answer makes Olivia draw her rapier again: and as the two of them riddle swiftly for six lines, we see once more why Shakespeare gave them almost anagrammatic names. Each dislikes hedging, in herself and others, each is fighting her way out of a trap with all her resources, and at some deep level they appreciate each other. At first Olivia deals with Cesario's stylish obliqueness a bit clumsily:

> If I think so, I think the same of you

and Viola does better, acknowledging what Olivia doesn't suspect:

> Then think you right: I am not what I am.

This is funnier for us than for Viola, and in fact all her discomfort at her job, her irritation with Olivia, and perhaps Orsino too, are welling up:

> OLIVIA: I would you were as I would have you be.
> VIOLA: Would it be better, madam, than I am?
>   I wish it might, for now I am your fool.

This should have led to closure, but instead it stokes Olivia's fire – Cesario is gorgeous when he's angry. Suddenly she sounds quite Jacobean, linking love and damnation:

> A murderous guilt shows not itself more soon
> Than love that would seem hid; love's night is noon

– her state can no more be hidden by the summer sun than could the Macbeths'. She develops the dark idea with a beautiful recklessness:

> Cesario, by the roses of the spring,
> By maidhood, honour, truth and everything,
> I love thee so, that maugre [despite] all thy pride,
> Nor wit nor reason can my passion hide.

In 1.5, Viola snapped the antiphonal tensions with the Willow Cabin speech, and now comic anguish has burst into a lovesong. From here on, Olivia's company will be as appealing as it was uncomfortable before – she has cartwheeled into the play's lyrical community. She is free.

The delighted outburst has taken her easily into the familiar singular of 'thee' and 'thou', and into rhyme as well – it is like Romeo and Juliet meeting at the ball and, through the strength of their feelings, going into sonnet form.[3] This version is more homespun than that: in particular, the first rhyme is used to deliver a delightful gaucherie – 'and everything' – as Olivia finds she can't think of enough things to swear by. It is difficult for Viola to honour this honesty with her own: for someone as unaffected as she is, it must be galling not to afford the candour. Olivia, who started the play veiled, can hide nothing any more; but concealment (for ever, as far as she knows) is Viola's major theme, her seclusion a nursed and perfected thing. She achieves something remarkable here by falling co-operatively into Olivia's verse pattern – an artery of absolute truth pulses inside a reply as oblique as lucidity can get:

> By innocence I swear, and by my youth,
> I have one heart, one bosom and one truth,
> And that no woman has; nor never none
> Shall mistress be of it, save I alone.

Perfect – apparently obliging, mystifying and beautifully constant. What will the graceful rejection provoke in Olivia? Flirtation. She brazenly suggests another meeting – because, things being as they are, she might yield to Orsino after all:

> Yet come again; for thou perhaps mayst move
> That heart which now abhors to like his love.

They both know what she has done – kicked open a naturally closing door: and so she is gone in a flash, leaving Viola stumped.

---

3 *Romeo and Juliet,*1.5, lines 97-110 in most editions.

3.2. According to that grandfather of Shakespearian editing, Nicholas Rowe, we now move into Olivia's house, but the rhythm of that is feeble on the stage. On film it might well be good to find Andrew woefully packing his bags in some little bedroom after observing the distressing events in the garden; but in the theatre, much of the distinction between the first and second half of this play is that the fragmentation of the former gives way to an uninterrupted roll of action, against a still horizon, with continuity of weather. Infuriated at his dismissal by Olivia, and enraged by what he has somehow seen (though we definitely won't want him to have been visible), Andrew storms onto a stage still hot, language for once tumbling out of him; and the benefit of his exploding on the women's heels is definitely worth one slight distortion – when he splutters

> . . . I saw't i' th' orchard

he has to mean here where he's standing, on this very spot.

He is definitely on his way: but then of course he is always going. In his first scene he realised it was the most sensible thing for him to do; after the party, leaving was as much of a threat as he could make it; and at the end of the play he will 'rather than forty pounds' he were at home. This is his best effort, and you can imagine, or see, his suitcase half-packed, coats struggled into and so on. And just as Olivia has drawn a heartfelt love from sexual confusion, Andrew's admirable decision this time is not based on clear-sightedness – he has misinterpreted the tense ebb and flow of the women's confrontation simply as a matter of Olivia doing 'more favours to the Count's serving-man' than he himself could dream of.

His splendid rage overflows its banks; but he is still needily credulous, and this gives Toby and Fabian their chance. Their team-work has progressed towards the telepathic since the deception of Malvolio. Toby spots the opening first:

> Did she see thee the while, old boy? Tell me that . . .

and when Fabian is faced with Andrew's absurd belief that Olivia must have had him in her eye throughout:

> As plain as I see you now

he immediately extemporises, quite brilliantly. He politely calls Andrew 'you' where Toby called him 'thee'; and this respect seems to give him an objectivity Toby lacks. Even so, the preposterous suggestion that

> This was a great argument of love in her toward you

is steep, even for Andrew – and Fabian had better watch his step:

> 'Slight, will you make an ass of me?

Meanwhile Toby can see that his young colleague[4] will need a moment's grace to improvise a justification for his brainwave, and he treads water with a maxim about judgment and reason – whereupon Fabian embarks on his brilliant riff. His twelve-line tirade consists of only three sentences, the first two of much the same rhythm and length, the third an inspired summary: Toby, for all his cunning, would not be capable of this, and it proves Fabian, in a single speech, to be a part worth playing. In its comic contrasts between Andrew's 'dormouse valour' and the brimstone that should now enter his liver, in the banging 'the youth into dumbness' with some 'excellent jests fire-new from the mint' and in its threat of Andrew's ending up hanging 'like an icicle on a Dutchman's beard', the speech is slightly reminiscent of the bright, turbulent style of Falstaff and Mistress Quickly in Eastcheap in *Henry IV* – and extremely funny when applied to the petulant scarecrow to whom it is addressed. And it is all improvised, very fast. Most of Shakespeare's characters, even the least gifted, are visited with tongues at some point, and here Fabian is blessed with the author's wild inventiveness. He even, unknowingly, hits on the key word 'accost' which caused Andrew such vexation in his opening scene with Maria: and Andrew will certainly make the connection, spotting his chance to do better this time. He can see that to go onto the offensive will be a lot better for him than to sit exasperated in 'the north of my lady's opinion' like some disgruntled ancient mariner.

Insinuated into the sequence by both his tormentors, and fatally courting him, is a silly linguistic affectation which flatters Andrew with worldliness: Toby describes reason and judgment as 'grand-jurymen since before Noah was a sailor' in the tone of one stating the obvious, and Fabian's Dutch icicle is a reference to the sufferings, recently published, of the crew on William Barents's voyage to

---

4   Of course Fabian, though called 'lad' by Toby, need not be young; but it certainly works well if he is, as it gives him an area of his own in the play, rather than a pale duplication of Toby's.

the Arctic in 1597. It all makes Andrew feel he is moving in a rarefied world indeed, part of a cosmopolitan group in constant debate of current affairs and precedent – so much so that he finds he can compete too, preferring to be 'a Brownist' rather than a professional politician. The Brownists were a sect publishing hell-fire tracts – and all Andrew knows is that, for the purposes of violence, they are better than politicians, if a bit too like the Puritans he hates. It all makes him feel clubbable and good, one of the select Inner Temple audience he is playing to.

The psychological insights in this tussle with Andrew's fragile ego are, on the whole, Fabian's: what comes easily to Toby is that most cruel form of comedy, a practical joke. In an inspiration that takes up where Fabian's left off, he visualises a ridiculous duel between Andrew and Cesario, quite happy to imagine the latter with at least eleven wounds, though of course there is small likelihood of that. The plan is gratuitous, sure in the event to humiliate one or both, and most unlikely to recommend Andrew to Olivia – who seems hardly to know who he is anyway. But the mixture of high Roman style in the challenge and apparent effortlessness in the doing works on Andrew, as yellow stockings did on Malvolio, so that he becomes great and ominous:

> Will either of you bear me a challenge to him?

Toby's vision of this document – a fearsome catalogue of taunts, both brief and expansive (the Bed of Ware – more worldly talk – was known to hold a dozen people[5]), at once witty, eloquent and rude (to use the intimate 'thou' under these circumstances will be a particular insult), to be issued from the splendid 'cubiculo' (not so much an inner sanctum as a small bedroom) – forms a vague and marvellous dream for Andrew, and he manages to forget that fighting is a messy business. Having had to be physically restrained from quitting, no power can stop him now from marching back inside like a bantam – his impulse hopelessly at odds with his capabilities and his appearance the opposite of what he imagines – even if he does remain rather anxious that his friends stay near at hand:

> Where shall I find you?

It has taken all of forty lines, and Fabian has certainly won his spurs in this dubious test of manhood. He and Toby have a moment's rest,

---

5   You can see it, eleven foot square, in the Victoria and Albert Museum in London.

and perhaps a drink; and Fabian's relative innocence – to him this is a harmless joke on a 'manikin' – is set brutally against Toby's extremism:

> I have been dear to him, lad, some two thousand strong, or so.

It is an enormous debt (two thirds of Andrew's annual income[6]) but Fabian, perhaps nervously, ignores this. He just wants to be reassured that there are limits:

> We shall have a rare letter from him; but you'll not deliver't

– but he gets only the comfort that 'oxen and wain-ropes' are not stronger than the duellists' cowardice; the harshness of Toby's lines about Andrew's bloodless liver, and his genial threat of cannibalism:

> I'll eat the rest of th' anatomy

leave no doubt of the toughness of his game. It is a rancid moment in the sunshine. In time, Fabian may learn the same bitterness: but, faced with it so soon after his moment of glory, he describes Cesario's cowardice rather timidly, perhaps backing off a little:

> . . . his opposite, the youth, bears in his visage no great presage
> of cruelty.

From the moment that the play's practical jokes began, Shakespeare has looped each new part of his story into the end of the last like a serial writer, with Maria, Toby and Fabian as the usual means. At the end of Malvolio's letter scene, Maria returned to release the pent-up steam. Here, Toby and Fabian, enjoying their success, have revealed important distinctions in their characters; and later on, in 3.4, the group will continually bridge the actions, toasting outcomes and furthering plans. At this point Maria, promising the reality of Malvolio in his wooer's gear, has essentially the same job as she had before, and the difficulty of sustaining it is still greater – it is all up to her for fifteen-odd lines, with virtually no supporting repartee even from Toby. Like the others in this scene, she is full of topical references, such as the 'augmented' map of the East Indies published in 1600 (the northern coast of what is now Australia was

---

6   Cf.1.3.22. Three thousand ducats is also Antonio's debt to Shylock in *The Merchant of Venice*. Meanwhile, in *Henry IV Part 2*, Falstaff has had 'a thousand pound' from Justice Shallow. These are meant to be large sums, but it is difficult to assess modern equivalents – and some uncertainty, passim, as to when Shakespeare meant pounds, when ducats, crowns, or talents.

included for the first time) – it had rhumb lines very reminiscent of the wrinkles around a person's eyes. Like the Dutchman's icicle, it's a terrific image if you know what it means, and pretty good even if you don't.[7] On the other hand, the Spanish word 'renegado' that places the unfortunate steward beyond reach of Christianity is obscure; and the fact that he is dressed like a 'pedant that keeps a school i' th' church' carries a number of lost meanings – teachers were at this time coming out of churches into proper school-rooms (except for some rural ones that Malvolio would not want to resemble), and cross-gartering, fashionable for half a century, was likewise out of date. One lost joke is all right, but three in a row make a director's fingers itch for the scalpel. Generally in Shakespeare (unless you are in the quite legitimate business of deconstruction, which lies outside the scope of this book), cutting is rarely a matter of excising whole episodes, which can be as destructive as slashing into some marvellous cloth, but rather of acknowledging our own shrinking vocabulary. The loss of so many of Shakespeare's beautiful words often leaves an audience enjoying just the surreal verbal collisions – the aura around the joke – or, as with Andrew's 'Brownist', sensing the faint light it sheds on his character. However, laughs like these, being more texture than logic, can die on their own breath.

Once you have decided which references lie below the waterline and should be cut, Maria's description of the grimacing Malvolio remains extremely alluring, even if a little long-winded: it needs to be fluently played, not broken up too much by her laughter, with the plotters more attentive than hysterical. The general prospect of better and better physical scenarios in the play is provoking a riotous linguistic invention to match, so that turbulent comic prose is washing round the lyric centre provided by Orsino, Olivia and Viola – and since Viola is implicated in the Andrew plot and Olivia in the gulling of Malvolio, we sense that apparent irreconcilables are approaching a juncture. But at this quickening point there are people we have forgotten, and Shakespeare changes the picture.

3.3.   Illyria has been for us the onomatopoeic home of self-deluding dreams, of romance and harmless folly: but there seems to be

7   In fact the two jokes are linked – the map included some of Barents's findings.

another version. Shakespeare refers to the place's other reputation both in *Henry VI Part 2* and *Measure for Measure* – where Ragozine, a 'notorious pirate' from there, loses his head to give the Duke an alibi. With some part of their minds, the Elizabethans thought of Illyria as violent, 'rough and inhospitable' indeed, a tense Mediterranean port where old grudges, such as Orsino's against Antonio, are not forgotten. You get the feeling of Marseilles or Naples, of cutthroats, seawalls and old ruined fortifications, where a man should certainly watch his back.

It is quite an awkward adjustment to bring Antonio back into the story: but then everything about him is awkward – his odd lonely character, his unsuspected passions. His and Sebastian's position to the side of the unfolding plot obliges both location and style to be changed for them, and the scaffolding of the play is rather badly exposed. Sebastian's contribution to the action has to be, for obvious enough reasons, held back till late: so if he is to stay in the mind's eye at all he needs someone to talk to, someone as separate as himself. That is Antonio, who also becomes a clothes-horse on which Shakespeare can hang a favourite theme – passionate friendship and its possible betrayal. By making Antonio into Sebastian's rescuer, he has already introduced masculine heroism, which will have another effect later in the play – the adjustment of the character of Orsino into a military leader so that Antonio can become a legitimate enemy of the state. It will be very startling for us, but rather good for the player of Orsino, keeping him this side of wetness. In the meantime Shakespeare can, through his outsider, treat the cloak-and-dagger, mean-street side of Illyria.

The trouble is that it happens just as the play is moving into rich comic gear, and a transposer's fingers twitch. Maria's excited report on Malvolio at the end of 3.2 could have been followed by his actual appearance in 3.4, and it is not as if the delay and change of locale increases the anticipation – in fact, it rather makes us forget, and the story has to be forcibly picked up again. I don't really see why 3.3 shouldn't be where 3.1 is, affording an open runway through the third Act. And how to stage this unexpected scene in the middle of Olivia's garden? Absolutely not a problem at the Globe, absolutely a problem for us. Of all compromises, the forestage is probably the best, in localised light. We can either find the two men at the moment of meeting in the street – a wonderful surprise for Sebastian and a great relief for Antonio – or already at the café table,

park bench, as you will, calming down, which is rather what the
opening suggests:

> SEBASTIAN: I would not by my will have troubled you,
>   But since you make your pleasure of your pains,
>   I will no further chide you.

Antonio, as much as he, has moved into harmonious, relaxed verse:
they are now more at home with each other than in the rather
congested introductory scene on the seashore. Antonio has followed
Sebastian into town, and though he acknowledges his desire was as
viciously cutting as 'filed steel', he swiftly tones down the violence of
his feelings, either not to hem in the young man or out of
embarrassment. So it was

> . . . not all love to see you

– no, really not, but, as much as anything, a disinterested concern
for a stranger alone in a dangerous city. This modest de-escalation
towards the 'willing love' that any decent person would show doesn't
fool Sebastian, but he has the grace not to tease his fretful friend.
Like the object of passion who pretends none of it is happening, he
concentrates on Antonio's kindness, and thanks and thanks him
with generosity and grace, while regretting that he is not in a
position to tip him:

> and oft good turns
> Are shuffled off with such uncurrent pay;
> But were my worth, as is my conscience, firm,
> You should find better dealing.

We are never free from this business of money and class, which we
shouldn't take simply as a convention. (How could we be – within a
few years, under James I, much of English life depended on an
intricate network of social obligation and debt.) Viola tipped the
Captain for making up a soothing story about Sebastian and for
keeping her secrets, and now her brother regrets, having lost
everything in the wreck, that he can't reward a man who clearly is
looking for no reward. It brings the scene to a slightly awkward halt,
and it has to restart conversationally:

> What's to do?
> Shall we go see the relics of this town?

Antonio demands that the young man check into some 'lodgings'
before he does any sightseeing, though in fact Sebastian is – a true

sign of youth – careless of where he will sleep that night. The fact is that Antonio has good reason to be circumspect, and his friend's touristic innocence forces the cause out of him: he is a notoriously wanted man. His modest account of his exploits against Orsino ('I did some service') only makes them more romantic to Sebastian, who becomes very considerate and tender, bestowing special *éclat* on the older man:

> Belike you slew great number of his people?

This assumption of the roles of anxious guardian and careless *protégé*, of hero and admirer, is a shadowplay for the two men's growing respect. Antonio decries himself again: it wasn't a matter of life and death so much as the fact that he alone 'stood out' when the time came for his faction to pay back to Illyria what they had taken. In fact, he probably understates – later in the play Orsino and his officers will paint a much more heroic version of his actions – but this may be all he wants to admit to for the moment.

Sebastian remains boyishly impressed:

> Do not then walk too open

– and a light reversal of their roles begins: no longer a helpless lover, Antonio is now the master, in charge of them both. He will find a good place to stay and order the dinner while Sebastian does his walking tour. He has in mind 'the Elephant' – which was in reality a few steps from the Globe Theatre itself: its patrons would have heard Viola's call of 'Westward Ho!' regularly from the boatmen.

Also, Antonio has the money, and so is in a position to be Sebastian's benefactor – a nice irony they will both appreciate. The purse (which will turn out to be a poisoned chalice) is an obvious benefit for a man whose

> store . . .

. . . is not for idle markets

– and Sebastian should spend it according to his custom. But he insists that he will be its custodian only:

> I'll be your purse-bearer and leave you for
> An hour.
> ANTONIO: To th' Elephant.
> SEBASTIAN: I do remember.

These are men of action, and the last line, split into three, implies a sudden rush off in opposite directions.

As before, the scene is short, and the actors should make just enough of it and no more: as they now know, these two parts won't come into their own till about ten p.m. But there has certainly been some movement in their relationship. Sebastian, like his sister, attracts a deal of affection, and despite the money business, you can see why – there is a guilelessness in him, a capacity for tender accord (and a manliness to come). His brief requiem for Viola in the previous scene had a grace that nobody else in the play except herself comes near: and he clearly inspires deep feelings in the man who has so riskily followed him.

He has also, most delicately, allowed the vulnerable Antonio to become strong, with a little hero-worship and by deferring to his need to take charge: Sebastian understands that it is love that makes Antonio such a fusspot, so he has given him the dignity of a job to do. It is the same delicacy that, in the earlier scene, made him try to spare Antonio the burden of being involved in his sorrows, especially as, having the same quality himself, Antonio hesitated to intrude. So it is mutual between them, and very distinct in a play which concentrates so much on self-absorption, false friendship and unfriendly passion. Both men carry their weaknesses with strength, dealing with each other with a mix of honesty and tact: among the love stories of the play, this one sets an example.

3.4.   A great firework is about to burst – more with the acceleration of a catherine-wheel than the whoosh of a rocket. Often farcical but without farce's inhumanity, the play's longest scene yet will add to other of Shakespeare's comic tours de force – the eavesdroppers' letters in *Love's Labour's Lost* and *Much Ado*, the lovers in the wood in *The Dream* – the extra skills of the weaver and braider, and a taste for physical clowning. As each story-line hinges onto another – Malvolio's to Andrew's to Viola's to Antonio's, with a major revelation at the end – the profligate ideas are nudged into a hazardous but conclusive logic.

It all starts, unpromisingly, in a mass of hints. Olivia declares:

> I have sent after him; he says he'll come

– and for a moment it is not clear who she means. Then we remember, from when we were last in this garden, Maria's cliffhanger about Malvolio's approach. However, this isn't he – Olivia is arriving with an eagerness that could hardly be inspired by Malvolio. Of course she means Cesario, who, after another 'final' parting, has been called back. Olivia has presumably done again what she did with the ring, that is, sent a messenger (but not Malvolio this time – he has been busy) hotfoot to intercept the page before he returns to Orsino. Viola won't like it, but it is still her job to obey. In point of fact, it is only some time later in the scene that Olivia's servant will return from the errand, having 'hardly' entreated Cesario back. So at this moment Olivia is anticipating – unless we understand her opening line, as critics rather desperately urge, to be a conditional clause with the 'if' left out: *if* he says he'll come, Olivia wonders,

> How shall I feast him? What bestow of him?

If it is an inconsistency, it goes unnoticed in the theatre – and indeed there are some others: why, when the convention of the aside means that no-one else can hear, does Olivia feel caught out ('I speak too loud') as Maria approaches? Why does she then want Malvolio to attend her – she will hardly welcome a chaperone when Cesario comes? When, in a moment, Malvolio arrives, she will object to his smiling because she sent for him 'upon a sad occasion'. What sad occasion – was she going to revert to the airs and graces of mourning for this third meeting? Unlikely – she is imagining a feast. Chopped as her logic is, in another way Olivia sounds very like herself: she imagines that promising young men can be bought either through their stomachs or with gifts.

The fact is that for Olivia to expect Malvolio to be 'sad and civil' is a good set-up, as we know the opposite is on its way. The expectation is high – disingenuously Maria hints at his 'very strange manner', thinks he is 'possessed' because 'he does nothing but smile', and feels Olivia might need a bodyguard. His arrival is very sudden, almost before we are ready:

> Sweet lady, ho, ho!

He is magnificent, surpassing expectation. Perhaps the yellow leg appears first, disembodied, or perhaps the Cheshire Cat Smile. Perhaps the trouser-leg needs rolling up before our eyes. As you wish. A stately entrance might be followed by a dash and a wild assault, or perhaps Malvolio proceeds with a deadly daftness towards his prey. Certainly, all his old maggoty self-doubt is gone. He is full of lightness and pleasure, with a special airiness to precede the awful intensity of lovemaking; and, whatever Olivia's reactions, they will provocatively confirm his sense of conquest. Her first response, oddly, seems to be to his smile rather than his more extravagant features:

> Smil'st thou? I sent for thee upon a sad occasion.

But Malvolio is safe in a paradise of his own, where even sadness can be turned to splendid account, and he can put up with – welcomes, in fact – physical pain:

> Sad, lady? I could be sad. This does make some obstruction in the blood, this cross-gartering, but what of that?

I would guess Malvolio has never used a phrase like 'what of that' before – in his old life every word had its due and worrying weight, so the three monosyllables are like wings. He is as translated as Bottom with the ass's head, but with far more new skills. So careful and scrupulous of late – and so suspicious of music – he finds he knows all the topical songs in this new world and can deliver them at will, his singing perhaps being of the same order as his smiling:

> . . . it is with me as the very true sonnet is: 'Please one, and please all'.

He finds he can construct nice antitheses:

> OLIVIA: Why, how dost thou, man? What is the matter with thee?
> MALVOLIO: Not black in my mind, though yellow in my legs . . .

– and he can pretend that he is only obeying orders:

> It did come to his hands, and commands shall be executed . . .

He is so confident, in fact, that he unhesitatingly responds to Olivia's invitation to go and sleep off his mania:

> Wilt thou go to bed, Malvolio?

with not a shadow of doubt as to its real meaning:

> To bed? Ay, sweetheart, and I'll come to thee.

He must be surprised that Olivia has been quite so quick to offer the inevitable, but then, in view of his style, what can you expect?

With who knows what terrible look in his eye, he might blow a stream of kisses at Olivia while effortlessly rebuking the servant class:

> MARIA: How do you, Malvolio?
> MALVOLIO: At your request! Yes, nightingales answer daws!

– and less like that musical bird than an affable steamroller, he just keeps quoting verbatim his articles of faith:

> Be not afraid of greatness . . . some are born great . . . some achieve greatness . . . and some have greatness thrust upon them

as Olivia struggles helplessly to get some purchase on it all. The worst thing for her, worse than the sheer moonstruckness of it, must be his sly sharing of some incomprehensible little secret between them.

Malvolio seems to proceed so harmlessly towards midsummer madness that the episode could be played with sublime charm, and leave Olivia with only the vapours of a bizarre dream. But there is another angle to think about, and it has to do with Maria's presence in the scene. Malvolio's increasingly eager rhythms could suggest something quite alarming. Whatever Olivia says or does, or doesn't say or do, inflames him as his garters do the flesh of his legs, cruelly bound for greater devotion; and even her decency towards him – 'God comfort thee . . . heaven restore thee' – sounds like a love-song. In his totalitarian certainty, he listens to no alternatives. Maria is there partly because the presence of the perpetrator makes it more fun, but also to cut him off if his chase gathers intensity – without that small constraint, the scene could even become a little unpleasant, with some of the claustrophobia, for instance, of Othello's and Desdemona's 'brothel' scene.[8]

Of course the trick is to integrate both effects, comedy and menace – and certainly Malvolio needs to maintain enough innocence for the audience to tolerate him when, in a moment, he contemplates his achievement. Olivia's desperate call for Toby (as if he could ever help):

> Where's my cousin Toby? Let some of my people have a special care of him . . .

and her kindness in parting (so different from the old days):

> I would not have him miscarry for the half of my dowry

are likewise unfortunate: they only reaffirm for him her loving

---

8 *Othello*, 4.2. In this pitiful scene, Othello locks the door, appoints Emilia as the madame, and bears down on his innocent wife.

cunning, and Toby's name reminds him immediately of how he has been told to treat that person.

Olivia and Maria (and a presumably astonished Servant[9]) escape to meet with Cesario, and once again Malvolio is alone in the garden with his letter. Women are unaccountable of course, but presumably this feigned horror and flight are part of the necessary chase: after all he endured months of contumely from Olivia before learning the tender truth. Malvolio knows he has shown an irresistible hand, or leg, but he does check his letter again, crumpled and worn out no doubt from reading and re-reading, to see how he is doing. He starts with accurate quotation:

> . . . be opposite with a kinsman, surly with servants . . . put thyself into the trick of singularity

but is soon imagining things that are not there, as to

> . . . the manner how: as a sad face, a reverend carriage, a slow tongue, in the habit of some sir of note, and so forth.

Fantasy has him for sure; and his triumph – 'I have limed her' – is in fact horrible, the image of a bird caught in a hunter's glue.[10] He insists that Olivia's word 'fellow' means not just a someone but an intimate mate, and three times thanks Jove, a pagan god, for giving him his sexual due. Everything 'adheres together' and he begins to go at such a gallop that language fails him:

> . . . no dram of a scruple, no scruple of a scruple, no obstacle, no incredulous or unsafe circumstance – what can be said? Nothing that can be can come between me and the full prospect of my hopes.

He may fling himself extravagantly on the floor or loll absurdly on the garden bench, but there is no missing the fascism that drives his airy rhapsody. He may feel like Romeo securing his love, but he sounds like Richard III catching the crown.

Still, he may well look good to us again by the time Toby, Maria and Fabian have finished their laborious exorcism routine. By good fortune of the plot, Andrew is not included, since he is at work on

9   Playing this chambermaid, a junior Maria, the actress has waited a long time for her one speech, with the dire responsibility of getting a laugh with it: she has to get her message out while absorbing the amazing sight of Malvolio.

10   Ursula says the same of Beatrice in *Much Ado*, but it sounds nastier coming from the male.

his challenge: the swift inventive rhythms required by this new *jeu d'esprit* would have been too much for him anyway, and his place in the magic circle of three has been taken by Maria. Their roles are reasonably distinct. Fabian favours the delicate approach of the counsellor, all sympathetic sorrow:

> No way but gentleness; gently; gently: the fiend is rough and will not be roughly used

– Toby professes the same approach but cannot prevent his brusqueness breaking through:

> . . . peace, peace! We must deal gently with him . . . What, man, defy the devil . . . Hang him, foul collier!

– while Maria, most infuriatingly, ululates with religious horror at his simplest remarks. Just as anything Olivia said to Malvolio had the effect of intensifying his libidinousness, now every reasonable request of his own:

> Let me enjoy my private. Go off! . . . How now, mistress?

is taken for a more fearsome proof of diabolical possession:

> Lo, how hollow the fiend speaks within him! . . . O Lord!

The three of them are expressing an Elizabethan enthusiasm for demonology that runs, more intently, through Hamlet's dealings with his father and floods *Macbeth*. Turned into a joke, the obscure material is not particularly funny to us:

> If all the devils of hell be drawn in little, and Legion [an unclean spirit] himself possessed him, yet I'll speak to him . . . What, man, 'tis not for gravity to play at cherry-pit with Satan[11]

– but it is just about kept afloat by the richness of the ingredients, and it is certainly a pleasure to imagine Malvolio providing a urine test:

> FABIAN: Carry his water to th' wise woman.
> MARIA: Marry, and it shall be done tomorrow morning if I live.

Throughout, the humorists need to sustain a snappy pace, and, since there is nothing like physical business to help a thinnish joke along, make witty choices of weapons of exorcism: garlic, salt, the

---

11 This was a very simple child's game in which cherry-stones were tossed from a little distance into a hole; but the fact of the hole directs us into the underground darkness where, according to folklore, Satan could indeed be a 'foul collier' – coalminers were feared as devils partly because of their blackened faces.

cross and so on. Malvolio's problem will be what to do with himself as the three flies buzz round him. Some of what is said is mightily consolidating for him: Maria, again the most effective psychologist, lets him hear that Olivia 'would not lose him for more than I'll say' (nicely echoing Olivia's own exit line), and he also gathers that Toby has been particularly instructed 'to have a care of him'. But there is not much for him physically to do for quite a long time, apart from trying to escape interference and maintain his *amour propre*. Not that that is so hard to do – their comedy is so broad that he certainly sees through it:

> You are idle, shallow things: I am not of your element . . . [12]

and his exit, in full moral sail but with yellow legs, has a certain Quixotic dignity.

The whole hard-worked exercise pays off in terms of character once he is gone. Pausing only for a good theatre joke:

> If this were played upon a stage now, I could condemn it as an improbable fiction

Fabian realises that there is a real danger of driving the poor man mad in the pursuit of comedy. To Maria, suddenly cold, that would be just fine:

> The house will be the quieter

– and as for Toby, only boredom will make him relent:

> . . . we'll have him in a dark room and bound . . . We may carry it thus for our pleasure, and his penance, till our very pastime, tired out of breath, prompt us to have mercy on him . . .

And there's the difference between the three, who for so much of the time operate as one. Fabian, decent, wanting not to go too far; Maria, with no sympathetic feeling for Malvolio at all; and Toby, positively warlike. If nothing else, the episode has re-stated three degrees of rancour.

This grimly sunny moment calms the action down a little, before it jolts forward and another man with a mission, Andrew, has his heartfelt efforts thoroughly mocked. The comedy is becoming noticeably broader and more gestural, and a visual treat is promised

12 The very word, by the way, dismissed by Feste earlier in the scene as 'overworn'.

with each new action – a high sun is beating down on these people, inflaming them to ever more extreme rituals when they should be having a siesta. For to repeat: the play has nothing to do with Christmas. Its true season is underlined by alliterations: first 'Midsummer madness', and now

> More matter for a May morning.

The exorcism of Malvolio and Andrew's challenge are so similarly weighted that they need to be played both for their similarity and, so to speak, their difference. The conspirators' act is well-practised by now: but Andrew is the far easier ride. He and Malvolio have both emerged from laborious solitudes, Andrew with his challenge and Malvolio in his stockings: where the latter thinks he has found a means to best his enemies, Andrew looks to the same group for companionship. These are the closest he can get to friends, these confident, sociable types: they seem at ease with the world, while he labours away with secret doubts. Like older friends at school, he can surely now depend on them for a fair assessment of his efforts: unfortunately, they are encouraging him to paint as deluded a self-portrait as they did for Malvolio.

As you would expect, Andrew remains as tightly bound by linguistic poverty as the steward is by his 'obstruction in the blood'. Introducing his work, he cannot even manage the correct ''tis' in reply to the question 'is't so saucy?', only repeating

> Ay, is't.

The proclamation is a fine satire on male bellicosity: funnier than the exorcism practices, it makes easy meat for Toby, Maria and Fabian, but it is technically as tricky for Andrew as they were for Malvolio. Again, what does he do? Practice kung-fu attitudes? Rival patience on a monument? Since the letter is really an appeal for acceptance from his manly friends, he will need constant reassurance: as he looks anxiously from face to face on almost every phrase, they must be sure to be ready with comfort as his eye alights.

There is an instinctive exchange of roles between Toby and Fabian now the challenge is written. This time Fabian simply backs up, keeping Andrew's delicate spirits from capsizing, while Toby takes the military burden, declaiming as if to Cesario himself. As with his discovery of Olivia's 'great argument of love', Fabian's tongue is almost too far into his cheek. For Andrew to hear his fine description of the document's 'salt and vinegar' promptly punned into

> Is't so saucy?

might alert even him; for his defiant

> I will waylay thee going home, where if it be thy chance to kill me

to evoke an ambiguous

> Good

is worse; and Fabian's insistence that his approach cleverly keeps him 'o' th' windy side of the law' when it obviously doesn't could stir a dim doubt as well. He is never quite sure about Fabian: and after all, it is not so much foolishness that is funny in Andrew as the occasional flickering of his intelligence.

Commissioned to be written 'in a martial hand', both 'curst and brief', the challenge will also be as frighteningly official to the eye as Andrew can manage, making up in manner what it shrinks from in content. Nevertheless, if you look at it as a single written speech without interjections, it is pure Aguecheek – full of attitudes struck and immediately abandoned, showing an overwhelming desire to please in the act of committing to hell. He will not be questioned on his motives:

> Youth, whatsoever thou art, thou art but a scurvy fellow . . . admire not in thy mind why I do call thee so, for I will show thee no reason for't

but then he immediately declares them:

> Thou com'st to the lady Olivia and in my sight she uses thee kindly.

There is some aggressive nonsense:

> . . . thou liest in thy throat. That is not the matter I challenge thee for . . .

but typical good nature in the assumption that he will probably lose:

> . . . if it be thy chance to kill me . . . thou kill'st me like a rogue and a villain.

(Is he or Cesario to be the rogue and villain?) Even the valediction:

> Thy friend, as thou usest him, and thy sworn enemy

is that of a man acting a part against his better nature. Meant to beef him up, the whole thing is enough to frighten Andrew out of his wits, as if he had glared at himself in the mirror: but it is not enough to worry Cesario, who, as Toby guesses, will realise 'it comes from a clodpole'. So the plan must be expanded: and as long as Andrew can be dispatched to a corner of the orchard[13] where he can 'swear horrible' (roaring, like the lion in the *Dream*, as gently as any sucking dove) his belligerence should be kept more or less afloat while the trickier question of impressing Cesario is addressed.

The repeating pattern – a deluded protagonist manoeuvred into folly – is pushing the play's ambiguities a stage further. In one way, Fabian, Maria and Toby are the voice of reason, our own route into the story, attractive amoralists who embody what we would wish for. On the other hand the cruelty is deepening. Malvolio is surprisingly good company in his new outfit, and his willingness to make a complete ass of himself in the name of love earns him a grudging respect; while Andrew's misplaced trust keeps him piteously vulnerable. We now see that Toby would keep one of them locked up in the dark for as long as he pleases and expose the other to a knife-edged sword. Whom to like? We peer at them all through Feste's many-coloured opal.

What's more, the next victim will be a real heroine, ambushed into a frightening conflict. For Viola to be brought to the duelling line, she has to be somewhere near at hand – which may, retrospectively, explain why Olivia started the scene by announcing that Cesario was on his way. Maria can now say that he is

> . . . in some commerce with my lady and will by and by depart.

This practical necessity may also account for the rather unsatisfactory little sequence between Viola and Olivia which now spills onto the stage, only to repeat their chronic theme – Olivia's sense of having betrayed herself and of not being able to stop, Viola's formal insistence on Orsino's business. The scene is frustrating: it is recapitulative, and, set where it is, has to sacrifice its own rhythm to the surrounding need for heady pace. Nothing much new has developed between them. Olivia's language remains a tussle between the emotional and the seemly; though behind it, there is, if not maturity, a finality in her tone, as if she were facing the inevitable. Her last requests are helpless, her pride collapsing around her:

---

13   This is the first recorded use of the word 'bumbaily', the wonderfully explicit description of a bailiff who comes up behind you.

> And, I beseech you, come again tomorrow.
> What shall you ask of me that I'll deny . . . ?

There is one lovely redeeming flash of humour in the midst of it all: if Cesario were to wear her 'jewel' as a parting gift, he will at least not be bothered by her insistent voice.

Cornered, Viola can only parry tersely, with stale fatigue – Orsino, nothing but Orsino, 'I will acquit you' of the rest. As she always does, Olivia asks her to 'come again' – but leaves her with a jab: just as her daylight was 'love's night', Cesario is the instrument of mortal perdition:

> A friend like thee might bear my soul to hell.

Poor Olivia – she may regret this as soon as she's gone. It is in the nature of this anguish that you can consign someone to hell but hope they don't get caught out in the rain: to keep their letter always in your pocket while storming around the room every few minutes, muttering at them. And sure enough, she will shortly summon Cesario back yet again.

But for Viola, relations have become intolerable, no more than a humiliating chase, and quite likely Olivia will have descended to some physical grappling as well. Escaping from her, she now turns to find a man putting a duelling weapon into her hand, with a jolt of portentous prose:

> Gentleman, God save thee.

What a day – it seems that it is not only Olivia who is unreasonably aggrieved, but some nameless 'interceptor'.

Toby, for whom there is no rest – whenever the action settles he must be there, improvising a new position – is now a military envoy, enough ceremonious ironmongery about him to turn the sunny garden into a misty field at dawn. He starts with a nice contrast: Viola's assailant is awaiting her 'bloody as the hunter' among the friendly fruit trees. He assumes the manners of the parade-ground, elaborating Andrew's prowess in a mixture of alarming polysyllables:

> . . . his incensement at this moment is so implacable that satisfaction can be none but by pangs of death and sepulchre

and military buckshot:

> Dismount thy tuck, be yare in thy preparation . . . betake you to your guard . . . Hob nob is his word: give't or take't.

We are deeply attached to Viola; but the more nightmarish this becomes for her, the funnier we find it. By now the comic rule that precludes real damage or death is secure – which is all the more reason for the emotions attached to them to be played for all they're worth.

The longish process of bringing Andrew and her to the point relies, as so often, on ever-more-inventive variations on one joke, and Toby, the imp well out of his bottle, shows an intimidating versatility. His usual taste in comedy is coarsely knockabout, but here he achieves a belligerent creativity, and a barking richness of language. Viola is swiftly stormed by his construct of Andrew as a sort of Exterminator, albeit in the guise of a carpet-knight – Toby can't resist referring to the lowly title, bought in return for no services. To Viola, he is all the more terrifying that way: this is someone who obviously doesn't bother with combat in the field, preferring to be 'quick, skilful and deadly' in well-chosen 'private brawl[s]' – in these he is a 'devil', with 'youth, strength and wrath' on his side and three mortal notches on his sword. Her language is steady enough but her knees have gelatinised, and she thinks to ask Olivia, of all people, for an armed guard. Perhaps she tries to make a run for it. Such pacifism is so unmanly that Toby is inclined to challenge her himself, as a traitor to the male sex:

> Back you shall not to the house, unless you undertake that with
> me which with as much safety you might answer him.

This prospect – and the outrageous unfairness of it – makes her, almost, stand up for herself:

> This is as uncivil as strange

and her vehemence – a touch of aggression at last – allows Toby to affect a considered compassion. As he marches stiffly away with a promise to find out what the real problem might be, Viola is left with some kind of lieutenant. She hasn't met this man before, and he just might be a friend:

> Pray you, sir, do you know of this matter?

However, instead of clarification, she finds in Fabian a poker-backed formality. He regrets that nothing she has heard of Andrew begins to compare with his reality:

> He is, indeed, sir, the most skilful, bloody and fatal opposite
> that you could possibly have found in any part of Illyria.

There go the knees again. However, this is a good man, not above a little unofficial sympathy:

> I will make your peace with him if I can.

The comic pattern requires that we now look at the other side. Editors get vexed by the Folio's directions for various exits and entrances at this point – and that the duel is suddenly to happen here, not at the 'orchard-end' – but it's all beside the point in performance. Practically, the accommodation of the two petrified parties and their seconds was an easy enough matter on an Elizabethan stage – there were pillars and wide distances to separate them: nowadays human masking by Fabian and Toby will keep Andrew from witnessing the diminutive figure's terror while the swifter process of winding Andrew himself up plays through. It is as if etiquette forbids the fighters seeing each other till they are in the ring – indeed boxers avoid eye-contact before the bell in just this way.

Andrew's Dutch courage has completely evaporated during his wait in the orchard; and of course Toby knows this prey (his smallest night-terror in fact) far better than he does Viola, so that he is almost relaxed and certainly very funny:

> I had a pass with him, rapier, scabbard and all . . . he pays you
> as surely as your feet hits the ground they step on.

For Andrew, it is all most unfortunate. If this glamorous opponent, a 'firago' always ready with the 'stuck-in', has even worked for the Shah of Persia,[14] it might be better to send him to hell verbally instead; on the other hand he seems to be enraged now, and will need mollifying. Andrew will make him an offer – his horse.[15] Toby is so at ease that, en passant, he spots the idea of stealing the animal for himself:

> I'll ride your horse as well as I ride you.

From the point of view of the pacifists, the stage has become a mad place, with men marching around, having whispered consultations and snapping their heels. With his aide-de-camp, Toby seems to be

14 The Sophy, meaning the Shah, was on people's minds (he is also mentioned at the end of Malvolio's gulling): two brothers, Sir Anthony Sherley and Sir Robert Sherley, had just published their memoirs of having served as ambassador and military advisor to him.

15 Grey Capilet thus joins a little family of Shakespearian horses, Lafeu's Bay Curtal in *All's Well* and Richard II's Roan Barbary, who are all touchingly memorialised by their colour.

brokering a ceremonial: it is no longer a matter of bloodshed but, on reasonable second thoughts, of a face-saving ritual. There is no longer much hope that they will

> kill one another by the look, like cockatrices

– but this way they can at least be made to face each other. As Viola prepares herself for this, Shakespeare pops in an aside for her, just for the fun of it – it is innocent enough in her mouth (though less so for a boy-actor) and it has an immediate smack of sauciness for his groundlings:

> Pray God defend me! A little thing would make me tell them
> how much I lack of a man.

Some Shakespearian fights – the big set-pieces in the Histories, and the ritualised climax of *Hamlet* – call for complex choreography: they are like pieces of music to be attuned to the action. Others, like Richard II's scrap with his murderers in Pomfret castle, and this one, probably start most successfully with improvisation. The combatants in both cases are amateurs, to say the least, and even the most sympathetic of fight designers might introduce a touch of inappropriate craft. If the actors begin by facing the situation as uncertainly as their characters and feel for what comes naturally, the designer's contribution will simply be to make the whole thing safe afterwards.

Dramatically, there is a particular danger in this fight, as it could be the wrong kind of anti-climax – only a certain amount of fun can be had from a duel that can hardly get started, and the lead-up to it, which provided most of the enjoyment, has been rather long. Apart from the text, there may have been final prayers, a tendency to faint, all manner of trembling in the sword-arm, even before the presumably hefty weapons supplied by Toby, massy and cold in the hand, have paralysed the fighters. All they can do in the event is vaguely try to co-operate. In fact the arrival of Antonio can interrupt proceedings at any time, and all the duel itself really needs is one good joke – their faces turned away in terror as they approach each other, or fright at the sound of the swords meeting – and, for my taste, one element of danger. For the situation is extremely perilous: fear is confronting the unfamiliar. Just as you might, crying death or glory, suddenly dive into freezing water and have done with it, there could well be a suicidal charge from Aguecheek that threatens real damage. If Viola were to duck and Andrew find himself confronting Antonio, all the better.

What is Antonio doing in Olivia's garden? Well, he could have been walking down the street (rather too 'open' for his own good), and seen it all over the hedge. His daring arrival to fight for love amidst Andrew's tremulous pirouettes and Viola's weight-lifting with her sword is like something from another planet – the real, murderous thing, verse recklessly pulsing to match. It is enough to make Andrew faint away with horror.

Toby's character now curves. Upset at the climax of his game, he is enraged, as if the real fighter in him has been called out by a worthy enemy. Taking Antonio on, he shows unquestionable courage; but it is also the start of his decline, the end of an extra-ordinary arc. It is hard to overstate the level of energy, resource-fulness and vigour that has been required of him since he invited Cesario to 'encounter the house' – it was a burden barely prepared for in the first half – and now, as exhaustion sets in for him as perhaps for his player, he has to draw his sword and square up physically as well.

Antonio brings with him a certain antithetical thumpiness which is quite tiring in itself after all the supple comic prose:

> ANTONIO: If you offend him, I for him defy you.
> TOBY: You, sir? Why, what are you?
> ANTONIO: One, sir, that for his love dares yet do more
>   Than you have heard him brag to you he will.
> TOBY: Nay, if you be an undertaker, I am for you.

The knockabout intrusion into the garden of further strangers – the Officers who have been stalking Antonio – has, as soon as it starts, to be subdued so that Andrew and Viola can have a moment of peaceful accommodation, made tender by great mutual relief. What Viola, not having heard Andrew's bribe, thinks he means by

> . . . I'll be as good as my word. He will bear you easily and reins well

is a question, but it is a pleasure to see these courteous and sympa-thetic people coming to terms – especially as they are now surroun-ded by the new official language of force. The arrest of Antonio, meanwhile, continues the formal heroics – he makes one attempt to deny who he is:

> You do mistake me, sir

– but is soon seen to be suffering from an unheroic emotion. Evading the Officers, and softening his diction, he makes a gentle approach to Viola, who he thinks is his beloved Sebastian. He points out that this is where love has led him:

> This comes with seeking you

and, perhaps because he hopes to bribe himself out of jail, asks for the money he lent him for sightseeing. His main sorrow is that he will be able to help less from now on:

> What will you do, now my necessity
> Makes me to ask you for my purse?

Mainly, of course, the request is there for the sake of what follows. Antonio takes the ensuing silence to be Sebastian's astonishment at the turn of events – at seeing him again, at seeing him so compromised. What he never expected, repeating his request, was

> What money, sir?

The stunning question is followed by silence, the missing half of a blank verse line.

To Viola, so recently relieved, trouble is starting up again – a wild stranger is for some reason asking her for bail. Perhaps time will untangle this as well. Meanwhile, her nature is generous – she will help the panhandler, extravagantly, with half of her 'present', a poor page now rather than the aristocrat who paid off the Sea Captain:

> Out of my lean and low ability
> I'll lend you something. My having is not much . . .

With the misunderstanding, the verse syncopates a little:

> VIOLA: Hold, there's half my coffer.
> ANTONIO: Will you deny me now?

Astonishingly for Viola, what is coming back is reproach: for some reason the man thinks he is entitled to more. He speaks of inexplicable 'kindnesses' he has shown her. If it were not, obviously, a mistake, it would be outrageous, since the one thing she cannot endure, she would like to say, is ingratitude. She is eloquent on the point – she hates the fault more

> Than lying, vainness, babbling drunkenness,
> Or any taint of vice whose strong corruption
> Inhabits our frail blood

but she is completely silenced by what follows, as the Officers begin
to press in:

> This youth that you see here
> I snatched one-half out of the jaws of death . . .
> Thou hast, Sebastian, done good feature shame.

There is a terrific counterpoint here between eloquent agony
and secret hope: Antonio's passion is forcing him into a lengthy,
sententious invective while something very quietly happens inside
Viola. The actor of Antonio has to be a little careful – he will soon,
brought face to face with Orsino, have to go over all this again, and
he might end up repeating his effects. Anger and pain need to be
balanced carefully, the first more prominent here than the second –
the grief lapping around his enraged bafflement hasn't yet developed
its full swell.

> In nature there's no blemish but the mind:
> None can be called deformed but the unkind.
> Virtue is beauty, but the beauteous-evil
> Are empty trunks, o'erflourished by the devil.

This is a somewhat formal version of two of the hottest Shakespearian themes: the ingratitude of friends and the wrongness in
nature that a beautiful form can veil moral corruption. To
Shakespeare it was a nightmarish obliquity: here it is set in the
mouth of the play's 'simple' man, and in a ludicrous context. For the
busy officers he does indeed 'grow mad': but we know that it is all
based on a mistake, a silly cue for a tragic emotion.

The sky has been growing overcast ever since Toby's practical joke
exposed the loneliness and unkindness on the play's underside: but
in the twilight a small light shines – Viola has heard a name she
thought forgotten. Unaccountably, she asks no question about
Sebastian – it is almost unbelievable, but oddly in character. Instead
she turns to us, forced, like everyone else *in extremis*, into taut
rhyming couplets:

> Methinks his words do from such passion fly
> That he believes himself; so do not I.
> Prove true, imagination, O prove true,
> That I, dear brother, be now ta'en for you!

Then she too names him, and the impact pushes her into a beautiful
definition of what, really, she has been doing all along – simply
keeping him alive:

> I my brother know
> Yet living in my glass; even such and so
> In favour was my brother, and he went
> Still in this fashion, colour, ornament,
> For him I imitate.

This is so lovely and unexpected that it makes the final spasm of clowning – Toby and Fabian malignly working Andrew one last time into chasing her for revenge – quite tiresome, though hard to cut for narrative reasons. Of all their linking passages, it is the limpest, overtaken by the play's events: Andrew, recently so human with Cesario, is now posturing stupidly again, and the lumbering prose of the others is two-dimensional:

> TOBY: A very dishonest paltry boy, and more a coward than a
>   hare . . .
> FABIAN: A coward, a most devout coward, religious in it.
> ANDREW: 'Slid, I'll after him again and beat him.

Who would have thought we would tire of them so suddenly?

But then who would have thought that this long ski-run, with its farcical adventures and virtuosic rhythms, would be veiling *Twelfth Night*'s forgotten purpose – Viola's journey through the maze to her brother? As she walks quietly towards her future, she has almost taken over the play. This has been a long afternoon, from the chiming of Olivia's clock to – perhaps – the lighting of lanterns now; but even if you do not set the scene against the correlative of time and weather, a great amount of ground has been covered with hardly a hitch. With gentle authority, Shakespeare has prepared the play for its epiphany: but first it must survive one of the toughest theatrical rites of passage there is – one of his fourth Acts.

ACT FOUR

Act 4 Scene 1–Act 4 Scene 3

4.1. Most machines have a weakness, or at least a stresspoint eventually discovered by their users. In the little world of a Shakespeare play, it is Act Four, or – because of course the Act and Scene divisions were arbitrarily determined after the event – somewhere in the preparations for the finale. It lies in wait, and it can't be escaped: the moment when, with all due respect, you begin to want to go home. There is, it is true, an appetite for the inordinately long theatre event that goes on even for days, but then the terms for the audience are understood to be those of siege and seclusion from the world, followed by a gratifying celebration of the survival of performers and audience. These comforts don't apply in a normal play when you feel that a story that should be coming to the point is in fact working to rule, as if we'd booked not for the show itself but for entertainment till eleven. Shakespeare is adept in these procrastinations: they may take the form of endless parleys and transactions before the battle when the battle is all we want, or a marking time because it is understood that the tragic hero and his audience need a rest from one another. *Henry IV Part 1* is of the first kind, *Hamlet* of the second. In *Richard III*, *Coriolanus* and *Lear*, even the weary protagonist doesn't escape the drawn-out process; in *Macbeth* he does, while the play abandons its headlong pace for a longish discursion, in England, on kingship. In a sort of reversal of this, Act Four of *Antony and Cleopatra* is really the play's climax, while Act Five needs all the willingness it can muster to convince you that Cleopatra's manoeuvrings with Caesar are as gripping as her wrestlings with Antony. The fact that we know that – at the outdoor Globe at least – Shakespeare's company had to have an eye on the arrival of dusk only makes you wonder yet again about the authenticity of the long texts we have and how they were assembled. Perhaps they were a sort of compendium of all the available material, to be selected from each time the play was put on. And perhaps, like Chekhov, Shakespeare should have considered the four-act play, or at least the half-an-hour-shorter play. If he were here, we would be warning him of the counter-attractions of television.

In the characteristic lull of *Twelfth Night*'s Act Four there will be plenty of good things, but only Olivia's meeting with Sebastian really advances the plot, and most of the jokes are repeats. Although the play is edging towards a romantic conclusion, its energy is now perilously hard to sustain. The early editors Rowe and Capell, re-acting to a rhythmic break as one set of characters leaves and the next enters, place this first scene in the street outside Olivia's house – but how, scenically, are we to do this with any fluency? In practice, 4.1 should be rehearsed as a continuation of 3.4. As if to invigorate the process, it starts with Feste, absent for a while from the play, chasing Sebastian. Pointless to enquire why the twin brother too is in Olivia's garden – he just is – but in general, where have these two been? Sebastian has been sightseeing before returning to the Ele-phant, and he will turn out to be less safe here in the garden than in town. You always feel that Feste might just as well be somewhere else as on the stage with us, pursuing a different life and a different identity: perhaps Orsino, out of the play for an even longer time, has offered him permanent work, singing folk-songs through the night; or he might have been somewhere quite other, perhaps working in the docks. These speculations may sound silly, but they matter very much to the players, and therefore in the end to the audience – for all that the Method has been mocked, many imaginative hares can be set running by an actor who arrives on the stage completely convinced of where he's coming from.

The farce of keeping Aguecheek worked up against Cesario is really, since Antonio's arrival, not so welcome any more: more than any horseplay, what has to be achieved in the plot now is Sebastian's face-to-face with Olivia. It is done by having Aguecheek make an ill-advised attack on the young man so that the ensuing scrap brings Olivia out of her house. Feste is thrown into the ring as a bonus, as stylish as ever and in some measure taking up the energy of the play from Toby. But he is irritable, and so is Sebastian, who has the manner of a tourist being bothered by a persistent local hustler. The joke, apart from the obvious mistaken identity, is that Olivia, like a hamster on a wheel, has yet again sent for Cesario, this time using not Malvolio but Feste, who is thoroughly disgruntled by it.

Sebastian's sophistication of speech strikes Feste very strongly: he remembers Cesario (from the beginning of Act Three) as prosey and unimpressive, and assumes he must have learned his new style from some patron – who has taught him to speak in verse, to be critical ('thou art a foolish fellow'), outspoken ('vent thy folly'), and patronising ('I prithee, foolish Greek, depart from me'). The affectations of the strangely changed page are worth a mock:

> Vent my folly! He has heard that word of some great man and now applies it to a fool. Vent my folly!

It is fairly clear to modern audiences that Feste is giving 'vent' the overtone of 'fart'; but his use soon afterwards of a word which has genuinely changed its meaning is more taxing:

> I am afraid this great lubber, the world, will prove a cockney

– a cockney being then a spoiled, foppish boy and little to do with Bow Bells.[1]

In the matter of tips, however, Cesario's 'open hand' is not much changed. To make him shut up, Feste now gets, as he thinks, a third gratuity from him which is in fact a tetchy withdrawal by Sebastian from Antonio's purse. As he does so, the low comedy arrives, maddening Sebastian further. The degenerating battle between Andrew and Cesario this time produces only a short laugh as the amazed Andrew, having got up the gander to offer Cesario violence, is beaten to the ground by Sebastian, who is in turn challenged by the trigger-happy Toby, as was Antonio. We could certainly do with a new joke. This scrappy farce forces Feste, normally so careless of authority, into a slight change of character – he sounds almost unctuous:

> This will I tell my lady straight; I would not be in some of your coats for twopence

and he hurries away. Andrew, who started the fight, threatens legal action, no doubt from a sitting position:[2]

---

1   In fact, the word's meaning was changing at exactly this moment – there are examples of both uses in 1600. Perhaps the double-meaning is part of Feste's joke.

2   Shakespeare, for who knows what reason, loves this particular legal plea, especially in the early years of the 1600s – there is a comic example with Constable Elbow and Froth in *Measure for Measure*, and a more sardonic one when Hamlet examines Yorick's skull.

> I'll have an action of battery against him, if there be any law in
> Illyria[2]

– and Sebastian, persuaded that he has fallen among feeble lunatics,
is easily able to break Toby's armlock (as Cesario could never have
done) and defend himself. Toby is as amazed as Feste at this new
vigour –

> You are well fleshed

and shows the same misplaced courage that he did with Antonio:

> Nay then, I must have an ounce or two of this malapert blood
> from you.

Enough. He has met a Waterloo more final than any duellist's
wound: Olivia, awaiting Cesario and driven past her limits, is utterly
incensed. She arrives and turns him into a sort of wild animal

> Fit for the mountains and the barbarous caves . . .

The threat of losing his place in the house sobers Toby up wonderfully, and he and his team slink away – Andrew still light-years from
presenting his suit and Fabian hoping he has escaped unnoticed.
And as Olivia turns to Sebastian, the play somersaults again.

Truth to tell, despite the felicitous situation I am not sure how
well Shakespeare has managed what follows. Olivia's tone to Cesario
is quite changed – it is almost as if she knew she was speaking to
a stranger. Her captious relationship with the page had reached
screaming-point: but now, as if such storms were just incidents in
their rewarding friendship, she calls him 'gentle' once more:

> I prithee, gentle friend,
> Let thy fair wisdom, not thy passion, sway
> In this uncivil and unjust extent
> Against thy peace.

Cesario is to come in for a little tea and sympathy, while she
complains about her relatives:

> Go with me to my house
> And hear thou there how many fruitless pranks
> This ruffian hath botched up . . .

It would have been more credible for Olivia to say 'the house' rather
than 'my house', as Cesario knows her premises very well. But at
least her confession of love has given her wings: the little joke earlier
about the jewel Cesario was to wear to keep her quiet is now

followed by another tender conceit – now that she is in love, she is like a hare startled out of a thicket by the least danger:

> Beshrew his soul for me,
> He started one poor heart of mine, in thee.

The fun of course is in waiting for the reaction. Sebastian turns to us, balancing sexual opportunism and genuine enchantment:

> What relish is in this? How runs the stream?
> Or I am mad, or else this is a dream.
> Let fancy still my sense in Lethe steep:
> If it be thus to dream, still let me sleep.

Whether madness, hallucination or anaesthesia, it is certainly a stroke of luck.

His short soliloquy is dead time for Olivia – feeling she is no further forward, she pleads from the heart again:

> Would thou'dst be ruled by me!

– and is suddenly liberated:

> SEBASTIAN: Madam, I will.
> OLIVIA: O say so, and so be!

Bereaved and shipwrecked, pestered by a clown and unaccountably embroiled in a silly brawl, Sebastian is offered a view of paradise by a perfect stranger: while Olivia, who has wrestled with an impossibly knotted rope for what seems a lifetime, finds it shaken free in a second. As they approach each other, it is very funny, and, suddenly, very touching.

4.2. It is said that Sir Donald Wolfit, the legendary English actor-manager (whose ego perhaps fitted roles such as Volpone and Tamburlaine better than it did Hamlet and Brutus), concluded that the scene in which Feste visits the incarcerated Malvolio disguised as Sir Topas the curate could not have been written by Shakespeare, for the simple reason that he, Wolfit, had particular difficulty learning it. The panache of adducing this personal hotline to the author is all the more impressive since he was playing Malvolio, and it is Feste who has the bigger problem. The Fool's text is impenetrable in many places and the whole basis of his behaviour difficult to swallow. But the Elizabethans were much preoccupied with madness, fascination and horror being mixed pretty evenly, and writers responded enthusiastically and more or less creatively. However, if Kyd's Hieronimo and Isabella (*The Spanish Tragedy*) and Shakespeare's own mad men and women are the authentic stuff of tragedy, there is a decline in the Jacobean period towards the gratuitous celebration of symptoms and effects – lengthy furls of phantasmagoric imagery are devoted to Webster's lycanthropic Duke Ferdinand in *The Duchess of Malfi*[3] and to Brachiano, poisoned by his own helmet in *The White Devil*.[4] There is also plenty of voyeurism in the writing of Thomas Dekker and in the sub-plot of Middleton and Rowley's *The Changeling*. Naturally the interest extends to how madness should be handled and whether it can be cured (the topaz stone was thought to be particularly helpful against 'evill thoughts and phrensie', hence Feste's curate's name).[5] The example in *Twelfth Night* is of course a simulation, since there is in fact no madman present, but Feste does guy the enthusiasm Londoners felt for going to gawp through the bars of Bedlam Hospital.[6]

To us, however, such a scene, a much darker version of the 'exorcism' performed on Malvolio earlier and conducted by a still more amoral man, is likely to seem cruel and exploitative and that's all. It is also completely unnecessary, containing only one narrative unit – Malvolio's attempt to get Feste to fetch him writing materials so that he can appeal to Olivia for his release. This moment is held back mercilessly while Feste develops his torture, which he would justify to himself either by the curiously nihilistic licence of his profession or by Malvolio's scathing comments on him way back in

3   Give me some wet hay . . . I do account this world but a dog-kennel.

4   Let me have some quails to supper . . . no, some fried dog-fish . . .
     Yonder's a fine slave come in now . .
     Why, there in a blue bonnet, and a pair
     Of breeches with a great cod-piece: ha, ha, ha !

5   He is also in Chaucer, giving his name to a Canterbury Tale, as

     a knyght . . . fair and gentle
     In battaille and in tourneyment . . .
     A doughty swayn
     Whyt was his face as payndemayn
     His lippes red as rose . . .
     He hadde a semely nose.

6   Another *Twelfth Night* icon, this scene has inspired the best efforts of artists – Nicholas Rowe's 1709 edition contains the first known illustration of the play (they are all in full Restoration fig), and Henry Fuseli later had Malvolio like some Old Testament casualty, Jeremiah perhaps, and Feste slightly godlike in a shaft of celestial light.

1.5. It is certainly extreme – performers may often wish that their critics would roast in hell, but confronted by the actual person, the poor dandruffy man just doing his job, they wouldn't normally expend this kind of energy.

Clearly Toby has been as good as his word – Malvolio is in 'a dark room and bound', wherever on Olivia's estate this is to be imagined. Perhaps a garden shed, perhaps an attic in the house. I have seen Malvolio imprisoned in a sort of subterranean cage, like an open sewer, so that all you see are his clawing hands and peering eyes protruding just above stage level; and in my own ESC production his face was lit but nothing else of him. But you may prefer to see his whole distressed body, straitjacketed or roped, chained to the floor like a bear at the stake. The only rule is that since Feste is about to play two characters, himself and Topas, Malvolio mustn't see him: so either it is very dark – in the stage convention whereby we can just about see but he can't – or he can be blindfolded (which means he can express nothing with his eyes).

Maria arrives with jokey props:

> MARIA: Nay, I prithee put on this gown and this beard . . .
> Do it quickly.

It is a little discouraging, this dressing-up game so soon after the knockabout in 4.1; but Feste's distinct style soon emerges. Left alone with us, he immediately runs through three typical modes: first, a satirical jab[7] when he seemed only to be horsing about:

> FESTE: Well, I'll put it on, and I will dissemble myself in't, and
> I would I were the first that ever dissembled in such a gown

– then difficult text that does mean something (but check the footnotes):

> . . . to be said an honest man and a good housekeeper goes as
> fairly as to say a careful man and a great scholar

– and, as Maria returns with Toby, the intentional nonsense he likes to use with Aguecheek:

> For as the old hermit of Prague, that never saw pen and ink,
> very wittily said to a niece of King Gorboduc 'That that is, is'.

This is a reversal of his infuriated 'nothing that is so, is so' in 4.1. Toby can find no reply beyond

---

7 Particularly at Puritans like Malvolio himself, who famously concealed their black 'Geneva' gowns beneath commonplace white surplices.

To him, Sir Topas.

Feste now applies his resources to making Malvolio (revealed in one way or another) wish he were dead. Punishing him as much for what he is as what he has done, he re-paints, rather as might Edvard Munch or Lewis Carroll, familiar figures in a terrifying light – the pastoral cleric as bloodsucker, the innocent fool as mental defective, between them making the man of some honour gibber. At first, Feste's approach is similar to Toby's and Maria's in the garden, hearing 'the fiend' speaking 'hollow . . . within him', but this time it is with the apparent authority of the Church:

MALVOLIO: Sir Topas, Sir Topas, good Sir Topas, go to my lady.
FESTE: Out, hyperbolical fiend! How vexest thou this man! Talk'st thou nothing but of ladies?

It is very depressing for Malvolio to hear this stuff again: he seems to be surrounded by religious fanatics. In fact Feste has more advanced psychological weapons up his sleeve, not to say the instincts of the professional interrogator: his brain-tampering is as accomplished as if he were asking a blind man to declare the points of the compass. He starts and continues on the assumption that the one thing he and Malvolio can agree on is that Malvolio is, quite bluntly, mad:

MALVOLIO: Who calls there?
FESTE: Sir Topas the curate, who comes to visit Malvolio the lunatic . . .

This will force Malvolio into repeated protestations:

Do not think I am mad . . . I am not mad . . . I say to you this house is dark.
FESTE: Madman, thou errest . . .
MALVOLIO: . . . I am no more mad than you are

– and the more he insists, the more any man might begin to wonder about himself. His language has some of the monosyllabic desperation of Lear:

O let me not be mad, not mad, sweet heaven

– or perhaps the anxiety of Hamlet when it occurs to him that his assumed madness might have taken him over. In Hamlet's case, of course, it is the consequence of his own tampering with the boundaries: for Malvolio, whose protestations of sanity are beginning to sound like a dementia, the insecurity has been cruelly forced on him. And in fact, the impressive thing about him, both here and when he arrives in the final scene, is his calm, battered certainty that 'what is, is'. By the time Feste has finished with him, all he really doubts is his ability to survive.

Taking it for granted that the obvious is untrue and the untrue obvious, Sir Topas invites Malvolio to peer at a completely self-cancelling picture: the house

>hath bay windows transparent as barricadoes

– that is, a natural source of light is as luminous here as an impenetrable wall of barrels; and the nonsensical image becomes appropriately ecclesiastical:

>the clerestories toward the south-north are as lustrous as ebony

– in other words, the windows in this peculiar house of worship are pitch black.

Malvolio perhaps understands this maddening technique, and he knows his rights – in simple monosyllables he repeats that the house is indeed dark, and offers to prove his sanity by what, were he dealing with a genuine pastor, would be a conclusive test: he will give intelligent answers to formal questions. What he gets back is a trick based on the doctrine of transmigration of souls:

>What is the opinion of Pythagoras concerning wildfowl?

Malvolio is relieved   he knows the old Greek idea that there is a risk that, in killing a small bird, you might 'dispossess' your grandmother's immortal spirit. His attitude to it is mature – as a good Christian he disagrees with the doctrine, and thinks 'nobly of the soul'. But now, madly, he seems to be dealing with a Christian minister who believes in paganism, in fact makes belief in it proof of sanity:

>Thou shalt hold th' opinion of Pythagoras ere I will allow of thy wits

and who then abandons him to his fate:

>Fare thee well.

But at least this horrible conversation, like a short exchange with the Inquisition, is better than the nothing before it and the new nothing that follows. As Feste, Toby and Maria watch, silence once more closes in around him like blackness, and his increasingly desperate cry:

> Sir Topas, Sir Topas!

echoes on and on before Toby quietly approves Feste's performance:

> My most exquisite Sir Topas!

Feste is indeed 'for all waters': almost the most alarming thing about the torture has been its effortless counterpoint between cascading words and overbearing silence.

Toby, who has given rather muted support throughout – 'A good knave . . . well said, master Parson' – is tiring quickly, and for good reason: he has seen the writing on the wall in Olivia's hand. He let Maria put together the Topas outfit alone, and seems only to be going through the motions, really wanting to be 'rid of this knavery':

> If he may be conveniently delivered, I would he were . . .

In fact, he will not bother to watch the second half of the act at all, but will wait for a résumé: Feste must now go

> To him in thine own voice, and bring me word how thou find'st
> him.

As he leaves, sour and disappointed, he invites Maria to his bedroom: whether this is for the first time or not, it may have a new significance – the politics in the house are changing, and we will shortly be told that the two have married. Maria leaves the play in silence, having done Shakespeare a small, neat favour: Feste might as well

> have done this without thy beard and gown; he sees thee not

– but Shakespeare wanted us to see them, and puts his excuse into her mouth.

Feste is left alone with his victim. Having played to the rather jaded audience of Toby and Maria, the pleasure is now all his own. Malvolio proceeds with a certain embattled dignity, Feste with ever greater malice – the actor of Malvolio must play hard and strong down the line, desperate and urgent, while the Fool dances perversely around him. For Malvolio's benefit, he will now be not just himself but a sort of caricature Feste – a wildly cheerful over-the-top funny man, chanting silly ditties[8] to a famous hater of both fools and music:

> Hey Robin, jolly Robin
> Tell me how thy lady does . . .
> My lady is unkind, perdy . . .

He affects not even to hear Malvolio properly (he has to call three times). At least, to Malvolio's relief, it is a familiar voice when it comes:

> Good fool, as ever thou wilt deserve well at my hand, help me
> to a candle and pen, ink and paper . . .

and he is even, comfortingly, addressed by name:

> Master Malvolio?

– only to find that this familiar figure is going on the same principles as the curate:

> Alas, sir, how fell you besides your five wits?

Still, he is scrupulously polite to Feste, confiding what he has been astute enough to realise:

> They . . . do all they can to face me out of my wits

and promises him everything he never did before – money, courtesy, gratitude for life. His hope now is for some sensible talk: he sees himself sitting quietly in his cell by candle-light, writing an elegant plea to Olivia. But the more lucid he becomes, the less he can shake off the bedlam:

> MALVOLIO: Fool, there was never man so notoriously abused.
> I am as well in my wits, fool, as thou art.
> FESTE: But as well? Then you are mad indeed, if you be no
> better in your wits than a fool.

Feste has him trapped and won't let go: the unhelpful helpfulness and the sympathetic tone drive his knife in further. Then he invents a third set-up, the return of the ferocious cleric to upbraid the jolly fool:

> [*As Sir Topas.*] Maintain no words with him, good fellow. [*As himself.*] Who I, sir? Not I, sir . . .

Feste is a radio performer before his time, and any acoustic extras he can devise – hopping noiselessly from one side of Malvolio to the

---

8   Actually written by Sir Thomas Wyatt as, typically, a lyric for a forsaken lover, so as subtly aimed in its way at Malvolio as 'Come Away Death' was at Orsino.

other for the two characters, then confusing him further by changing the sides – will make up in skill for what they lack in humanity. The poor fool 'shent for speaking' by Sir Topas seems to make common cause with Malvolio – he's a God-fearing man, and, rebuked by the Church, there's nothing more he can do. Imagine Malvolio's desperation: his friends are less help than his enemies. Feste may make him seem to hear the cleric's footsteps receding; and at last, after a little more unhelpful sympathy:

> . . . are you not mad indeed or do you but counterfeit?

he agrees to get pen, paper and ink, before leaving, satisfied at last – with surely the scariest and silliest of his songs, perhaps improvised on the spot. He peoples the dark house with the crude medieval figures of the old morality plays, maddening Malvolio further with jagged, jingly nonsense:

> Who, with dagger of lath,`
> In his rage and his wrath
> Cries 'Ah, ha' to the devil,
> Like a mad lad,
> 'Pare thy nails, dad?'
> Adieu, goodman devil.[9]

The whole scene has been like some long, unnecessary expiation – a vengeful private account settled with only the virtuosity of its performance to recommend it: even Haiyuza's Mr Sataki would have to admit that this is where the laughs run out. After such a tilt towards darkness, it will be hard for the play to recover. Indeed, the oddest sense of alienation has developed by the time Feste leaves: and since Malvolio cannot, we are left, wordlessly, with him as the light fades, in a sort of lopsided diminuendo. Not only are our sympathies seriously muddled, but in a sense we have lost contact, watching, as if down the wrong end of a telescope, someone completely absorbed in playing two false identities in front of a man who can't see him. In a way, Feste has prefigured two characters from *King Lear*: the Fool himself, whose riddling and snatches of song both settle and disorientate the King, and Edgar, who paints an imaginary landscape (with crows and samphire-gatherer) on Dover cliff for his blind father Gloucester. However in Feste's hands the imagery has become as wild as that of Edgar's abandoned

---

9   The 'old Vice' may have been the devil's son, one of whose jobs was keeping his father's nails trimmed.

alter ego, Poor Tom – and, unlike him, he has effectively shut the audience out.

4.3. A personable young man, the heroic version of our heroine, steps into the mayhem, as he did once before into his sister's perplexities. But not to take us into a different world: instead he repeats, in broad daylight, the bedlam theme, since he too is persuading himself he is sane. There is air, and Sebastian can breathe it; he can feel the sun's warmth; he holds in his hand a pearl with Olivia's fingerprint still on it. But these things are more vivid than they were before, and not only because he sees them through love's eyes: 'mad' and 'madness' recur three times in his speech. Malvolio's nightmare has stayed in the ether a little – and distraction is being seen, as through Feste's opal again, in its different colours, from enchantment through to mania.

Sebastian fears the unknown, and to grasp it, he needs the help of his friend, whose disappearance alarms him:

> Where's Antonio then?
> I could not find him at the Elephant,
> Yet there he was, and there I found this credit,
> That he did range the town to seek me out.

There is just no certainty in Illyria: people lose each other as they might in the forest of Arden, and they can be attacked by idiots or unaccountably taken up by beautiful heiresses. Nothing that is, is. Sebastian's feelings are kept in a precarious balance – he may take the stage lyrically, supported by music, but the sun may be setting and the shadows long around him; and by the time Olivia arrives, though he's marvelled that

> . . . this accident and flood of fortune
> So far exceed[s] all instance, all discourse,
> That I am ready to distrust mine eyes

he still hasn't said he's happy.

His speech is in fact highly technical, a sort of gentle tirade. Few actors enjoy considering the formal shape of a passage of verse too early in rehearsals, but with this one it is difficult to postpone – its structure is tightly tied to both storytelling and mood, and quite demanding. Cautious deductions and reportage occupy the first seven lines, holding back the excitement and insisting on narrative logic. The query about Antonio's whereabouts begins half way through a blank verse line, and so needs to spring, however incongruously, from the previous words rather than being preceded by a pause for thought.[10] The sublime panic that then sets in as Sebastian realises how far what has happened lies beyond any reasonable mistake makes his verse suddenly race, the ideas tumbling over themselves: his eyes are liars, he must argue with his own argument, he's mad, no, she's mad, she can't be: it's all, well . . . unreadable. This main sentence lasts for thirteen lines before reaching a full stop, which itself (line 20) sits in the middle of a verse measure and therefore has more of the function of a comma – as does the one following halfway through line 21. So this is a run of fourteen lines in all, a clue to the work it is being asked to do, which is to build not so much to a climax as to further inconclusiveness:

> There's something in't
That is deceivable.

Circling his problem, Sebastian hasn't got very far, but the player has travelled some distance. If the speech comes to a peak too early, as it can around the fifteenth or sixteenth line, the energy will drain away and let Olivia down badly on her entrance. The acceleration mustn't smooth out the changes of thought either, but leave them sharp and unreconciled. Shakespeare's flexibility is being lent to an ordinary person again, and the ordinary person playing him needs to become an iambic athlete, a fast thinker aware of breath control – and as any singer will tell you, even in the most minor operatic challenge you can't leave anything to chance.

Well, the irritated actor may say, before we get onto all that, what are the facts? What happened inside the house? Remembering Olivia's professed habit of buying more oft than begging or borrowing, has she 'feasted' him, and what exactly has she 'bestowed' on him? Well, we never know whether Hamlet and Ophelia have slept together either. For the moment, you take your choice – either to have Sebastian seriously rumpled and Olivia straightening her clothes as she rushes on with the embarrassed Priest, or to concentrate on the implicit. In the language, where Shakespeare settles everything, the

---

10   Again, there are a number of theories about the iambic pentameter, but we can surely agree that any pause in the middle of a line has to be very short, or the pulse will be lost, as if a musical bar had been interrupted. Shakespeare always allows the second half of a line to bounce off the first, or alternatively leaves it tacet and starts another.

hurdy-gurdy effect of Sebastian's speech, which threatened to spin
the play off its axis again, is now quieted by the mature and practical
tone of Olivia, who means to elevate the bizarre state of affairs to
something good. Sebastian is to go 'into the chantry by'

> And underneath that consecrated roof
> Plight me the full assurance of your faith . . .

For her, one life has been changed into another, as love will do, but at
the speed of an astonishing dream. She is a high-minded woman and
she has given enough of herself to want the gift sanctified, but her
lines have a lovely peacefulness in them – within which Shakespeare
continues to develop her character. She has a new willingness, for
example, to admit a weakness: she needs the marriage in order

> That my most jealous and too doubtful soul
> May live at peace

and her tender insecurity warms the formal tone of the arrangements.
Trained to control, she is now quite happy to accede to someone
else's needs:

> He shall conceal it
> Whilcs you are willing it shall come to note . . . [11]

and even her self-consciousness has become a gift – she will use her
position (never quite forgotten) creatively, and when the time comes
they will have a big celebration

> According to my birth.

At a stroke, Sebastian has exchanged economic dependency on
Antonio for the benefit of marriage to a richer partner. More and
more, we are quietly invited to consider him next to (and now
approaching) his sister, whom we know far better. She seemed to
forget him as soon as she arrived at Orsino's, even though we know
now that her passionate attachment never died. Sebastian in turn let
her be, soon after he was taken up by Antonio – he has made no
mention of her since, and now, forgetting Antonio, he is ready to
throw his lot in with Olivia, as Viola presumably would with Orsino
if she could. But it is hard to see him as an opportunist: his destiny
has been sweetly prepared for by his sympathetic qualities earlier,
and by our knowledge that no brother of Viola's can be all bad.

---

11   You might want to change 'whiles' to 'till' since that is what it means; but you forgo a
small alliteration – 'whiles you are willing' – if you do.

It is also possible that this is the scene, rather than at any more obvious opportunities earlier, in which to deliver some precise image of Sebastian's genetic link to Viola. I heard a story recently of two completely dissimilar twins, whose lives went in quite different directions, but who not only married women with the same name but who both had the mannerism – their only one – of sneezing in a specially loud way, for effect. That would not be it, but the sharing of just one habit by Viola and Sebastian – a gesture, a way of laughing, a characteristic hesitation – will have a tremendously direct effect, if it is chosen carefully, *very* carefully, and introduced very lightly.

The precipitation of events gives this brief scene undoubted charm, and Olivia has banished her shadows. With the slightest hint as to who will finally wear the trousers:

> heavens so shine
> That they may fairly note this act of mine

they approach each other for the second time, mutually impressed with their seriousness, and move calmly off to seal the great change of circumstance – led by an old friend, the Priest, who has lived through a lot without speaking. He will have his turn soon, but for the time being he must just keep a good clerical face on.

ACT FIVE

Act 5 Scene 1

5.1. Feste again, not pursuing but pursued and in complacent charge:

> FABIAN: Now, as thou lov'st me, let me see his letter.

It is hard to spot, but this is a missive Malvolio has managed to get off to Olivia with the pen and ink Feste helped him to, and Fabian is very anxious about it. The lid may be blown off the conspiracy – so although there is very little time for the plot in this fast little routine, Fabian's need must be sharply played. Feste, on the other hand, is invulnerable – although he mocked Malvolio more cruelly than anyone, he didn't conspire against him, and in fact ended up helping him. What they don't know is that Malvolio is now the last thing on Olivia's mind.

> FESTE: Good Master Fabian, grant me another request.
> FABIAN: Anything.
> FESTE: Do not desire to see this letter.
> FABIAN: This is to give a dog and in recompense desire my
>   dog again.

This dog would have set the Inner Temple audience by the ears[1] – they would have known that a certain Dr Bullein, who was related to Queen Elizabeth, once agreed to make his sovereign a gift of his favourite pet dog, which she fancied: when she said he could have anything he wanted in return, he of course asked her for the dog back. A Feste with good connections. Without this topical push, the joke flaps in the wind, rounding off the exchange but hardly a big laugh.

   Suddenly Orsino is here, quite unexpected. What has brought him out, anxious as an anchorite in daylight? Too much inactivity

---

1 None more so than our old informant John Manningham, whose diary entry is our source for the following story.

perhaps, even by his standards. Cesario has failed in both his missions, and has been unsettlingly absent – detained by Olivia, embroiled in the duel and then mistaken for Sebastian before returning to base. Stalemate and general unease have persuaded Orsino that he should straighten up and conduct his own business. Viola may seem a little subdued and formal by his side, back in the garden where she has had so much trouble: there could even be a little estrangement between them, the air heavy with all she hasn't told him.

Orsino in Olivia's territory, the key to the Malvolio plot in the hands of the Fool, Viola with a man she loves about to confront a woman who loves her – and Sebastian just out of sight. We can feel the final reel engaging, and not only because of the time – most of the questions now are not a matter of If, but How.

Presumably the Count is looking his best and, now the moment has arrived, he is in a genial enough mood. He is friendly and open-handed to Feste, who takes full advantage. Touching lightly on the theme of insincerity which haunts this part of the play (Antonio will be back in a moment), he declares himself better pleased with his enemies who tell him he is an ass than with his friends who flatter him, because

> . . . by my foes, sir, I profit in the knowledge of myself, and by my friends I am abused . . .

He camouflages his moral – perhaps it was a bit harsh – in a little verbal dance:

> . . . so that, conclusions to be as kisses, if your four negatives make your two affirmatives, why then, the worse for my friends and the better for my foes.

There is always a certain amount of spare matter with Feste, spark-ling filaments around his nut-hard truths.

In fact he is looking for a mendicant's royal flush. In all his begging in the play, he has never managed a third tip from the same person: after singing 'Come Away Death' he had the delicacy not even to double his money; with Cesario in Act Three, he hung about for a third coin but only halfheartedly; and so annoying was Sebastian he couldn't be much bothered. He is putting real effort into Orsino, sensing a propitious moment, and pulls out a refrain he probably has always at the ready:

tertio . . . the third . . . the triplex . . . one, two, three . . .

– but Orsino, his nerves perhaps showing a little, draws a princely line, at least until a message is sent to Olivia:

> If you will let your lady know I am here to speak with her, and bring her along with you, it may awake my bounty further.

Feste hangs on a little longer, or perhaps starts off and returns – he must explain that this blatant desire for money is not greed (he is a poor man) – but he draws a blank.

Fabian could leave with him, still nagging him for the letter. But there is much to be said for full attendance on the stage, so that everyone witnesses each story-line even if they are, frustratingly, forbidden to speak. This last scene of the play (400 lines long, as complicated as *Measure for Measure* or *Cymbeline* but better delivered than either) is bravura dénouement, and it depends a little on group complicity: everyone turns up by chance in this garden all at the same time, and then has to shelve their own dilemmas and listen to the others.[2] They will at least observe some odd conjunctions – Orsino face to face with Toby and Andrew, Antonio sharing the stage with Feste. This is one of the rare cases when a director will do well to sit down and work out the choreography in advance. Fourteen people to be disposed on the stage with some kind of grace – even my sensitive Japanese cast needed help. In general, actors don't much like being told where to stand in this automatic way – they feel gazumped and powerless and may stop thinking – so how to achieve your plan while keeping the players inventive is a diplomatic matter. You can't perhaps insist on the details every day, but sometimes simply let the scene mill about freely, content to keep the end result at the back of your mind – and of course the actors' intuitions will refine it anyway. Sooner or later there will be an authoritarian moment: an actor may appeal for help, there is always the question of visibility, and if all else fails, a lighting plot that pins everyone down to one place and no other.

---

2   Harley Granville Barker, in his preface to the play (one of his lesser achievements), described its last scene as 'scandalously ill-arranged and ill-written . . . the despair of any stage manager'. In general, Barker had an astonishing gift for being half-right. For him, Feste should indeed be old, but only to emphasise that he is 'one of life's self-acknowledged failures' (really?). He believes Shakespeare started the play as 'a passionate love romance for Orsino' but then changed his mind; in general he wants more in 'the Egyptian thief' key – 'that fine fury'. He once commented to John Gielgud that Toby is a man 'who disdains to be drunk on anything but vintage Burgundy'. What happened to the burnt sack?

Nothing is turning out today as Orsino expected: having overcome his own anxiety and then dealt with Feste, he is now faced with something quite extraordinary – his old enemy Antonio, under arrest and announced only by an excited Cesario:

> Here comes the man, sir, that did rescue me.

Orsino's brain spins, and so does his language, into a sort of heroic jingle:

> That face of his I do remember well;
> Yet when I saw it last it was besmeared
> As black as Vulcan, in the smoke of war.

It is all suddenly stertorian, a bit *Henry VI Part 1*, and the play wobbles a little – it is the necessary price of tying Antonio into the plot again. In this rhetorical mode, the Officer tells Orsino something he surely already knows:

> Orsino, this is that Antonio
> That took the Phoenix and her fraught from Candy,[3]
> And this is he that did the Tiger board
> When your young nephew Titus lost his leg.

This, from the author of the Willow Cabin Speech and the spice-box dialogue of Maria and Toby. It seems particularly dangerous to introduce the unfortunate Titus, with his pompous Latin name, into a play which debunks high seriousness to such good effect.

The fact is of course that Orsino is only a romantic by default: he is supposed to be a governor and warrior, and he can revert. All the belligerent clatter almost drowns something more human – Viola's mediation, depth of feeling hidden as usual inside a gentle rhythm:

> He did me kindness, sir, drew on my side,
> But in conclusion put strange speech upon me,
> I know not what 'twas but distraction.

Orsino doesn't seem to hear this – to him Antonio remains

> Notable pirate! Thou salt-water thief!

Pressed for an explanation of what he would agree was 'foolish boldness', Antonio tells his plaintive story, accurate in every detail to what we have seen of him with Sebastian. But it is undermined by a deep sense of victimisation. Brooded on since his arrest, his misfortune has become monstrous, 'a witchcraft', in which a man can give

3   The capital of Crete (now Khania), not Kandy in Sri Lanka.

> . . . love without retention, or restraint,
> All his in dedication

but still become

> a twenty-years' removed thing
> While one would wink.

It is almost embarrassing, this naked confession in front of Orsino and his staff – even though, did he but know it, Orsino understands this sort of thing quite well. It is also as unadorned and factual as perfected sorrow can be: if his onslaught on Cesario earlier was mainly shards of fury, Antonio is now helpless, enfeebled. Still Viola says nothing, though it must all be proof conclusive of what she most needs to know. To Orsino, the story is dismissable nonsense, except that it exacerbates a nagging uncertainty about his ambiguous page.

In this scene, whenever someone occupies the stage and comes to the point, he has to be bundled off – Feste had to make way for Orsino, Orsino for Antonio, and now he too has to be parked:

> Here comes the Countess; now heaven walks on earth.

It isn't easy for Orsino: at the moment his attention is drawn to Olivia, his ears are ringing with the news that Cesario has been with Antonio at every moment he has also been with him:

> But for thee, fellow – Fellow, thy words are madness;
> Three months this youth hath tended upon me.
> But more of that anon.

The awkward repetition of 'fellow' and the conventional 'more of that anon' show the difficulty he is having. He certainly hoped to be better focused as he confronted a woman around whom he has spun such a fantastic mesh that it was always going to be hard to see her features clearly.

Olivia has lost her husband, within moments it seems of having got him to the altar. Perhaps she rushed him a little, and he has bolted: he is certainly nowhere to be seen. Almost as bad, Feste has been in to tell her that the wretched Orsino is waiting for her in the garden. It is like having some tiresome old suitor at your wedding reception. She asks the distinguished visitor, without the slightest courtesy, what he wants:

> What would my lord but that he may not have

– making herself, for the sake of it, something less than human:

> Wherein Olivia may seem serviceable?

Her choice of adjective turns her, with wonderful sulkiness, into a sort of household appliance.

And then she sees, standing beside him, her bridegroom. It seems he has done the most insulting thing – left her within a few hours of marriage and gone back into the duke's service:

> Cesario, you do not keep promise with me.

The beauty of this is that because she has got the right name for the wrong person, it strikes both Orsino and Viola as an outrage. It is as if the Queen had simply ignored some visiting dignitary to talk to his fascinating secretary. Viola's 'Madam!' contains (if possible) both shock at the sullen rudeness to Orsino and her own bewilderment at being accused again. Orsino, who has been waiting months for this moment, manages half an overture:

> Gracious Olivia –

before being swept aside once more: in an inverted reply, she tells him he'll have to wait until she gets her answer from Cesario:

> What do you say, Cesario? Good my lord –

But Viola won't have it – she is Orsino's servant and he is a prince, entitled to talk if he wants:

> My lord would speak; my duty hushes me.

Invited by Viola's manners to observe good manners of her own, Olivia turns her frustration onto Orsino and flatly insults him in front of the whole company:

> If it be aught to the old tune, my lord,
> It is as fat and fulsome to mine ear
> As howling after music.

Orsino simply cannot cope with this. It is heard by Antonio, by Olivia's attendants and his own officers: compared by his love to a yowling tomcat, he is as shamed as Antonio was a few moments ago. He manages to stay coherent for long enough to denounce her as an 'uncivil lady' (true) to whom he has offered faithful devotion (true), but with his impotent:

> What shall I do?

he begins to break. Olivia reverts, infuriatingly, to a mealy etiquette, perfunctorily inviting him to please himself as long as he keeps his dignity:

> Even what it please my lord that shall become him.

You can almost see her mock-curtsey.

What we know of Orsino is that this sort of thing, almost any contradiction in fact, sends him off like a sky-rocket; but we might want to restrain him as the old lurid violence begins to bubble:

> Why should I not, had I the heart to do it,
> Like to th' Egyptian thief at point of death,
> Kill what I love . . . ?[4]

Feste was right to sense something mortal in Orsino's appetites – from dying for love he now thinks of murdering for it. He will destroy Olivia, like Othello seeing nobility in a savage decision – or rather, he would, had he the heart to do it. However he does have the heart, in order to spite her, to kill his page, especially as a new poison is taking hold of him – his problem was after all Cesario, who seems able to be in two places at once and to have two plans as well. It is this 'minion' who 'screws' him out of his rightful place. With an ugly violence to match the ugly words, which he can't improve with a neat couplet, he determines to

> . . . sacrifice the lamb that I do love
> To spite a raven's heart within a dove.

He does say that he loves her – and so much does Viola love him that she responds erotically:

> And I most jocund, apt and willingly,
> To do you rest, a thousand deaths would die.

Heroic violence arrived with Antonio: now brutal comedy is fizzing beween the romantics, in Viola's recklessness no less than Orsino's intemperance and Olivia's bad humour. Their adrenalin has propelled Shakespeare's language into a different key and timbre, the most sustained of the scene so far. In some way the style combines the high passionate courtliness of Marivaux with the timing

---

4 The 'Egyptian thief' figured in a story in an old Roman anthology then recently translated, interesting its English audience with its passionate pagan absurdity: a man set on by robbers turns on his captive, with whom he has fallen in love, and tries to kill her but misses – the translator is fascinated that these marvellous 'barbarous people' could kill the ones they loved in order to see them in the next world.

and rhythms of farce: the comedy is there – just – waiting for its chance, but the old mechanism of mistaken identity is also being used to provoke extreme feelings. They have to be played on the line, at full tilt, with precision and energy, since any pause for reflection will deflate the whole nitrous balloon.

And of course they crystallise into rhymes, acting as bar-lines in the rush of music. Without faltering, Viola breaks away – and almost forgets her assumed character:

> OLIVIA: Where goes Cesario?
> VIOLA: After him I love,
>   More than I love these eyes, more than my life . . .

but, with energy pouring out of her, she still manages one of her gender paradoxes:

> More, by all mores, than e'er I shall love wife.
> If I do feign, you witnesses above,
> Punish my life for tainting of my love.

Hearing this, Orsino doesn't exactly listen, but at least he doesn't speak; and Olivia must make what she can of it – but fast. Her husband loves not her, but his employer, so much so that he would go blind and die for him. She is 'detested' and 'beguiled' indeed, but she pointedly uses the familiar 'thou' as Viola storms back at her:

> VIOLA: Who does beguile you? Who does do you wrong?
> OLIVIA: Hast thou forgot thyself? Is it so long?

The rhymes splatter like pebbles on a roof. The business of thinking to call up the Priest, of instructing a servant to get him and of the servant going, have to feel as if they occupy no more than the half-line the idea is given, and the crescendo continues:

> ORSINO: Come, away!
> OLIVIA: Whither, my lord? Cesario, husband, stay!

– at which point the brakes screech on. Orsino, surely to God, needs a moment to take this in, and we're allowed to laugh at last.

At the beginning of the scene, as Olivia, Orsino and Viola converged, their commotion produced a sort of chaos, the metre breaking down in a flurry of counter-demands; now they have become like pistons in an engine. A trio of argumentative instruments, the actors aim to perform emotional acrobatics with formal perfection, and the shading of farcical virtuosity in their work will be much appreciated. As the scene's furious exchanges now slow down, the rhymes break up again, and an unhappy mean is reached as Olivia more or less begs Cesario to stay with her. That way, he will have nothing more to fear from this savage man:

> Fear not, Cesario, take thy fortunes up;
> Be that thou know'st thou art, and then thou art
> As great as that thou fear'st.

The slight modulation allows the Priest to arrive with the right sense of consequence. Olivia now speaks to him in five lines without a full stop, while his part consists of addressing the company in a single sentence of eight – and the rhythm is appropriately solemn from them both:

> OLIVIA: Father, I charge thee by thy reverence
>   Here to unfold . . . what thou dost know
>   Hath newly passed between this youth and me.
> PRIEST: A contract of eternal bond of love,
>   Confirmed by mutual joinder of your hands . . .

It is a perfect little oration in the maddest circumstances, with a nice ecclesiastical joke at the end:

> And all the ceremony of this compact
> Sealed in my function, by my testimony;
> Since when, my watch hath told me, toward my grave
> I have travelled but two hours.

His job imperturbably done, he withdraws into the shadows, leaving a time-bomb ticking. Its first effect is to make Orsino far more fluent and powerful than he was before. Regret has soaked into his rage, as it did for Antonio, and his malediction of Cesario has a semblance of dignity. He gives it the only thing he can, his poetry:

> O thou dissembling cub! What wilt thou be
> When time hath sowed a grizzle on thy case? . . .
> Farewell, and take her, but direct thy feet
> Where thou and I henceforth may never meet.

Poor Viola, twice cursed: funny play, that tampers with our emotions but leaves us with a distant sense that everyone will get their deserts in the end. However any kind of finale is postponed by more pain, so real it is comic – the completely unexpected arrival of the broken-headed Andrew to take the play over from Orsino (who joins Fabian, Antonio, Olivia and Viola in a critical mass).

He is calling out in the most ordinary, desperate prose:

> For the love of God, a surgeon!

– and, although he needs attention himself, he is really doing it for his friend, whose trouble is greater than his:

> Send one presently to Sir Toby . . . H'as broken my head across,
> and has given Sir Toby a bloody coxcomb too.

It is always a pleasure to see Andrew, but the laugh of recognition will halve or die when we see the difficulty he is in. It is in fact fascinating to watch an audience at this point in the play if it is going well. Everything is half funny, half horrible; and we certainly never expected blood, for all Antonio's machismo and Orsino's sound and fury. The altercation Andrew describes is not the one we witnessed, but a further fracas at some point after Olivia has taken Sebastian in and married him, and it accounts for the latter's absence since. The one good thing is that Andrew at last meets Olivia, though hardly in the way he'd hoped back in the days of buttonholes, serenades and new-minted French. She turns out to be very kind:

> What's the matter?

– whereupon he subsides into childish sorrow:

> I had rather than forty pound I were at home.

If it were Toby listening, Andrew's plaintiveness would be ignored, as it was when he confessed that he was adored once; but this time due attention is paid:

> Who has done this, Sir Andrew?

– and he is allowed to explain that the 'dishonest, paltry boy' he so confidently took on turned out to be a Zorro:

> The count's gentleman, one Cesario. We took him for a coward,
> but he's the very devil incardinate

(he means incarnate).

Even under Olivia's protection, Andrew jumps out of his skin at seeing this fire-eater again:

> Od's lifelings, here he is! You broke my head for nothing, and
> that that I did, I was set on to do't by Sir Toby

– which is true, if a little craven. Viola has now been accused, in swift succession, of disloyalty to a friend, breach of promise, betrayal of professional trust and assault and battery.

It goes without saying that a director has had to continue thinking ahead: these confrontations are very enjoyable, but hopeless unless they are well staged. At the point of Andrew's entrance, Orsino and Viola are fast on their way out, and Olivia is trying to stop them, either by chasing them or imperiously holding her ground; Antonio and the Officers are still there (a real nuisance, this, but necessary); and the Priest and any other attendants (and probably Fabian) are fully engaged, expressing much with little means. As soon as Andrew saw Olivia, he surely went to her; and then Orsino's voice:

> My gentleman, Cesario?

took his eye across to his 'attacker'. And now that Toby and Feste (and perhaps Maria, hurrying out of the house in a panic) spill on, they need to take the centre of the stage. Stop the rehearsal here, and work backwards: that is, look at what you've got, decide how it could be improved, and then see how the better positions could have been achieved in the preceding few moments.

Sending Andrew on first has been Shakespeare's way of beginning the separation between him and Toby, normally never out of each other's sight, in preparation for their final moments. Andrew in his distress has become quite voluble – can hardly be shut up, indeed – and he complains at Cesario:

> Here comes Sir Toby halting – you shall hear more; but if he had not been in drink he would have tickled you othergates than he did.

He himself will stay close to Olivia for the time being. Orsino can see that Toby is some sort of 'gentleman'; and indeed Toby starts by expressing himself quite delicately, rather philosophically, aware that he has, by some drunken logic, come face to face with the Duke of Illyria:

> That's all one. H'as hurt me, and there's th' end on't.

But his gallantry doesn't last long:

> Sot, did'st see Dick Surgeon, sot?[5]

He often calls Feste 'sot', and indeed the word can mean fool as much as drunkard. According to Feste, the doctor, like Toby, is the

---

5 Dick Surgeon thus joins the Thames boatmen of Act Three, and Yaughan the Bankside barman who is to fill a stoup of liquor for the Gravedigger in *Hamlet*, in the local army of Londoners in the plays' shadows.

other kind, so there is no hope there. Nobody quite knows why his eyes are therefore 'set at eight i' th' morning' – or indeed what a 'passy measures pavin' is: the best guess at the latter is that it is a stately Italian step with a swaying motion to it, slower than a galliard, so that Toby's imagining of the intoxicated surgeon has been fed through his own predilection for the dance. The disgraceful picture allows him to follow up with an outrageous claim:

> . . . I hate a drunken rogue

– which is perhaps delivered as a manly sidelong confidence to his new friend the Duke.

Andrew, of course, is waiting for some acknowledgment of his kindness in going ahead and alerting everyone to Toby's troubles – some sentimental companionship would be enough:

> I'll help you, Sir Toby, because we'll be dressed together.

However, courtly or not, Toby is in his cups and seething – Andrew's spaniel smell exasperates him, and his mask suddenly comes off:

> Will you help? An ass-head, and a coxcomb, and a knave, a thin-faced knave, a gull?

Andrew can only gape: it is stunning. We knew it would happen one day, and so did he perhaps. Allowing the awful moment to register, Olivia bustles them off and out of the play, their story quite over.

Astonishingly, two of the three Tobys I have directed at first tried to turn these last lines of his into a description of Toby himself, as a final bitter piece of self-loathing. But they most definitely aren't – they are about Andrew. However, such mistaken convictions should be recorded, as they may say something about the working relationship between the two actors. It is almost too late for it, but here is a word to the wise. Toby, don't resent Andrew, even though he gets most of the laughs while you do the hard work – he is Stan Laurel to your Oliver Hardy, and his reactive comedy can't fail. Meanwhile you must motor your way through tough stretches of plot and congested dialogue – but you will (truly) get great credit for your generous work from an audience that senses that yours is the play's most arduous part. And another word to the wise: Andrew, tolerate your Toby. He may be older and more easily puffed-out than you, especially around the time of the duel, and overall he is putting out a lot. His beady eye may alight coldly on you from time to time, and he may drop a cold blanket on your finest inspirations, but be patient. You have to get on. *Au revoir.*

The departure of good humour leaves a vacuum, to be filled by a miracle. The narrative link between the exit of Andrew, Toby and Feste and the arrival of Sebastian is obvious enough: Sebastian has realised what he's done in physically attacking someone (Toby) who is now an in-law of sorts, and he is hastening to apologise to his wife, whom he still only knows well enough to address as 'madam'. Technically, the entrance is a little tricky, simply because it comes on top of an exit which threatens a hiatus. If Sebastian arrives hot on the heels of his victims, their choice is either to stay and marvel that they now have two pugnacious enemies; or to scatter inside, a movement which will distract from what is surely going to be a heart-stopping moment for the rest of us. Equally, the comics are not going to be specially welcome if they stay to witness the whole last movement. If Sebastian can anticipate his entrance a moment, arriving discreetly so that it is only the sound of his voice that swings our attention to him, that is one way. If Olivia's dismissal:

> Get him to bed, and let his hurt be looked to

reveals Sebastian immediately behind Andrew and Toby as they move off, that can also be exciting and stylish. What nobody can afford is dead time, so some elision has to be found between the shambolic exit and the thrilling arrival.

The skill of doing things in this order is immediately evident: Andrew and Toby have formed a bitterly funny bridge between the loveless wrangling conducted in the name of love by Olivia and Orsino, and the true miracle of family restoration. Also, part of Andrew's function has been to release a quality in Olivia – and very tentatively in Orsino – that we have not seen before: a proper aristocrat's care for the third estate. By asking Toby how he was, Orsino began to participate in events outside himself, and Olivia, though as incensed as ever by Toby, is developing some sympathy for the underdog. From now on, she will be inclined to get to the bottom of things for fairness's sake. Both these characters, in fact, are being prepared for what they must become.

For all the structural cunning, however, the arrival of Sebastian, exactly at the long scene's half-way point, may cause such a change of tone that it feels like the beginning of part two. Connected though he is to what we have just seen and heard, he is now, so to speak, both expected and a shock. His manners are graceful, and Shake-speare skilfully introduces 'the brother of my blood' in his second line as an oblique preparation for his meeting with Viola. Quite what huge offence a drunkard and a fool can have offered him that he must retaliate a second time and break their heads open is hard to guess; but it does present this tender man, here for the gentlest of reasons, in as pugnaciously manly a light as possible, like a soldier come to play a love scene. He is met with a stunned silence, of course. Mistaking this for offence, he manages to become more intimate with Olivia:

> Pardon me, sweet one, even for the vows
> We made each other but so late ago.

More staging decisions for the director – or rather another check-point that the last series of decisions was right. Sebastian doesn't appear to react to Orsino's lines (which he wouldn't understand):

> One face, one voice, one habit, and two persons –
> A natural perspective, that is and is not!

– so Orsino shouldn't be in his eyeline. Sebastian's next port of call after talking to Olivia is Antonio, whom he greets as if that were his greatest good fortune – and it his friend who guides him towards his real stroke of luck:

> An apple cleft in two is not more twin
> Than these two creatures

- so that, as Antonio and Olivia stare at Viola, Sebastian follows their gaze in the silence of the empty half-line. To see himself.

The astonishing thing that now happens to him and to his sister has thus been salted from the start by a comedy too gentle to debase it – by the fight that required his apology, by the wit of Orsino's reaction, by Antonio's blunt astonishment and by Olivia's relish at seeing two beauties instead of one. Viola characteristically remains silent, tensely balancing our pleasure. At this famous moment, touchstone of the production's sense of control, the laughter should stop dead, as if turned off by a switch, just as Sebastian's eyes meet his sister's.[6] As they step carefully into the unknown, Sebastian, fearful of some inconceivable mistake, uses his reason as a rein:

---

6   All other sounds too. I have always turned the soundtrack (birdsong, cicadas) off at this moment – you don't notice it's gone, just hear a new kind of silence.

> Do I stand there? I never had a brother;
> Nor can there be that deity in my nature
> Of here and everywhere.

Stepping-stone to stepping-stone. A little of the feeling Sebastian is holding back seeps into the singing rhythm of

> I had a sister,
> Whom the blind waves and surges have devoured

– and having matched music and metre precisely to his emotion, Shakespeare restrains him again for the sake of caution:

> Of charity, what kin are you to me?
> What countryman? What name? What parentage?

That could be Hamlet on the battlements, facing a ghost. Viola meanwhile has reached the other end of her spectrum – the opposite point from her despair when she saw her life as a blank. But she is as careful as her brother, identifying herself as if under oath, like him allowed only one small surge of emotion, on the same image:

> So went he suited to his wat'ry tomb.

Again like Hamlet, she dreads a visitant, there to fool her in Sebastian's habit as he lived:

> If spirits can assume both form and suit
> You come to fright us.

The fear is competing with a rising hope; and Sebastian accelerates the pace, picking up her incomplete line in a cluster of consonants – he is, as she says, a spirit, but one living in his own body:

> A spirit I am indeed,
> But am in that dimension grossly clad
> Which from the womb I did participate.

His puzzle is only that he seems to be addressing a younger brother; but he is beginning to suspect the truth, and he abandons his slight wordiness, letting his hope ring a little:

> Were you a woman – as the rest goes even –
> I should my tears let fall upon your cheek,
> And say, 'Thrice welcome, drowned Viola!'

Her name at last, for the first time in the play. It is a wonderful coup and its music fills the theatre; and as if it were a talisman of new good fortune, it is triumphantly repeated twice within twelve lines.

Patience on a monument, smiling at grief, Viola becomes herself at last, with time and place no longer her enemy, and our hindsight confirms her glory.

The twins' talk, gently antiphonal, dwells on details of the most domestic kind – that mole on their father's forehead they both wondered at (and prodded as they sat on his knee), the awful day of Viola's thirteenth birthday, 'lively' in both their souls, when he died too soon. The lovely piece of music ends with Sebastian repeating almost word for word Viola's phrasing, twin for twin:

> VIOLA: And died that day when Viola from her birth
>   Had numbered thirteen years.
> SEBASTIAN: O that record is lively in my soul!
>   He finished indeed his mortal act
>   That day that made my sister thirteen years.[7]

It is as if using the same words makes them more certain, but still the proof is not complete:

> VIOLA: If nothing lets to make us happy both
>   But this my masculine usurped attire,
>   Do not embrace me, till each circumstance
>   Of place, time, fortune, do cohere and jump
>   That I am Viola . . .

The only thing Sebastian doesn't know now is why she is disguised. For the first time since she was last a woman, taking her great initiative on the beach, Viola takes charge of events and lays out a plan. Everything must be explained, point by point, before they will allow emotion to wash through them; and only as she describes her great gap of time:

> I was preserved – to serve this noble count.
> All the occurrence of my fortune since
> Hath been between this lady and this lord

does she allow the outside world back into their charmed circle of two.

Sebastian, re-directed towards Olivia by Viola's line, realises what else has happened: Olivia meant to marry his sister, and his arrival has saved their skins, allowing the female and the male to curl naturally towards each other. His tone could be exuberant:

---

7 It's sometimes noticed (though not usually in performance) that Shakespeare seems to be forgetting that the two are twins as he identifies Viola's thirteenth birthday, rather than their shared birthday, as the day of their father's death. Not proven – it could just as well be a generous concentration on her alone for the immediate purpose.

> So comes it, lady, you have been mistook.
> But nature to her bias drew in that

– but if he plays it that way he will immediately have to modulate to something more sympathetic, sparing her the grotesquerie of what she has tried to do. He assures Olivia that he, the gallant headbreaker, is in fact a virgin like his sister ('a maid and man').[8] The delicately moving comment, unnecessary, manly but innocent, rests for a moment, until Orsino ventures in as sensitively as his temperament will allow. He assures Olivia, fellow-ruler, that everything is all right, since Sebastian is an aristocrat – he has now realised that this page of his, with his surprising fluency and ability to stand up for himself, must be One of Us:

> Be not amazed, right noble is his blood.[9]

Orsino also wants part of the action, and sees no reason why he shouldn't. Where the 'perspective' of the twins at first offered a divided image, it now makes sense, and he stakes his claim. He is a little bluff, trying to propose to a girl who is still a young man:

> Boy, thou hast said to me a thousand times
> Thou never shouldst love woman like to me.

Viola does the work for him, promising the most ferocious constancy, distilled by her long patience. Her style is both sweet and violent – her loyalty will be as absolute, as intolerant as the molten fire deep in the sun. Orsino still cannot quite see who she is: although he offers her his hand in marriage, she has only recovered her name so far, and her trousers and shirt, or doublet and hose, hang from

8   The subtlety whereby a small detail reinforces the impact of a bigger one is entirely typical. When Macduff loses his family in *Macbeth*, his grief for his country jostles with his own sorrow and even seems as great. Shylock combines his pain at his daughter's flight and the loss of his money likewise.

9   In Shakespeare grace and status often sound like the same thing – 'blood' meaning temperament as well as stock, 'noble' being both intrinsic and inherited. Later in his life some outraged humanity drove Shakespeare's art towards an accidental socialism, probably at odds with his own practices. While he was writing sympathetically about the Citizens' desperate need for bread in *Coriolanus*, there is evidence that he was himself storing large quantities of malt at his house in Stratford's New Place for re-sale during a time of starvation. And having declared in *Lear*:

> So distribution shall do undo excess
> And each man have enough

he seems to have ended his life on good terms with those Stratford landlords who enclosed their estates, damaging communal interests. Oh dear.

her like a tatty old costume. It turns out that she cannot even get at her 'woman's weeds', because for some completely unexplained reason Malvolio has had the Sea Captain who was looking after them arrested 'upon some action' and placed 'in durance'.

This is so vastly improbable that one can only gape. But the fact is that it is Malvolio's turn now, and to tie him into the action as effectively as Sebastian was, he is be made into some Stalinist Public Prosecutor, intimidating ordinary citizens and thereby achieving some remote connection with Viola. Olivia in any case waves his prosecution of the Captain aside, insisting in the general happiness that the latter be released, without in fact enquiring whether he has done something wrong or not. An audience is so complicit by now that it will hardly mind all this contrivance. The penalty for it is that Viola cannot recover her clothes until Malvolio has been dealt with, and perhaps not then; so the attractive option of her leaving and returning as a woman isn't really on, and Orsino will seem to have a boy on his arm for the ceremonial general exit.

Coming back to earth after the twins' reunion, you certainly feel a slide and bump. The real beauty of their duet was its emotional chastity as they tentatively sketched in their feelings, leaving spaces between the pencil lines. Catharsis at this point would be difficult to build on, whereas some restraint allows the rest of the play to happen. We should do as Viola says, and postpone her embrace with Sebastian until the very final exit; otherwise, everything ahead – the reorganising of the marriages, all the business that Feste, Malvolio and Fabian have yet to do – will have to push against a slurry of other feelings. So even this great climax, like every other critical moment in the scene, is deferred.

The difficulty is that nobody else looks very good from now on. Orsino has gauchely broken in with his talk about Sebastian's social credentials, Olivia has overriden Malvolio's actions without knowing their reason, and she even seems to have forgotten the encounter with the yellow-stockinged steward that caused her so much human concern at the time:

> And yet, alas, now I remember me,
> They say, poor gentleman, he's much distract.
> A most extracting frenzy of mine own
> From my remembrance clearly banished his.

Yes indeed. Shakespeare probably doesn't intend us to be critical – he is only struggling to tie the bits of his plot together by whatever means he can. A director can choose either to let the audience recognise that process, or imply a little scepticism about these rulers. And now Feste sets about making another cabaret turn out of Malvolio's predicament.

To ease his return to the play, Malvolio gets the build-up of a Shakespearian letter: it is the one Feste has long held onto, perhaps out of cruel relish and despite Fabian's blandishments, and which he now acts up extravagantly:

FESTE: 'By the Lord, madam – '
OLIVIA: How now, art thou mad?

For once he has misjudged his audience: a longish prologue about holding 'Beelzebub at the stave's end', several irritating quibbles and an impression of Malvolio the madman is what neither the assembled company nor an audience needs at this stage. He accordingly loses the job to Fabian.

With a few exceptions, letters are a great bore in Shakespeare, but this one is animated by our knowledge of Fabian's predicament. It is said that physiologically we read only every few words on a page, our eyes scanning rapidly backwards and forwards to assemble the rest of the picture, and this Fabian will certainly be doing now. Sentence by sentence, he doesn't know what lies ahead – he may find himself and his group nailed publicly by Malvolio's extremely coherent complaint. He is in luck: though Toby is mentioned, neither Andrew or Maria or he himself is. Nevertheless the cat is out of the bag:

I have your own letter that induced me to the semblance I put on

– and, as Orsino interjects, this is hardly a madman's style. In fact, Malvolio's tone towards Olivia is strikingly new throughout – quite accusing:

I doubt not but to do myself much right, or you much shame . . .

and defiantly dignified:

Think of me as you please.

If his demeanour when he arrives is to be like this, Fabian will have some fast talking to do.

A moment of time has to be filled while Fabian fetches Malvolio, and it is best done by re-confirming the marriage arrangements, which create an alliance between two ruling parties – Olivia presents herself to Orsino 'as well a sister as a wife', and to Viola, with whom

she has travelled so far, as a sister-in-law. It will all be celebrated by
a reception on the right scale, Olivia once again drawing attention to
her position and wealth; and Orsino, with a certain delicate wit but
at some length, repeats his proposal to Viola:

> Your master quits you; and for your service done him,
> So much against the mettle of your sex,
> So far beneath your soft and tender breeding,
> And since you called me master for so long,
> Here is my hand; you shall from this time be
> Your master's mistress.

It is accepted in silence, and Viola says no more in the play.[10]
Perhaps she is forestalled by Orsino seeing Malvolio, and must delay
her answer. How he inflects his line:

> Is this the madman?

will depend on what he sees coming. Malvolio might have been able
to get into a hurried version of his normal clothes, in which case he
will seem most unlike a lunatic, but he may still be in strait-jacket,
pyjamas or rags, perhaps with one stubborn yellow stocking rucked
round his ankle. Either way, what is striking is his dignity: not a
sense of stage consequence but real self-respect, not the false pride
of the official but the straight back of the victim of torture. The actor
in fact has to do something quite new in the part – in a sense not to
act at all but to be, presenting a simple identity that shames everyone around him. It is much the same effect as when Andrew arrived
with his head broken, another moment whose tragic pulse threatened the merry dispositions. Malvolio alone now speaks with a
'modesty of honour', the poor crumpled letter he is not to be parted
from in his hand. For the first time in the play, he is in verse, and it
immediately carries weight and conviction:

> MALVOLIO: Madam, you have done me wrong,
>   Notorious wrong.
> OLIVIA: Have I, Malvolio? No.
> MALVOLIO: Lady, you have. Pray you, peruse that letter.
>   You must not now deny it is your hand . . .

---

10   This silence has been commented on by critics; but really Viola has fulfilled herself now,
and I don't see much significant about it. It is certainly not like Shakespeare's other great
silent betrothal, that of Isabella to the Duke in *Measure for Measure* – now that truly is
ambiguous, and perhaps a chilling example of the male in control; as is its verbose version –
Katharine's ambiguous Hymn to Him at the end of *The Taming of the Shrew*.

Try it energetic and angry: it will be petulant and diminishing, and you won't like it. With the right measure of calm, the speech becomes a reproach – of us, too, for laughing at Malvolio's bedraggled glory. He comes straight to the point in front of everyone, and spares himself nothing. Given his fundamental mistake, his account of his wrongs is absolutely precise, as of someone who has gone over and over the matter – even if it creates a furtive remembered pleasure for us. There is nothing of the old man left – even the touch of superiority on

> . . . Sir Toby and the lighter people

is pretty much a quotation from the letter. His tone is convinced and justified. Why, in a single sentence of ten lines and a concluding phrase, did Olivia lead him on, giving him

> such clear lights of favour

– why did she ask him to

> come smiling and cross-gartered to you,
> To put on yellow stockings . . .

– why, in fact, did she lose control of her business so far as to allow Toby to lock him up and torment him with Sir Topas, so that he became

> . . . the most notorious geck and gull
> That e'er invention played on.[11]

Three times he asks her, why?

This elevation of a great comic construction into the lucid dignity of iambic pentameters is something of a masterstroke. Some on the stage will look at the floor, some of the audience smile without laughter. But the fact is that Olivia has done him no wrong – though she is guilty to a degree of bad governance, and she did forget about him when he was most vulnerable. At least her verse falls in sympathetically with his as she gently breaks his mistake to him. For some reason she immediately recognises Maria's handwriting as Malvolio didn't, and the thing is exposed in a flash: like a hanged man Malvolio falls through the trap. He is not only betrayed, but an even greater geck and gull than he feared. She builds up his case for him,

---

11 This great word 'geck' is a piece of dialect straight from Shakespeare's home county of Warwickshire, where it still exists.

finishing with the intimidating language of the law – he has been practised on, and

> when we know the grounds and authors of it

– which she more or less already does – he will be both plaintiff and judge. It is a quite improper offer, long after the horse has bolted: she is washing her hands of the whole business, and the prospect of Malvolio sitting on his own case and meting out punishment is daunting, since he has always had the accused in his sights. So Olivia's arbitration leaves something to be desired: she is not yet the ruler she may become.

And none of the original plotters are there to explain themselves to the kangaroo court. Fabian intervenes, a courageous servant taking Olivia and Malvolio on by, quite inaccurately, assuming the blame and exonerating Maria. His speech is a fine exercise in damage limitation. He has the good sense at the start to emphasise the general happiness of 'the present hour', which he, the merest onlooker, has so enjoyed, and which, with luck, will lead to a general atmosphere of tolerance. The blameless Maria only wrote the counterfeit letter 'at Sir Toby's great importance'; and Andrew of course is not significant enough to mention. The whole thing was merely a reproach to Malvolio for his

> stubborn and uncourteous parts

(which is putting it mildly); and in any case, they could all have been wrong even about them – these characteristics were merely things

> We had *conceived* against him.

The surprising news is that Toby was so delighted with Maria's draftsmanship that, in pure excess of pleasure, he has married her – which only proves how good-humoured the whole thing has been. Listening, we realise that this hasty action must have been performed by the busy Priest after hitching up Sebastian and Olivia, and it has a further meaning: the marriage will put a wall of sorts around the couple, who may now amount to more than the sum of their parts in the household.

Fabian respectfully rests his case. His whole account, in its essence true but completely mendacious in detail, 'plucks on' not just 'laughter' and 'revenge', but a sort of aghast sympathy, particularly in Olivia. She has to decide whether the malice was sportful or the sport malicious. As far as the

> injuries . . .
> That have on both sides passed

go, Fabian and the others have had the sport and Malvolio been driven half crazy. Her response is indecisive:

> Alas, poor fool, how have they baffled thee.

The word 'fool' no doubt means victim here, or could be the affectionate term with which Lear describes Cordelia (probably) at the moment before his death. But Feste hears it and steps in. He stands for the opposite of Fabian's diplomatic instincts, and will have more revenge still. He quotes back at Malvolio the part of the letter (which in fact he has never seen) that has most inflamed its victim:

> Some are born great, some achieve greatness, and some have greatness thrown upon them

and then humiliates him further – he who thought he had finally reached the bottom – with the news that he himself was Topas. None of it would have happened, he would have Malvolio know, had he not been put down as 'a barren rascal' in front of Olivia. Bitter and brilliant, Feste crowns this with his finest aphorism:

> the whirligig of time brings in his revenges

and Malvolio's cup finally empties. Where can he go, whom can he look at, what can he even begin to say? Everyone watches, even those who studiedly didn't before. He has caught the comprehensive range of his unpopularity in a flash. Humiliated before the people he doesn't know (Orsino, Antonio and Sebastian), he is hated, it seems, by everyone else. This might make him quite clear and quick-witted, so that his answer comes at speed; or he might need a moment to absorb it all. Whenever it happens, the exit he is given almost audibly breaks the fabric of the play, as does Shylock's from *The Merchant of Venice*: he will be back, in some way, in person or as a just punishment, to revisit a company that now resembles a clutch of snapping dogs. It's a verse line – just – but very syncopated, with an untypical directness in the elision of 'I will':[12]

---

12   Neither Malvolio nor Feste has been given the chance to react to the fact there are now two Cesarios on the stage. Feste could just about absorb the sight without comment: it would be a bold production indeed that gave Malvolio a moment to see, perhaps at the very end, that the codling Cesario has multiplied. It is so against theatrical expectation that it might be worth trying.

I'll be revenged on the whole pack of you.

He goes, darkness closing like a tide behind him. I think there is a pause: nobody quite knows what to do. Olivia is in charge, but a bit lost, her inexperience still showing – she can only protest, borrowing one of Malvolio's adjectives:

He hath been most notoriously abused

– but nothing follows. Orsino comes to at last, showing some of the instinctive class of the prince to strengthen her – it is not strictly his business, but obviously something must be fixed:

Pursue him, and entreat him to a peace.

The red herring about the Sea Captain may serve at least to get both sides talking, restoring a degree of formality to the ashamed steward. Fabian, who gets all the rotten jobs, is dispatched to make this difficult overture. We may feel that Malvolio is not open to negotiation, but Orsino is sure it will all be fine. The time is 'golden', and he himself will not leave till the two marriages are celebrated, and all disharmonies dissolved.

The one who is forgotten is Antonio, still under arrest, still short of his purse, watching his beloved Sebastian reunited with his sister and well married. John Philip Kemble (Drury Lane, 1815) wrote some extra lines for Orsino here, and I must say I favour most of them, if not the sentimental conclusion:

Go, officers,
We do discharge you of your prisoner.
Antonio, thou hast well deserv'd our thanks;
Thy kind protection of Cesario's person
Although thou knew'st not then for whom thou fought'st,
Merits our favour; henceforth, be forgotten
All cause of anger: thou hast a noble spirit,
And, as Sebastian's friend, be ever near him.

These marriages certainly have something perfunctory about them, as if the fantastic contortions of the plot had made the characters into puppets. Olivia is perfectly happy with the exchange of Cesario for Sebastian, even though, for all she knows, the brother may have none of the attractive inner qualities of the disguised Viola; and Orsino is released from obsession as completely as if Viola had waved a wand over him. He gets the formal final word, greeting his 'fancy's queen' – a phrase he might just as well have used of Olivia –

but Viola remains silent, she who would have died for him. Perhaps romance has been seriously compromised by the demands of comedy: the fulfilment of marriage seems shallower here than the friendships it brings, let alone the bonds of blood. Orsino and Olivia will certainly be better as relatives, as Orsino seems to acknowledge, their obsessiveness more harmless that way than in the lists of love. Their new union is a lighter version of what we recognise now as the one uncompromised desire running through the play, for the reunion of Viola and Sebastian. That has really been the point.

The comics have been noticeably swept away behind the door, like the dust that Puck disperses with his broom in the *Dream*, though it is tempting to incorporate them in some way in the finale. Which leaves the troublesome vapour of Malvolio. If the play could be said to hold any final meaning, it would lie somewhere between him and the twins – between relationship and isolation, between the natural responses of blood and the barren imaginings of the solitary. Love was distorted in Malvolio's hands – though no more so than in Olivia's and Orsino's – and achingly natural between Viola and Sebastian. As if words would only weaken the force of their final embrace, the form is entirely broken and the play ended with a song, sung by the play's other solitary, binding audience and actors together.

Most unusually. The King of France bids a brief farewell to the public at the end of *All's Well* ;[13] Puck hardly steps out of the play as he blesses the newly-wed house; Rosalind, inciting the men and the women by different means to applaud at the conclusion of *As You Like It*, exploits the theatrical ambiguities of being a boy playing a woman who has also played a boy. But none of them do it with music. However, since *Twelfth Night* declared its business with its very first line, and has been punctuated throughout with songs, a musician now re-codes the play. He will summarise not the story but the nature of the underlying ritual – as always suggesting something about who he is but still not explaining. What he gives us is most odd and melancholy, made pretty by pleasant repetitions. His song counterpoints the play's spontaneity – the sense in which these events could only happen once, perhaps at a Feast of Fools – with one of life's endless certainties, continual rainfall. As a man's life runs through, in four ages, the one thing you know is that the wind

---

13   With a reminiscent line: the actors will 'pay'

   With strife to please you, day exceeding day.

will blow and every day the rain will fall – not all the time, but at some time, sooner or later, every day. When Feste was a boy

> A foolish thing was but a toy

– his silly actions were dismissed as just silly, because he was a child – and the rain came down. When he was a man, such foolishness was seen as a kind of wickedness for which the gate could be shut against him – and the rain kept coming down. When he married

> By swaggering could I never thrive

– but however modest his behaviour, the rain continued. When he grew old, he fell down drunk, and it still rained.[14] And speaking of age, it rained at the beginning of time – but what can anyone say about that? The thought stops, hanging oddly over a play with little sense of the past. Perhaps there is silence. The idea is tossed away, as if too difficult, and today's audience is simply asked to come back tomorrow.

Robert Armin, the company's new comic, may have written this song for himself – it is very much like one of his Fool's songs in *Lear* later – but Shakespeare certainly accepts it as part of his design. A quietist message from a professional joker, it gently restores the audience to itself, its overall gesture perhaps the 'What You Will' of the play's subtitle. It also repeats a small persistent phrase: to the drunken Toby in Olivia's first scene it was 'all one' who was at the gate, as it was to him when his head was broken at the end; to Feste too, confronting Malvolio, the fact that he played Sir Topas was 'all one'; and now the all-one-ness summarises the entire experience of the evening:

> But that's all one, our play is done,
> And we'll strive to please you every day.

In other words, forget but don't forget. We fail in our job if we don't show our audience the door; we also fail if they really do forget us once they're outside. In this meeting in no-man's land, rather like the vaudevillian's downstage patch where he can confide in the audience, the man we called Feste stands between the play and the street, a ghost from the story who is not quite one of us either. There

---

14   This fourth verse is a fearsomely difficult bit of text, best absorbed in the music; I've read yards of commentary, all equally desperate. Something's got 'corrupted', as if a transcriber (as can happen with song lyrics) is trying to reproduce something on the page that he has only half-caught from the song's performance.

are many ways of presenting the song (the only thing it mustn't be is sentimental): the cast can be reintroduced, and even the casualties – Andrew, on his way back to his country estate, and Malvolio – join in; or the singer can be left mediating between us and their shadows in typical solitude. And at last we notice that Feste is no longer Feste: he has gone through the stages of a man's life in his song, from the cradle to the grave, and then looked back to the creation of the world. The darkness gathers. Who is this man we are watching? As he looks back at us, William Shakespeare's shoulders shrug. Hey, ho. It is as you like it, all one, and what you will. The rain keeps coming down, but the theatre, with your blessing – and as long as the world's Malvolios can be kept in check – may somehow keep going.

CONCLUSION
Chicago Shakespeare Theater, 1995

CONCLUSION

Chicago Shakespeare Theater, 1995

TO NAN ZABRISKIE AND DONALD EASTMAN
DESIGN OFFICE
CHICAGO SHAKESPEARE THEATER
CHICAGO
ILLINOIS
September 1995

Dear Nan and Donald

I want to look at *Twelfth Night* from an American point of view if I can. I should explain that I've done the play twice before, in different countries, so I'm arriving with some luggage – things which always work for me. But we have midwestern actors this time, and we need to use their imaginations, not some assimilated idea of old England. I hate seeing Americans trying to be like the RSC – what for? So this will be a mixture of what I know and what I'm guessing at.

The central structure of the play is Olivia's household – sometimes it looks as crazy as an M.C. Escher, but when the weather runs high we cling to it like Sebastian to the ship's mast. Her house is sustained by many people and sustains them in return – everyone knows their place exactly, even as they risk it or try to improve it. In American terms, it's more Edith Wharton than Scott Fitzgerald – this is old money, relaxed privilege and leisure, no taint yet of the parvenu. So could this be Long Island, on a great estate calmly surveying what the Atlantic breakers throw at its feet? I did think of the South, but then you get implications that are a bit hefty for the play. But imagine Boston Brahmins, or New York in the twenties, and the underclass could be Irish immigrant – and Feste's music Celtic rather than blues-based. I'm looking at Ron Keaton for the part, a really good singer (in fact he looks a bit like Van Morrison) – he's nervous as hell of doing Shakespeare but I think he'll be fine. I can see him with a gipsy band – fiddle and guitar, plus hand-drum and bass. We've got Rokko Jans to do the songs – he does David Mamet's film scores, so that's really good. Andrew Aguecheek is the rich outsider – maybe a Plantation Dandy up from Virginia, looking for a Yankee bride. The other strangers are Viola and Sebastian and Antonio: the twins could even be Canadian, shipwrecked on their way south – but only if they can get comfy with the accent. Antonio a Mexican? No, too smartassed.

You know the stage at the Ruth Page of course – I must say the sooner Chicago Shakespeare get out of rented accommodation into their own theatre the better. It looks rather difficult to me, like a long tongue stuck out at the audience with that little toy proscenium (like an Elizabethan inner stage, but not enough so) behind it. Also there's a rake to the stage, which has no virtue when the audience is on three sides – it suggests the customers in front matter more, which spoils the point of having them all around. Donald, I know you've used different levels on your sets there before, very ingeniously, but I'd rather not – for me it's too small a space, and a lot of architecture will crick too many necks. Maybe the floor could be tiles, breaking into a rough driftwood feel downstage – you should never forget the sea in this play. Nan: soft-soled shoes for everyone, please!

As far as exteriors are concerned, here are some things I don't like: pretend leaves and pretend trees and pretend grass. To suggest the garden all we need is a facade that looks both ways – maybe some ironwork with a little doorway set into it. Lit from the front, it'll be the outdoor wall of Olivia's house; but backlit, we're inside the house looking out at bright weather. Orsino's palace and the seaside need to be found some other way, mostly with light. Orsino's world all cushions, probably, very closed in but very opulent.

More soon.

★

LONDON
October 1995

Home from tonight's show, open a bottle, and do some auditions by videotape. That's the way we're having to cast, and looking at this heap of Fedexed packages, I wonder if I've made a mistake. I can't get to Chicago to do auditions as I'm playing in Ronald Harwood's *Taking Sides* every night in London – have been doing so since the day this summer when Barbara Gaines's invitation to do *Twelfth Night* arrived. Barbara is the founder and director of Chicago Shakespeare, and her phone calls wouldn't take no for an answer: I was impressed, even though I'd never heard of a director choosing his cast electronically. But she is invincible, and something about her reminds me of Bogdanov and myself at the ESC.

Her company, like many good ideas, shouldn't strictly have happened. Having been working as an actress in New York and Chicago, she sustained a serious knee injury, and during a long period of recovery began to call in some old college friends for Shakespeare workshops, and finally to see if there was good reason to form a new group in this, one of America's busiest theatre cities.[1] Chicago Shakespeare's first show was *Henry V* , and, ten years later, they have clearly done a remarkable job. They have covered nearly half the canon – not just *Lear*, *Much Ado* and *Othello*, but the rarities, *King John*, *Troilus*, *Cymbeline* – playing to midwestern theatregoers who had previously to go for Shakespeare to the Guthrie at Minneapolis or to wait for the occasional revival at the Goodman Theatre downtown. Come to that, it's hard to find some of these plays in England either. All this out of a rented, odoriferous and electrically unsafe ballet theatre, the 300-seat Ruth Page on Dearborn and Clark, near the John Hancock Building on Chicago's Gold Coast. Barbara directs most of the shows, with one annual import like me for contrast. They have a very strong subscription base and are invariably sold out, so everyone is happy, and new sponsors, wooed by a strong Board, seem to be queuing up – in Chicago, business will still chase a good arts idea. The dream is one

---

1   It's typical enough – in Chicago college graduates often stay together, raise money and do it themselves, unlike their English counterparts, who are inclined to leave such enterprising ideas in their empty beer glasses. Although the scene seems to be dominated by the legendary Steppenwolf – to which loyal alumni such as John Malkovich and John Mahoney return regularly like golden-winged homing pigeons – about ninety companies are at work in Chicago any given night, mostly small, many very good.

day to build a two-auditorium custom-built home for the company downtown:[2] meanwhile I have the comfort of being sponsored by the Sara Lee Foundation (yes, the cake and pastry people), and of a great practical advantage: although this is a repertoire theatre, the company do not rehearse a new show until the previous one has closed, at which point the theatre is shut up so that the skeleton at least of the new set can be on the stage throughout the rehearsal period. Luxury indeed.

Back in London, *Taking Sides* could clearly run on beyond its planned six months, and my commitment to Chicago will bring it to a halt, which embarrasses and displeases me. I am attached to the show and correspondingly dyspeptic about *Twelfth Night*, which is not at all fair on Barbara and her people. But I don't want to touch the play for a third time without a team I really like, and it's hard to get the measure of what's available – will we be able to call on the best actors? The company pays them well over Equity requirements, but how wide does their net spread? Are they as good as Stratford Ontario? I know Barbara allows herself a star from New York from time to time, but is this an admission of defeat for a Chicago ensemble? At the moment the videotapes are offering only one Toby Belch and two Malvolios to choose from: I sit down with the remote control, half-hoping for the worst.

★

TO NAN ZABRISKIE
COSTUME DESIGNER
CHICAGO SHAKESPEARE THEATER
October 1995

Dear Nan

Yes, Olivia's mourning lace should be very fine, the finest Irish lace we can afford: go to Borovicks in Berwick Street while you're over here. As you know, the National and RSC Hire won't help you much

2   Throughout this account I am using the Company's new name – Chicago Shakespeare Theater – though it was only assumed when their ideal was realised in 1999, and they opened with *Antony and Cleopatra* in their new premises on Navy Pier, surrounded by Lake Michigan. Thirty million dollars had been raised and the theatre built in two years, and it opened on time. It was a triumph for Gaines, for her company (especially her Executive Producer Criss Henderson) and the city of Chicago – and food for thought.

except with the the poor characters – most of their grand stuff has done a season or two and won't look too good. We'll have to make as much as we possibly can, rather than hire. For Olivia in the second act, I like very much your silk chiffon and pleated satin, and your book on the Gibson Girls is an inspiration, I must say. After all, Gibson didn't so much reflect a real world as invent a lovelier one, so that a whole generation rushed to join the soirée, aspiring to something that only existed in Life Magazine. Something about that is like Olivia. We'll give her that lovely soft mussiness in the hair. The ideal American girl! Now I just have to find the right tall actress with a straight nose and a square jaw.

Malvolio should wear a morning suit with starched dicky and carry a hat. Moustache-trainers might well work with his nightshirt in such a small theatre. I think a hairnet might be a good idea too – he wants to *subdue* his hair! Fabian I think should be a footman – stockings and breeches and waistcoat. Yes, plus-fours for Toby (and a pocket for his brandy flask at all times) – a cavalry outfit for the Duel. Andrew is tricky – but I like your co-respondent shoes (or maybe spats?) and pink waistcoat. How about an ivory-topped walking-stick? Andrew's and Toby's drunk scene could feel like a clambake – sou'wester for Toby, Andrew's trousers rolled up and a barrel of shells. For Orsino's functionaries – well, it's only Valentine – I like the wing collar and brown suit. Likewise Maria in bustle and bib and apron. All of Olivia's household should have black mourning armbands in the first half, even Toby – it's the rule. Both Maria and the Waiting Gentlewoman should have light black veils like Olivia – they'll all wear them when Cesario arrives and can't tell which is which – they'll look like three sibyls. Orsino needs a sort of naval dress uniform at the end, having been slobbing around for the rest of the play. Feste can be put together anyways – whatever Ron and you pick up – he is to himself alone, a self-assembled man. Antonio, too, is a bit of this, a bit of that, as long as he doesn't become a riot of scarves and berets and gloves and purses. Viola as Cesario and Sebastian – well, it's a practical problem that Shake-speare doesn't help at all with: just make them look attractive. Let's say they were at supper just before the ship went down, in nice waistcoats and flannel pants (check Viola's from behind though – if she looks too female congratulate her and give her a jacket).

★

TO: DONALD EASTMAN
SET DESIGNER
NEW YORK
October 1995

Dear Donald

A blue court chair with clouds on its cushion, a yellow ballet shoe sitting alone in the sand-dunes – I like your images very much, even if we end up using just the dunes: you've caught the feel of the play. These mauve Cape Cod seascapes too, unnaturally calm on either side of a storm, beautiful and ominous. I like the Hamptons house as well – very rough knotted wood panels, the clapboarding incredibly fragile, like bark – blue wisteria outside, heavy draperies and Corinthian columns in the drawing room, louvred shutters – we should definitely use the shutters, they're a much better texture than my metalwork. If they're small enough, there could be countless little shutter flaps for Olivia's house – we could organise them as we fancy each night to let needles of sunshine in. Think how these different surfaces will take the light! Olivia's world is intricate, but Orsino's is on a flatter plane – his panels could be mirrored to reflect himself, and you don't know if it's day or night. I'm only telling you what you've already done! I'd still like the proscenium facade softer, less assertive – we're looking at it all evening. Many thanks – go on sending me whatever comes to you: this is great dreaming-time.

*

LONDON
November 1995

'Hi Michael, this is my body'.

One by one, I glare at them, fingers twitching over the fast-forward button. They come brightly onto camera, turn north, south, east and west, and do their stuff. At least they endure it: American actors take the humiliation of taped auditions as a matter of course, and you might not get the English to do the same. They sell themselves pretty hard, hitting the play's emotions flat on the nose because there's no director there: it's all OK but not outstanding. No prickly sense of professional status, at least: most are as ready to accept the Sea Captain as Malvolio just to keep working, but on the other hand there are quite a lot of Sea Captains. Suddenly, Sarajane Avidon pops her head round the edge of an empty frame and whispers urgently: '*Michael Pennington*! *Sure* wish you were *here*!' Mischief, frustration and eagerness all in a phrase, and she hasn't opened the script yet. Ample and fiftyish, Sarajane is the right Maria for Howard Witt, who seems inevitable as Sir Toby as he's the only one being proposed. He's certainly strong, gruff and jolly, but I can't tell if there's bitterness in there as well, as there is in most middle-aged actors if they'll own up to it. I could ask for another tape of him to find out, but we've already gone through that with Malvolio. Having stipulated that the steward be not a comic turn but a man haunted by love, I got a tape of Greg Vinkler, seemingly playing Angelo or Macbeth with Malvolio's lines. Casting had insisted he's the funniest actor in Chicago: looking now at his second, lighter version I realise that indeed he may be. As well as Keaton, stumpy and unsentimental, for Feste, I settle on Vinkler, Witt and Avidon; on Lisa Dodson, who has beauty and poise, rather in the English manner, for Olivia; and on Henry Godinez, who suggests the Hispanic frenzy of Orsino. Frank Farrell, with a permanent air of low-level anxiety and more than a passing resemblance to the Scarecow in *The Wizard of Oz*, walks away with Aguecheek, much as Kato did in Japan. I realise with a shock that satellite selection could work, the only problem being the dog in his London manger. The remote control dangles lifelessly.

A bigger worry is my work permit: there's no sign of it. We're approaching the last week of *Taking Sides*, and I'm supposed to rehearse in Chicago on the following Monday. If the papers don't arrive, my colleagues here will be out of work for nothing, and I wildly imagine myself lying low in London for six weeks, and then boasting about how well things went in Chicago. Except that my own life has gone pear-shaped and I haven't got a home to hide in anyway, so I have to go somewhere. The only dark logic to finishing the play is that Dan Massey has been off for a week with shingles and we can't imagine him coming back soon. He has been battling with cancer for ages: watching him build his triumphant perform- ance as Wilhelm Furtwängler against his illness has been inspiring, and shingles at this stage is like some *buffo* curtain being dropped on his head. But I suppose it means we've finished the job: the understudy will play out time, and I do have to go. If immigration agrees. And if they do, I don't want to meet an eager American company with any kind of bad grace: I must give myself a talking-to.

CHICAGO
15 December 1995

A Feast of Fools perhaps, and me the biggest. Everybody but the cleaners has turned out for my opening discourse, for which I'm barely ready. So I flash a hand rather than show it – instead of the iamb and the feminine ending hot from the Stratford foundry, they're getting *The House of Mirth* and *The Age of Innocence*. Not that Shakespeare, with his at least seven veils, ever ventured the explicit social criticism of Edith Wharton, but still it is there, like a small bug in the machine. And certainly some of the exchanges between Lily Bart and Seldon in the first novel and Archer and Ellen in the second flicker as brightly as those of Olivia and Cesario. However, that's enough American literature: there's bound to be an expert somewhere in the room. I ply a disingenuous tentativeness, promising to test these no doubt naive ideas.

As I introduce everyone (some know each other hardly better than I do), special tribute must be paid to the two musician-actors, Jay Voss (hammer dulcimer and various guitars) and L.J. Slavin (fiddle, flute, mandolin and saw), who, hooked out of the blue Chicago night into the hail-fellow-well-met world of theatre, need the welcome most. These introductions are an elementary courtesy,[3] if tinged with showmanship: however, I know my limits and didn't try it in Japan. Don Eastman rises to present the model of his set, sitting eagerly beside me like the shaggy dog which, as a night-reveller, he does resemble: I mention his enthusiasm because Don was the collaborator I was least sure of. Breezily self-confident on the phone (after propounding an idea, he would invariably apostrophise 'Nice, huh?'), he always gave me the impression of having too much work on. In fact he is full of talent, has exquisite taste and is painfully sensitive: his main worry at the moment is that I might be upset that his design asks me to forgo an upstage entrance for the actors. Mine meanwhile is that he still feels Malvolio's Letter Scene should happen not in the garden but in the ballroom; and also that the erected set looks to have been built too cheaply – plywood panels are unlikely to slide smoothly.

The triumph of videotape: we read the play and it is well cast. As an actor, I am almost infuriated that it could have been done this

3   A surprising number of directors ask their new companies to introduce themselves, which is agonising and creates a suspicion that they have forgotten their own casting.

way: but for a director it is a great relief. Each new character, from Orsino to the Officers, sings out like a bell, and I feel something stirring in me at last. On the other hand, it is a bad hair day. After much deliberation I have chosen a new actress called Elyse Myrto for Viola, against contenders who were more established but whose approach seemed a bit technical. Elyse had great freshness and an uncanny resemblance to Chris Gerson, the most likely Sebastian, and what she lacked in experience would surely be balanced by Lisa Dodson's as Olivia.[4] However, there has been some rumbling. Elyse's agent has Californian dreams for her, and he has forbidden her to cut her hair to Cesario's length until the dress rehearsal, feeling she might need it until then. Need it for what, I asked, glimpsing a red rag? Why, for commercials, the agent has said. But I'm not about to release her from rehearsals – this, after all, is Viola. Well, we're talking Hollywood, and in that case the agent (not the chivalrous English type that lets the client decide), will pull her from the show. Nice knowing you, we say.

In the end Elyse, who really wants to do the part, has defied this Rasputin (which shows a deal of balls at her age, in that place), but today it transpires that she does visualise Viola sporting her own current strawberry rinse. For one thing, this is asking a lot of Chris Gerson, who is meeting her, as Sebastians do, at least half-way. Mmm. Meanwhile in another corner of the room, Howard Witt (Toby) is declining to shave his all-purpose Shakespearian beard to achieve the much more specific period look Nan and I want – big sideburns meeting the moustache above a clean-shaven chin. Being of the same trade, I can interpret that this senior-actor gesture may have little to do with beards, and manage to fix him with a mixture of flattery and intimidation, sadly ruminating on the consequences of our not agreeing the point. Observing this, Elyse agrees to a more natural hue. There are many appreciative *moues* at all this muscle-flexing, which has given me no pleasure at all: I retreat for an early night.

For a week before Christmas we all slither to work across parking lots smooth with packed ice in bright sun that doesn't prevent your face peeling off: the actors variously, I from the nearby comfort of the Delaware Tower Apartments, Chicago Shakespeare's staff along the doubly dangerous route from their offices at Cabrini Green, at

---

4   It was the opposite with the ESC: how many ways can this play's glove stretch?

that time one of the most desperate inner-city precincts in America. Walking in and out of a stifling blanket of heat at the Ruth Page, which manages to smell simultaneously of mice and doughnuts, I wish I had that great gift of the experienced director – getting away cleanly. At either end of the day there will always be somebody wanting a bit extra, out of surgery hours: the brilliant Rokko with a new musical segue, Howard with a character thought, Chuck Constant (the Priest) raising a point that's interested him in my book about the ESC. I am dismayed to find that, at this nervy early stage, Chuck seems to be the only actor with physical grace on the stage. This is what the videos didn't show, and an elegant Priest doesn't quite cover the play's needs. Looking at several varieties of ungainliness, I wonder how much of the play we could do sitting down. For their part, I think the cast are disappointed by the read-and-block approach – it is certainly conventional (and the exact opposite of how we went to work in Tokyo): but here we have three weeks only of rehearsal, followed by a whole week of technicals, followed by two weeks of previews, so we need some architecture early. The room is rather full of specialists, eager to be unpopular in a good cause. Christine Adaire (Vocal Coach) keeps an ear on Frank Farrell's Southern accent as Aguecheek, hearing tin sounds that I can't, touches in Myrto's and Gerson's Canadian, and tries to move Ron Keaton from first- to second-generation Irish immigrant. Like Chuck, Kate Buckley (Verse Coach – subtle distinction) is an Anglophile, a terrier murderously pouncing on missed beats and neglected end-stops as if they were black rats. These people are very good, but you can have too many experts, and everyone is rather nervous.

Myself, I feel both over-prepared and unfamiliar, as if I had once known a lot about this play but had forgotten it. Everyone looks at me, all the time. Greg Vinkler tensely: he is weathering a crisis of the heart, and Malvolio is very important to him. Like Nakano in Tokyo, he is a favourite (eleven shows for Chicago Shakespeare and director of his own company in Wisconsin); but he seems to underestimate his own talent, tending to lean on things that have worked for him before. In the Letter Scene he is already out hunting for comic business – as if the impending yellow stockings and cross-garters were not enough. When, like a hateful headmaster, I call him to order for some excruciating invention, he has an endearing way of slapping his own wrist in rebuke, as if he had fallen prey to a secret vice.[5] We agree to concentrate on inventions that are Funny (characterful), not just Funnyish (gags) – the distinction becomes a company mantra. Meanwhile a picnic basket will bedevil him with a host of small tasks – a cheese-knife to be cleaned, a sandwich to be carefully unwrapped, a bottle of Chardonnay to be opened without splashing his suit, napkin, banana (ah, blessed banana): he becomes so busy timing the lines to the complicated business that he acts unselfconsciously and lovely things come through. He even dusts the bench with a handkerchief before he sits on it, and proposes the hint of a Jewish accent to suggest Malvolio's immigrant origins – it's a good idea.

Some of Greg's anxiety I certainly understand, since Don's set doesn't work at all for this scene: having persuaded him that we should be outdoors, in line with the text, I haven't found the resolve to argue that everything is in the wrong relationship. Sometimes, over the years, I've thought that where Andrew, Toby and Fabian hide doesn't matter, sometimes that it does. The only reasonable places for them here are in narrow crannies – room for one person only – a long way upstage of where Malvolio will conduct his monologue, so that they will have to shout across him to each other as well as beyond him to the audience. With the best will in the world, all this is hard for Malvolio to ignore. Does it matter? We grind to a halt, procrastinating.

In fact, the leads all start out struggling – Vinkler with his comedy demons, Godinez with Orsino's sexuality, Farrell (Aguecheek) with the great burden of being foolish, Keaton (Feste) with the archaic language, and Witt (Toby) with his congested text – all of them straining to entertain before they know who they are. How could it be otherwise? Rehearsing throughout on the set, on the stage, might seem to be a blessing: but there is a strong argument for staying in an unsexy rehearsal room, stepping through imaginary door-frames and observing the masking tape on the floor, until the actors have really convinced themselves. A stage is always a hot spot, even at ten o'clock in the morning; and being on it too soon can be to re-live the performer's oldest nightmare (we all have it before an opening): being in front of an audience not only having neglected to learn the

5 Later, having entirely conquered this scene, he will decide to trip over a step on his exit: it's terrible, but then I reflect that Beerbohm Tree did the same thing on his first entrance. I am truly sorry to say that once I had returned to England, Greg broke his ankle in the process of furtively reinstating one of his gags.

lines, but having forgotten to put any clothes on either. No wonder the principals are stumbling about like new-born calves. I wish I didn't have to push them so hard.

On the other hand, the play's satellites shine with instant brightness – Adrianne Cury as the Waiting Gentlewoman, who, because she must have a name, I am calling Molly; Chuck Constant's cherubic Priest, his nose now in John Barton's *Playing Shakespeare* between his entrances; and Jack Sanderson, a round actor who can't help being funny – which makes him great as the Waiter in Antonio's and Sebastian's café scene (measly tip), but more of a liability as the honest Sea Captain. Jack refers to me as 'the Wicked Weaver', but I don't see much warp and woof yet – except, as usual, in the music. We spend a long night recording Rokko's wonderful new settings (eventually issued as a CD) at the WFMT Radio Station. Jay Voss is gently learned, a bit like Stefan Grossman, equally at home in jazz, blues, country and bluegrass: you might imagine him making defiantly unprofitable albums on the history of folk music, but in fact the piratical-looking L.J. Slavin is the studious one – he has spent large parts of his life documenting old-time musicians in the Appalachian backwoods, and does a very successful schools programme on the early settlers' music. (Towards dawn, I wildly promise to get his home-produced album, *Zilldog Dance*, distributed in England, a task well beyond my powers.) Their enthusiasm throughout – many times coming in to watch rehearsals when they weren't needed (but also, being musicians, sometimes not being around when they were) – was to make me rejoice. We come out with an infectious jig on the penny whistle for Malvolio's and Viola's ring chase, an almost unplayably slow waltz for 'Mistress Mine' – and a determination that the interval jam session will feature the Priest on concertina, Valentine rendering a chorus like Howard Keel, and finally L.J's hilarious musical saw.

One inessential – I'd like to call it a grace-note – before the holiday. When Toby disrupts Olivia's measured deliberations with 'a plague o' these pickled herrings', he may be living up to his name, but this burping drunk is old business, and it bores me. Could not the emission be top-down rather than bottom-up? I look at my company of serious American actors devoutly regarding the English Shakespearian: they begin to gape. On request, a few shy raspberries bravely simulate the unique sound. Toby can do an accompanying pelvic shift but, since he has to speak, not the noise – which ought to come from behind some discreet and unobserved hand. Who will get the job? Kurt Naebig, who thought he'd joined to play Fabian, leads the field. Happy Christmas, everyone.

★

A thoughtful holiday, in minus twenty degrees of windchill and still bright sunshine: Lake Michigan is frozen to maybe forty metres out but a light sandy beach blows up drily at its edge, and as you come out of the skyscrapers' shadows you must shade your eyes. Surrounded by gifts and Christmas decorations from these most generous people, I am frankly homesick – if you can be, without, for the time being, having a home. I have the impression that for them the plight of the visitor in his rented apartment, rather than the play, has been the leading Green Room subject, while I have been thinking my uncharitable thoughts. The Body Shop's Christmas incense billows through the apartment, and the tree groans with things not only for me but for my son Mark – who, condemned to travel the world with his father's *Twelfth Night*s, has arrived for the holiday with his girlfriend Caroline.

While they go to midnight mass in Holy Name Cathedral, I force myself to switch off *It's A Wonderful World* and at last think positively about the play, to which we will return almost as soon as the bells stop ringing. The nuclear structure of *Twelfth Night* is like a daisy-chain, ghosted by an alternative one. Each character is circumstantially linked to another, but has, did they but know it, a deeper need for someone else. At the opening, Orsino is like a limpet on Olivia: but he is immediately followed onto the stage by Viola, who, setting out for his court, implies another possibility for him. By her position, Olivia is enmeshed in formal relationships, but her wild attachment to Cesario runs a tripwire for her entire household. Apparently secure, Toby is in urgent need of Andrew and Maria. Viola's attachment to Orsino confuses her link with Olivia, and she is always shadowed by her brother. She thinks Feste is 'a merry fellow' who cares for nothing, but in fact she's wrong. Sebastian longs for his sister but is distracted by Olivia. The most precarious characters, sympathetic just because of their weak connections, are Andrew, who depends on a false bond with Toby; Antonio, inadvisedly enthralled to Sebastian; and Malvolio, fixated on Olivia. All of the latter nearly fall out of the play, or do so.

I have a feeling that this essentially uncluttered production could bring all this out well, but it would be surprising at this stage if the relationships were very vivid: the actors are naturally intent on establishing themselves, for themselves. Ned Schmidtke, for instance, having reflected on Antonio's lines:

> In nature there's no blemish but the mind:
> None can be called deformed but the unkind

wants to give himself an actual blemish – a milky contact lens – next to which the deformity of Sebastian's spiritual treachery will seem worse. And – wouldn't you know – Howard is wondering if it isn't Toby who is the 'coxcomb', the 'thin-faced knave' at the end. Discouraging them both, I felt badly – Ned was prepared to pay for the lens himself and Howard was sincere – but of course both are self-engrossed ideas. Eventually the actors will define themselves by the energy they give to each other.

Looking about, I can see half-developed faces, like dim cameos on a family tree. Next to Ned, Chris Gerson as Sebastian, seemingly straight off the Chicago street (albeit more uptown Evanston than the Loop), feels too overheated in a contemporary American way – it's all right as far as it goes, but, faced by the marvel of Olivia, there is too much of 'weigh-heigh, my lucky day' in his reaction and nothing moonstruck. In the same way his response to his lost sister is too flip. As in many young actors, his masculinity masks a childishly generous heart that he doesn't yet trust. With Myrto, the problems are similar. Viola is loved by young and old alike in the theatre, sharing the qualities of both: but Elyse is inclined to stamp her foot in moments of vexation, and her general manner is coltish going on petulant. Her dealings with Henry Godinez's Count seem a bit Palm Beach, Orsino's difficult personality not working a deep response in her: and his attraction to her Cesario comes out in bursts of over-innocent high spirits. Godinez is very handsome, with long curly hair and a dazzling smile, a serious and energetic actor slightly embarrassed by the determination of designers to show his chest whenever possible – matters which Nan Zabriskie is making worse with a lace ballet shirt and pleated cream trousers. Meanwhile Lisa Dodson, who with Greg Vinkler indefinably leads the company, is resistant to playing Olivia as abrasively as I would like, perhaps because she has done a number of Shakespeare's heroines – Ophelia, Imogen, Hermione – and Olivia is a different, less lovely matter. I may have to negotiate with her, accepting some softness in return for well-placed stabs of temper.

On Boxing Day Mark and Caroline disappear to the big second-hand clothes market on Belmont Street (which seems to me not much different from Camden Town, but what do I know); and before returning in, I hope, top gear tomorrow, I look for some kind of norm in videotapes of Barbara Gaines's past shows, which feature many of the same actors. The productions use the limited space of the Ruth Page very inventively, finding a direct rapport with the house, and they have feeling and sweep. But for my taste there is not much of what you might call politics: that steeliness without which new Shakespeare can feel like a softish form of avant-garde – and which makes *Julius Caesar*, for instance, not so much an heroic tragedy as an obsessive study of the way republicanism and totalitarianism stalk and imitate each other. It's an odd thing to feel, since Barbara's *King Lear* a few years ago had beggars all over the stage, emphasising what Lear had 'ta'en too little care' of, and her *Henry V* ended with film of the Vietnam War Memorial in Washington listing its 59,000 dead, with the King's name, formerly on a great banner, dissolving to take its place among them as Henry V Closser. In this and in other ways, there is no question about the excitement Chicago Shakespeare is engendering. However, the good intentions seem to me to get skewed by something in the actors' training, which encourages them mainly to tap into primary emotions, so that their approach to the text is not particularly intelligent or graded. Often they miss the status contests that flicker even in domestic scenes – well, that's very English. I go with Barbara to a preview that Ian McKellen is hosting of his and Richard Loncraine's film of *Richard III:* he is startled to see me rise to my feet so far from home to salute it, thinking for a moment he is being stalked. At dinner, Barbara worries about how to find an image to 'release' her forthcoming production of the same play: Ian, actor now rather than producer, gently points out that maybe the text itself will take care of that. Equally gently, Barbara stresses that she is only aiming at what he has just done; and that anyway our engrained English sense of scruple in Shakespeare is like a distant rumour to her people. True enough: though we may resist it, English actors of my generation have absorbed first a tradition, and then its modification in the hands of directors like Peter Hall, Trevor Nunn and especially, because of his consuming concern for the matter, John Barton.

I hope we carry all this lightly, as McKellen does in his adaptation of Richard's character into twentieth-century terms and as I hope to with this *Twelfth Night*, but still it is there, mother's milk re-flavoured year by year.

Just as in Tokyo, I realise I am pining for some English modulations, nostalgic where I meant to be heretical. There is, to be sure, a certain *loudness* all around: in *Twelfth Night*'s love scenes the effect is enthusiastic but not at all erotic. But I did want this to be an American production – Shakespeare's language is packed with words and idioms that arrived with the founding fathers and have become exclusively American (like 'liquor', 'garbage' and the construction 'I'll have him do such-and-such'), and I am very distrustful of any worshipping at the English shrine.[6] At the same time, something's irritating me. Same old bind – I want Japanese and American energies together with the lovely benefits of English nuance.[7]

Back to work, determined to take the pressure off but release the hare. We warm up with Toby's small personal explosion over the pickled herrings. A lively debate begins, in the best traditions of the Actors' Studio: clearly, everyone has been thinking over Christmas about the matter of farting. How much *control* is Toby exercising? Is he colluding in the shocking moment, passing his point of no-return with drunken relish? In any event, come along, ladies and gentlemen, we're talking about pickled herrings, this is not a matter of roses, after all. We try it again, and all nostrils twitch – all at the same moment. No, such a thing takes time, snaking its way around the room. When does it reach you, Chuck, and what is the Priest's opinion of it? You're the last victim, Adrianne, nearest to the door – that's right, ever so discreetly, slide it open an inch or two. But – to summarise – *should* we do it? And in an *Olivia* scene? And is it Funny, or only Funnyish? Well, it'll go well at the children's

---

6 American self-confidence is supreme in modern work, but much less so in Shakespeare still. Even Al Pacino, a great screen actor, owes something to Olivier when it comes to Richard III, as Marlon Brando did as Mark Antony.

7 In general, the very best actors are the same everywhere, while the merely good reflect the tendencies of their own background. And American English simply doesn't modulate as much as British. One of the difficulties faced by an English actor learning an American accent, for instance, is abandoning English shadowplay – the multiple qualifications, deferrals and obliquities we use to work ourselves in and out of conversation – and learn instead to come in strong with the thought, pursuing it to the end of the sentence without a lot of variation.

matinées. Howard himself somehow becomes the arbiter. There is an attractive puritanism in him: he used to edit out his suggestive moments as Pandarus in *Troilus and Cressida* for the schools performances, happily reinstating them in the evenings. But he agrees that this gastric firefly is something different, a touch of nature that makes the whole world kin. It stays in.

If the play works like a daisy chain, the links are a series of highly charged duologues. Viola and Olivia have their three, pitched in different keys – from an alert *en garde* to high tension to a clumsy uncoupling. It is a cliché to compare good acting to tennis, but it is often true. When it comes to

> OLIVIA: . . . Where lies your text?
> VIOLA: In Orsino's bosom.
> OLIVIA: In his bosom? In what chapter of his bosom?
> VIOLA: To answer by the method, in the first of his heart.
> OLIVIA: O, I have read it: it is heresy. Have you no more to say?

the sense of a rally is obvious, and the actors have to get their reactions up to championship speed. But it's also true when the style is *legato:* exciting as it is to see two players at the net slugging volleys at each other, you really appreciate their craft when they're both stuck at the base line, looking for openings, negotiating in a state of delicate heat. In the theatre, the tension can be sharpened by arbitrary direction, as if the umpire had commanded the players to stay back. As they engage, Elyse and Lisa instinctively close in on each other; but what if they were forced to opposite edges of the stage – the one trying to escape, the other hoping to hold on to her but at arm's length? To hear a line of Shakespeare, charged with need, arcing across some distance rather than being hammered into the face, is to feel the arguments become not petty but glorious. The body always *wants* to do something – the resistance imposed on it and its effect on the voice are the interesting things.

Some other points. Since every line is triggered at speed by what the other character says, the one rule is to pick up your cue, and then you can refine your thought in the act of expressing it. The heat of listening is as great as the heat of speaking, and the mercury mustn't drop. Don't stroll aimlessly about, feeling you should keep on the move for the audience's sake – it becomes as deadly as if you just stood there and recited. Making a fierce speech at your partner, then showing an angry face to the audience, won't do. Why look at the customers? They can see you. If ever they need to watch both your faces simultaneously, any alert director will fix it.[8]

As I lecture on like this, Elyse is offered a highly-paid commercial and asks for a day off. Sorry, can't do it. I also hear that Kevin Rigdon (lighting designer), whom I am impatient to talk with, is coming into Chicago for only two hours tomorrow: he is designing for Corin and Vanessa Redgrave in Huston, their schedule keeps changing, and he is in thrall. Barbara, it's impossible, please find someone else. She checks three or four alternative designers without success, then finds that Kevin's assistant, a zealous and delightful graduate called Shannon McKinney, will be good enough for the job if necessary. After much nagging, Kevin will now give us *four* hours tomorrow, but I'm not much reassured. It is the New Year, and I have wrecked my own cast with a particularly good party:[9] but it is starting with trade toughness, like the first rehearsal.

In this spirit, Barbara tells me candidly the show is not sexy enough yet and the staging a bit dull – I respond to the second point if not the first. To have Malvolio tied to a ballroom chair for the Sir Topas scene was fine on paper, but in practice it's not cruel enough. However, both the ESC and Tokyo solutions – the vertical coffin and the prison of light – seem too aesthetic in this theatre. We tie him with long diagonal ropes, running downstage left to upstage right, downstage right to upstage left, in a particularly nasty twisting bind: he has no control at all and the slightest flick of a rope will send him toppling. Is it practicable without damaging Greg, and what kind of ropes? The flicks must of course be mimed, and Greg time his own falls to them. Donald Eastman is as absent as Kevin now, back in New York on another show and cut off in any case by blizzards running up and down the East Coast. Thank God for a local ship-

---

8   We did this with the Willow Cabin speech, when Viola assumed the pose of a strong (male) protector standing behind Olivia's chair, her hands nearly on her shoulders – and both were able to show us what they felt, unguarded. A touch of backlight lifted the speech, so that it glowed a little with accidental pink.

9   Here at least the daisy-chain was inspired, as in the luckiest of open houses: the numbers never too few or too many, from six in the evening to three in the morning, as if those leaving had sent the next wave, waiting in the freezing street, inside. I had done a ton of food and bottomless champagne, but it was multiplied tenfold as everybody brought trollies as well. It was good to become a waiter rather than a Significant Figure, and to observe true natures. Frank Farrell so passionate about African pigmy hedgehogs that, believing them rare, he recently bought two, only to find that they breed so fast that he now has thirty; Greg a political radical; Gerson a rock and roller – it was our day of licensed folly.

chandler – the coarseness of the mooring-ropes he supplies suits our makeshift air, and they look as if they could cause serious burns.

Earlier, watching the waves of the revellers' party divide for Malvolio, I cannot deny, as with all the other set pieces, some comedy-fatigue. Tim Davies's night-cap with bobble or Seiya Nakano's face-mask? No, this time just a nightshirt almost down to the knobbly knees and unfortunate slippers; but what to do with Toby's and Feste's Funnyish singing, while Malvolio stands and watches them? Best to hand it over to the actors: they haven't done the play three times. Andrew is the last to see the steward approach, still dancing foolishly around with a blanket while the others freeze – finally Frank collapses giddily at Malvolio's feet. I elaborate this offering: why doesn't Andrew make a swift upwards inspection under the nightshirt, then sit up with that expressive gesture of the thumb and forefinger that suggests he has spied something absolutely miniscule? Having only just got over the pickled herrings, the cast gape at me again – these American actors are so *respectful*. But I like the Bankside lewdness creeping into our proceedings. It occurs to me, in a sweeter vein, that some warm secrets might be germinating in this dark house. As the company drifts away in the anticlimax after Malvolio's departure, Fabian and Molly happen to take the same exit and he slips his arm round her shoulder as they disappear from sight.

Things are not going so well between Andrew, Toby and Maria, and I am getting small deputations from each of the actors in turn. It is somewhat to be expected: my brief to them hasn't been clear enough   all three are hovering somewhere between charm and documentary, and not quite trusting each other. Back to the beginning. Maria's job is the smooth running of the house's inside and underside – and her rancour against Malvolio is, initially at least, the deepest: she pursues vengeance almost as far as Feste does, and further than Andrew or Fabian ever would. It happens that in this production Olivia and Malvolio are of an age, and Sarajane as Maria evidently a decade older: Olivia can thus be easily regal with Malvolio and a little less so with Maria, who might have looked after her (just as Feste entertained her) as she grew up. As senior Waiting Gentlewoman, Maria is like the Mistress of the Queen's Bedchamber, in a relation to Olivia both intimate and subservient. The moral nub of her story is that, by imitating her mistress's writing, she seriously abuses her confidentiality – her anger has led her into this

betrayal, and she has to slip back into the shadows to avoid account-
ing for it. Sarajane, who made me spill my wine at her audition,
turns out to be frailer than I expected, and, like Greg, lacks genuine
self-confidence until she has practical details to work with – whereas
Howard and Frank as Toby and Andrew are a degree more improvisational, gaining more laughs in rehearsals. Sarajane should take
heart: she is completely convincing as Olivia's duenna, and her
being of an age with Howard promises to make their partnership
natural and effortless.

Toby of course takes Maria for granted. It is hard to imagine this
man showing kindness to her, or indeed any emotion untouched by
self-interest. But then, with the single exception of Viola, there is
hardly a character in the play who doesn't pursue their ends with
notable greed: you notice Toby's banditry more because it is not
veiled by poetry, foolishness or the knockabout effect of mistaken
identity. He uses not only Andrew but Fabian, so impressed by him
and in the end so shocked by how far he will go. Whenever Toby
flags, the younger man serves him brilliantly – only to find himself
alone when explanations are due. In fact Toby hates his existence,
which seems to offer him nothing: he is propelled to marry Maria by
a fatigue and despair entirely of his own making. Bargains are struck
throughout life, in beds and elsewhere, and this is his: it has been
settled long ago that she and he are as linked as a nut and a bolt.

At the moment, the setting up of Andrew's duel with Cesario is
stuck rigid, and there is sorrow in the air. A bit like Kato, Frank
Farrell has discovered an ability to flop to the ground as if a puppet-
master had withdrawn his hand, and he has timed it for the most
hyperbolical description of Cesario's murderousness – 'they say he
has been fencer to the Sophy'. But Howard doesn't like it, and, with
an ominous courtesy, questions what Frank is doing – it is hard for
him to pick Andrew up again with one hand, handle all his duelling
props with the other, and still keep the text going. Frank is puzzled
as to why this problem should arise. Here we go again. Maybe my
fondness for Andrew has again become too evident to Toby. I have
also just significantly bruised Howard by asking him to execute a
quick change into full Cavalry fig just before this point, which in the
Ruth Page is impossible without a great din and disturbance. Not
only that, but he and I have just snapped at each other in the first
rehearsal for the rather complicated curtain-call. So attention must
be paid. It is true that no Toby should be made into Andrew's comic

slave: on the other hand, this fall of Frank's is not just Funnyish, it's really Funny.

Frank has his own, rather beastly problem to attend to. He is a natural eccentric, in his big round glasses that make him look like a startled heron, and his comedy at its best comes off with a beautiful lightness: but I've tied him up in this emphatic Southern accent, the riskiest thing in the production. My idea was that Andrew's trace element of aggression would be well served by a few redneck intonations – I thought it would be fun (and Funny), and Frank has certainly enjoyed his evenings studying Bette Davis in *Jezebel*. But I can see the problem. Andrew's appeal is human in a rather inhuman world, and an audience has a sneaking feeling of kinship: I'm always preaching that the part is all there on the page, that Frank shouldn't do too much, that if an audience senses he is *entertaining* them, everything will go cold and lumpy. However this quite distant accent makes him stick out a mile and is thick with effort. Best perhaps to forget the redneck and concentrate more on making him a soft, chesty Virginian gentleman, deferential and more mild-mannered than Andrew sometimes is.

As usual, the refrain of 'Mistress Mine' sees Toby and Andrew off to bed after their party, and Orsino's band begins to mill around: Valentine on double-bass, Fabian (in the wrong household, but Feste must have brought him along) as rhythm guitarist, the Priest on penny whistle. Providing a professional anchor, L.J plays a wailing fiddle, and Jay a twelve-string guitar spangled with harmonics. All of them wear those Gatsby caps (a bit ahead of time). We've come a long way from the ESC's Spanish guitar and bodhran – not to mention the traditional whey-faced Feste. This is a singer who can pulverise you at a moment's notice at no apparent cost to himself: and like many virtuosos he appears very offhand. Ron Keaton, in an agony of uncertainty every time he speaks, is supremely self-confident when he sings, knowing he can catch the heart. He has assembled red sneakers, a pair of very wide and therefore rascally pin-stripe trousers, and, for no special reason, a red sash over an evening dress jacket: he also has a big hand-drum slung on his hip, which he will play with a stick. As he begins, Orsino, in a black shirt this time, grips Cesario's hand – and, most unfairly again, I wish Henry Godinez weren't such a pussycat. Despite his sultry looks, he is giving off a rather fairminded distress, in mild waves. I feel I need more bad manners: but this is such a familiar reaction that I also wonder if my thinking has been misguided.

In the same way, I wonder if I am wrong about Olivia. After three productions, I am still struck at how remote a character she is: perhaps I am seeing her through my own prejudices. It seems to me that her habitual withdrawal into a privileged position when faced with the unknown is disagreeable and unfunny. Her rebuke of Malvolio at the start is unnecessarily shaming, her sympathy for him at the end barely blood-warm; her affection for Feste is a bit tepid too; her obsessive attraction to Cesario is not marked by kindliness, and her securing of Sebastian is ecstatic without being moving. She is nicest to Andrew – when she finally focuses on him. The key in which you play the two rulers affects the tone of the whole play: a Strindbergian Orsino or a glacially uncompanionable Olivia could paralyse it. Nevertheless, I distrust the dollops of charm needed to make them palatable – it lowers the play's standards. I hope that a tremulous self-consciousness – how shall she set things up with Cesario, how shall she dress – will be enough to extenuate Olivia, and an admirable recklessness to humanise Orsino. And I hope Lisa and Henry are right to trust me as I nag her to snap and riposte rather than to melt, and him to draw jagged, unlyrical lines.

In fact, by the usual mysterious process, the play is beginning to swell. Even without contact lenses, Ned Schmidtke's Antonio hurls himself into the arms of Chris Gerson's Sebastian with virile impetuosity, and achieves surpassing happiness at a café table. Ned arrived with us with an old-fashioned American swagger as if he was wearing very big heavy boots – chaps and spurs too; he seemed to sit with his legs too wide apart, and grin too much and too broadly. Now, a loyal and affectionate man himself, he has realised that love denudes Antonio: blundering into Olivia's garden, he faces Orsino's police vulnerable, somehow spindly-legged, surprisingly unequipped for their bruising maleness. Earlier on, his beaming face over coffee and schnapps is excellent – he gives Sebastian his whole purse as if it were a few pence or no more than a cigarette, and Chris Gerson receives it as if it were twice its real value. In their first scene, Chris is moderating his tearaway attitude: tweaked by the beautiful dulcimer theme Rokko has done for him, he breaks down not so much at the memory of his drowned sister but at the fact that, while speaking of her beauty, he somehow forgot for a moment that she was dead.

A brief call before the dress rehearsals on That Other Pickled Matter – would Toby perhaps pass the blame, or does he leave things, so to speak, hanging in the air? In the event he departs quickly, his place taken by Malvolio – standing just where Toby has been, the steward cannot miss the bouquet. Disgusted, he looks around for a culprit: the stage is quickly full of demurrals, but Olivia's Priest is a little slow off the mark and loses the musical chairs. Everyone glares at him: that's the way. We've got it.

Having postponed a decision until now on whether Malvolio should come back at the end, I'm inclined to think for the third time it's a good idea: I muse aloud to the cast, hoping the clinching image will come from them. If Olivia's household is Old New York, perhaps in some future projection Malvolio represents the new world – a railroad millionaire back from the West, perhaps, at home in Tiffany's, consuming conspicuously. Greg could certainly be such a *nouveau riche*, his life made comfortable at last by less successful immigrants. Thoughtful faces all around – is this an American idea too far? Well then, let's have Malvolio simply come back at the end of Feste's song, and improvise what he thinks of it. Hearing 'We'll strive to please you every day', Greg declines to tip him and snaps off the lights. Absolutely right, and Nan Zabriskie rushes out for a camel coat with a fur collar and a white scarf, white gloves and a stick, as if Malvolio was calling in on his way home from the opera. It fits, and I don't mention that the gesture is exactly what Tim Davies did for the ESC.

But then, a director's job is always to say the same things over and over and over again. However, I'd forgotten how hard on the calves the job is. Up and down, down and up, clowning a bit, running forward and then retreating fast before the fresh advice can die. The performances are quite advanced, so the preview period seems a bit long – the cast, bucked by a good reception from the start, are beginning to move about much better, though the text is still bedevilled by inaccuracies. Most of the work now takes the form of catching these, and of practical tidying. The lighting in particular fills out. I want a heat-lightning effect in Viola's shipwreck, the light without thunder that flashes when a distant storm is fitfully subsiding: this leads not to a sorry-can't-do but, since this is Chicago Shakespeare, to a city-wide search for the right lamp. Steppenwolf lend us one – it has to be operated manually, splashing small explosions of light along the cyclorama. (We identify four different lengths and intensities of flash and tie each to a word of text, each of them separately cued.) Meanwhile, as in Japan, the floor isn't looking good, and it seems impossible to see the delicate tiles of the interiors without being distracted by the driftwood on the forestage. In his brief sojourn, Kevin had hurriedly patched a few circuits but had by no means used the theatre's extensive range of instruments: we're left with broad fields of light but little ability to kill one area and isolate another. Replugging it all with Shannon, whose enthusiasm is worth all Kevin's briefly-glimpsed panache, we manage to deaden everything but what we want: transformed, Olivia's early scenes begin to look beautifully like a portrait in a distant frame, surrounded by darkness.

It is now so cold that a man with a frozen moustache is shown on the television news pouring water from a boiling kettle into the street – it freezes as it hits the ground. Technical fidgeting is punctuated by various homilies to the cast, cheering or corrective. Before the last preview[10] we agree that pace and flexibility are almost everything in a house this small: the audience will get the point quickly and expect still greater speed of thought from the actors. So if you're going to pause, you must be damned sure why, and the worst reason is shortness of breath. Tyrone Guthrie's advice that an actor should be able to do seven verse lines without reflating may be a bit hoary, but then, supposing you wanted to and found you couldn't? The public will also be put off by heavy cheerfulness – these characters are touchy, fullblooded and unstable, and even honest men like Antonio are like mercury. Remember the changes of scale – the moments when Shakespeare takes off like Concorde from ordinary speech into supreme metaphor, and as swiftly lands again. In conclusion I carpet the cast for still being loose on the text and even a little smug about what they're offering, and am rewarded by a most generous speech of thanks, enunciated by Howard and cheered by all. The air fills with the first sadness of separation: it seems they have even looked forward to the note sessions. I'm asked for last-minute warnings, but that's it. Breathe deeply, and no slow walking, please. Good luck to all.

Sitting in a remote corner of the building with Barbara Gaines and a bottomless bottle, I escape the heady purgatory of the first night, a ceremony which a director can influence only with encouraging

10   It's the last opportunity. Apart from the odd desperate show that rehearses right down to the deadline of its premiere (and may well end up a hit as a result), the director's job has near enough ended with the last preview: the actors generally need a clear and independent life for the last twenty-four hours, as they begin to grow away from him.

smiles. My book *Hamlet – A User's Guide* has just come out, and Barbara asks me to come back in the fall and direct that play. I wonder. She has already invited Michael Bogdanov to come and do *Timon of Athens*, which certainly promises a reunion but, I should have thought, more than enough expense for her. Looking in on *Twelfth Night* like a truant at selected moments (I know the scene timings by now) I can feel the temperature rise steadily – Andrew's and Toby's jig, Malvolio and Viola chasing through the streets, the pickled herrings (a nail-biting moment – have you ever blown a raspberry in a state of nerves?), even an unexpected laugh of anticipation when Sebastian says he is going to Orsino's court – now *that's* attentiveness.

I always knew that when Viola leaves after her soliloquy with the ring, an audience would jump at the sight of Sebastian stepping into the pool of light she has left: what I didn't expect was Elyse's rapport in the preceding speech. We rehearsed it with a certain despair, but now it is like falling off a log for her, as it was for Hirota – quite instinctive and discreetly sexual. Inexperience has its own beauty, and I hope, tresses restored, Elyse does well in California. 'Come Away Death' and the silence following it, Viola and Orsino silhouetted by backlight and unknowingly destined for each other, is lovely; the Letter fine, the Stockings too, and the Duel. On 'This is the air; that is the glorious sun' Chris Gerson, on impulse, hurls himself flat on the ground in a gesture at once abandoned, silly and ecstatic, like *Twelfth Night* itself. In his hands, it is not only the reunion with his sister that is moving at the end, but the moment afterwards when he turns to Olivia and declares his virginity.

Frank, Sarajane, Henry and Ned have hit their best form. Lisa Dodson's Olivia is enchanting without sentiment – she gasps with pleasure at the forbidden impact of Cesario, throws herself across her stately chair, jumps up, spins deliriously on her heels and grabs her desk, then caresses the chair as she wishes Cesario had when she was in it. I've learned something about the part from her: combining force with vulnerability, this is someone who will play Cleopatra. Howard Witt, too, is a revelation. Paradoxically, nerves make him authoritative, every syllable precise and tight with meaning: without losing a single laugh, his is a real study of a wasted life still fighting for life – it could be Chekhov. The same nerves have made Ron Keaton's singing as electrifying as when a jazz singer finally cuts loose: the rawest emotion just held by rhythm and pitch. Well, you can trust a Celt when it comes to the point. Kurt Naebig, gravel-voiced and with a startling look of Mickey Rourke, gets a special American rage into Fabian, most helpful in all the plotters' explosions of excitement; and at the end he sees his mentor Toby for what he is. Greg Vinkler smells his audience like a wolf, but, suppressing the showman in himself, is markedly economical in his yellow stockings. One of his moustache-curlers falls off, which is one of those things that happen only on first nights. The curtain-call is, as they say, a blast.[11] Just as in Tokyo, everyone is better than they've ever been on this fraught occasion: we could be in business.

The show turns out to be a substantial hit: it goes on to win some Jeff Awards, the Chicago equivalent of New York's Tonys. The *Chicago Tribune* calls it 'radiant . . . the best locally-produced Shakespeare in years' and describes the set as an Elizabethan courtyard; meanwhile the *Sun Times* thinks the 'revelatory' production takes place in Charleston, run down after the Civil War, with only Aguecheek retaining his accent and Viola and Sebastian as Yankees stranded in the defeated state. At least none of them worry about the propriety of Malvolio's final return: ah, not to be in pernickety England. Professor Martin Mueller at Northwestern University writes to Mayor Daley that this is the best *Twelfth Night* he's seen in his forty audience years and urges him to go – which, astonishingly, he does: later, he will support the company's search for a new home. He apparently laughs like a drain at the pickled herrings: this may not be of the same order as the British Ambassador weeping in Tokyo, but then maybe it is, and it is surely good enough for me.

A midwestern welcome is a byword: no East Coast neurosis or Californian narcissism here. If you do something that is liked you will be stopped in the street by strangers asking you, impractically, to stay. For a few days I do workshops and give lectures – but eventually, life awaits even in the dead of winter, and I have sad English business that can't be postponed. Leaving a truly-grieved cast for the airport, I have the feeling of quite intense ties being

---

11   This is a variation on the animals going in two by two (taking care to acknowledge that there is an audience on three sides) and each bow is tied to a precise beat of music. It is a genial and rather natty piece of choreography I must say, in that it appears to be based on the ensemble – except that as the barn-dance snakes and weaves, the principals do have a way of ending up in the middle. And in fact the musicians end up with the best call, which nobody can object to.

casually snapped, and the oddest sense that far more than two months have passed since *Taking Sides* finished, and I grumpily came away to what has turned out to be a love-match for us all. It is so cold at O'Hare airport that the liquids controlling the panel electronics in our 747 freeze and we sit on the runway for four hours, between one world and another: all the enthusiasm back in the city, like a band playing in the distance, begins to recede, and I feel stranded.

★

TO: PROFESSOR MARTIN MUELLER
NORTHWESTERN UNIVERSITY
CHICAGO.
London, February 1996

Dear Professor Mueller

How nice to get your letter. Of course the opening scene of *Twelfth Night* could be played more benevolently, and Orsino with less neurosis. Olivia too. I suppose the editor of the latest Arden edition, seemingly quite a Malvolio himself, would say our show exemplifies the 'trend in twentieth-century production which may be called anti-romantic, a trend towards extracting the potentially ironical and ridiculous in Shakespeare's dramatic situations, which I regard as wholly regrettable'. Well, as you like it: I haven't myself found Shakespeare to be soft on human folly, have you?

Anyway, I was charmed by your letter. I must say that one of the pleasures of being a 'Shakespearian' these last years has been the new amiability between scholars and showmen: nowadays the two parishes only quarrel about where the stage pillars in the recon-structed Globe Theatre in London should authentically be. Of course, there were always a few director-scholars qualified to work both sides of the street, such as the great John Barton, whom you rightly admire, and who has been something of an *agent-provocateur* in these matters. Over the years he has rewritten much of *King John* and the *Henry VI*s, and long ago I saw his princely eyes gleam as he declared to a group of scholars that, were he to do *As You Like It*, he would straight away write himself the scene of Duke Frederick meeting the old religious man in the forest, and cut something less interesting from the play to make room for it. Their fluttering fans were like some overplayed production of *The School for Scandal*, but their aghastness was genuine enough; however the same scholars might reproach you nowadays for letting *Hamlet* run for more than three hours, and most actors know a Good Quarto from a Bad.

You're very kind about *Twelfth Night*. It is not the fashion, as Rosalind might have said, to hear the director praise his own work – but since you ask my opinion, here is what I hope about the show, and even believe. I brought an inauspicious attitude of mind to it, but it's been the most satisfying version for me, not necessarily performance for performance but in the overall balance. The devotional and playful aspects of the text both seem to have been extended, it has a healthy dash of rudeness and some humanity. A director's life impinges on his work as much as an actor's, and some rough and tumble in mine may have shadowed the comedy but doggedly lightened the darker parts. But then this was a most generous company: they arrived with great slicks of adrenalin but then applied themselves to detail and nuance – sometimes exact phrasing too, though I must say that their verse lines, like Titus, were inclined to lose a leg from time to time. As a result, deep feelings hung on small hinges. We are all fools: every day they showed me just how foolish, using their own foolishness. And Chicago theatre's sense of ensemble served a play of eleven leading characters better than when I did it in Tokyo, for instance, where the intricacies of status inside the company jarred a bit on the smooth running of things.

And this remains the trickiest of all plays, a thing fashioned by a great cabinet-maker that you must reproduce without a single drawer jamming. The more you ply Olivia's world with natural detail, undercurrents and rivalries, the more of the moments you enjoyed will follow – Toby and Maria leaving for their honeymoon, Andrew packing up his yellow teddy-bears before anyone sees them, the pickled herring joke. (You know, I don't think I could have done that one in England – it wouldn't have been a surprise, and might even have seemed mannered – but it was possible here because audiences still seem delighted that Shakespeare can stoop so low.)

But as a director you've to be careful: the high sensibility and smarting pains of Orsino's story, and of Viola/Sebastian's, turn in the timeless suspension of a dream; and if Olivia's world is too fat with politics, it can be difficult to bring the other towards it. I'm sure you agree the design is conscious: the play swells with tragedy (loss at sea, the violent sorrows of Antonio, madness stalking Malvolio) but collusive fantasy thins its blood, without quite making it weightless. In this knockabout world in which the heart keeps stopping, you can encounter infinite riches by candle light, and occasionally great blasts of cold air threaten the flame. Above all, and heretically, Shakespeare implies that erotic love is completely haphazard, completely deceitful and illusory – kiss the portrait and you die – so any neat disposition, as of the couples at the end, is a joke. What's the deep meaning of that? It's terribly troubling in one way, and 'all one' in another.

You know all this! Thanks so much for writing.

All the best,

Michael.

★

TO BARBARA GAINES
CHICAGO SHAKESPEARE THEATER.
London, February 1996

Dear Barbara

Thanks for your news. I'm glad the *Hamlet* book is selling well with your audiences. But I don't think I should direct the production: oddly enough I've nothing to say. I also think the best service you can do for your Hamlet is to give him a director who hasn't played the part himself, even a generation ago in another country. If I were you, I would take your *User's Guide* in one hand and your big stick in the other and do it yourself.

The fact is that *Hamlet* has died on me, and *Twelfth Night*'s not far behind. That's Shakespeare – you've had it for good, until one day you read a newspaper, or sit in a waiting-room, and recall a beautiful phrase, and the whole business starts again. The plays fill up with our own experience, year after year: but at the moment I feel like one of Shakespeare's old mistresses – an old limp rag after thirty-five years in the service.

The thing with this playwright is that you're always out of date with yourself. I can tell you what got me excited as a kid; of how I think the best speaking can be both lean and beautiful; of how I once approved of cutting and then of not cutting. Being with the RSC in the 1970s was like some privileged pilgrimage – sleeping, eating and breathing Shakespeare with a clear conscience; then we did things with profound conviction in the ESC in the 1980s that I'm not sure I still believe in – our ruthless egalitarianism lowered our best level without raising the game, and it became hard to play a glamorous lead who was politically incorrect, like Coriolanus. The fact is that Shakespeare wrote star parts, and quite a few caricatures of working men; but we claim him as a liberal and believe in ensemble, or say we do. I do know that, at one time, finding a consensual approach to doing Shakespeare was a big issue that everyone discussed: in these unregulated days, the interest seems rather quaint.

And it's all written on water, of course. To be honest with you, I was shocked by the last performance of *Twelfth Night* I saw before I left. First of all, by my own work. I know the play is multi-faceted, but I counted eighty louvred panels behind Olivia, and a further thirty on the floor. But then I saw a tape of my ESC production five years ago and there must have been several hundred. Horrible – you were looking at this aggressively tessellated thing that made the actors unimportant. In Japan we had broad planes and washes of colour – much cleaner – but I seem to have regressed. Not only that, but after a week and a half the performances seemed to have collapsed. Now I know why I don't direct more often: it turns you against good, honest actors. Having got to the point of really talking to each other with those old words, they were now looking at the audience, striking attitudes and expostulating. For the first time it all sounded like a foreign language – single lines of verse being broken into three or four phrases, so you couldn't catch the sense. I presume this is my fault – I kept saying it all, but I can't have convinced them. Why couldn't I have left the actors with a deeper belief in what we were doing? And Viola's trousers need pressing. I know what happens when the show is up and running: the director goes, it becomes 'your own', you get more confident, it all 'grows'. All as it should be. But now I saw this nacre of over-confidence, all this 'freedom' spoiling our plan. Can you keep an eye on it, please? Do keep them fluent, talking quicker than they think they can.

Whatever you do you're dissatisfied five minutes later. That's why all Shakespearians dream of a moratorium on him – he's just too much, and you keep changing your mind, about how, why and if. At certain times I've become convinced that the only point in doing one of the plays is if there is somebody in the audience who has never seen it before, or somebody on the stage who never expected to play it – ever greater virtuosity in advancing the pleasure of the converted seems a smaller and smaller reason. And in fact many of my own highlights haven't been in a theatre at all, but through watching Shakespeare's transforming power in the hands of people who never imagined him to be a friend. I once saw a twelve-year-old in an ESC workshop at a London comprehensive required to play Capulet making that terrible attack on his daughter: the boy suddenly understood his father's baffled generation for a moment. That was worth everything. But then I also remember a woman on an inner-city estate doing Juliet's Nurse partly in Shakespeare and partly in Jamaican patois, and a high-security prisoner playing Caliban, his poetry a tangible defiance of the fact that he couldn't see over a wall a few feet away, couldn't even walk out of the room. At these great subversive moments, you can hear springs snapping – it is not a matter of a theatre aesthetic but of common coin.

But Shakespeare gives not a day's wage to the unemployed and only momentary hope to the prisoner. Everybody needs him, even the fortunate; and I'm glad to say that making a whole Shakespeare work night after night is still a job for the professionals. People pretend that they go to these plays for small reasons – they've heard the director's spin is cheeky, it's on the school syllabus, they like the lead actress. But I think we know how deep our need is – for the harmonisations of *Twelfth Night* or *The Dream*, for the vitality of *Antony* or *Henry IV*: and think of the astonishing silence that can prevail at a good *Hamlet*. It follows that there probably still is such a thing as a Shakespearian actor – it sounds like something out of the nineteenth century, but it remains a respectful soubriquet, just. It is as much to do with the ability to think quickly aloud as with the grand manner, and more to do with athleticism and alertness than a huge vocal tessatura. More than anything, with aligning your temperament. There are no introspective characters in Shakespeare, not even Hamlet – everything is based on the need to speak. His people are as afraid of silence as if they were on the radio, and they define their ideas on the move: unlike most of us, their thoughts are never thicker than their words. Very occasionally we meet a slow-witted character – one, in other words, of about our own speed – like Aguecheek, or Constable Dull in *Love's Labour's Lost*, who, accused of having 'spoke no word all this time', admits that he has

'understood none neither'. Like them, an audience after a Shakespeare may believe it has 'been at a great feast of language and stolen
the scraps' – in fact they feel cheated if they don't.

Habitually achieving all that may be what defines the actor (or
director) as a 'Shakespearian': and many such mulishly resist the
classification – it sounds too priest-like, too excluding. But it is silly
to, rather like denying one's own marriage. Like a marriage, a
lifelong engagement with Shakespeare will be marked by periods of
ecstasy, of boredom, of outright acrimony, of separations that seem
final but aren't; but there's no point in denying that it exists. We're
like oxen struggling in the shambles. And a good thing too – look at
the bludgeoning inarticulacy of prime-time TV, our degraded
vocabulary, the sensual deprivation of the Internet, all the
'liberation' that isolates us – will our kids still be able to hold each
other's gaze, let alone talk or tell a story? Well, your young customers
will. I got your Press release and I'm amazed at how much you're
doing with schools – I didn't know. You don't need my advice at this
stage, but all I say is, do what you need to for them – modern dress,
anything – just don't let them sense an establishment design behind
it: that beyond the entertainment lies an awesome masterpiece they
must now Go Home and Read. They can smell that a mile off. And
actually, I think we should welcome the fact that Shakespeare is
what he's become for many of them, a screenwriter. After all, that's
probably what he'd be doing now – not campaigning for theatre
subsidy, but enduring the indignities of the movies (he did survive
two whimsical monarchs) and pocketing the money. The advantage
for the kids is that by the time they've watched Romeo and Juliet (on
their videos) between the battle lines of Cambodia, Richard III
cutting Hastings up in a Wall Street boardroom, and the Witches
wasting Macbeth, they're Shakespearians whether they like it or not.
The language has been printed in them, in their own argot, through
conventions they understand. The next thing is to get them into a
theatre, where they're breathing the same breath as the actors, where
sometimes they *are* the actors. They can *be* it, almost causing the
thing to happen, not just having to sit in the dark, being simulated
at. This generation are both lucky and unlucky – all their access
offers them great opportunities, but also invites them to regress, side
by side in front of their screens as they sat as babies with their
unshared toys. With the work you're doing, you're attending to the
endangered chip in young people's brains that uses language to co-

operate, to maintain a vital restraint, to qualify selfish violence with a little mutual attentiveness. That's where their hope lies.

Ours too. The more sophisticated our tools become, the deeper our anxiety that we might have nothing to say, less to desire, our fluency run dry. We need the same light, the same sense of the wind behind us, and to remain as dumbstruck as the kids. Shakespeare is the big reassurance – after all, he was possible. While we work with him, the language keeps kicking, and we may even inherit his self-transforming condition, feeling too that our

> nature is subdued
> To what it works in, like the dyer's hand.

All the best for your *Hamlet*. I'm glad Michael Bogdanov is confirmed for *Timon* – give him good luck from me, and warn him: these actors now know the difference between Funny and Funnyish. Oh, and tell him – his patient has recovered, and I won't be giving up the day job. He'll know what I mean.

As ever,
Michael.